Courage and Country

**James Shields
More Than Irish Luck**

By

J. Sean Callan

ISBN: 0-9759351-0-0 (Paperback)

Library of Congress Control Number: 2003098493

Published in Lake Forest, Illinois by IrishQuill Publishing
PO Box 955, Libertyville, IL 60048-0955
Email: irishquill@aol.com. Tel/fax 847 735 0811

Printed in the USA

James Shields as he appeared when he was Senator from Minnesota in 1859.

Dedication:

To Clair

a source of inspiration

Table of Contents

Foreword

I first learned of General James Shields when the Historical Society of Lake Forest and Lake Bluff, in the Township of Shields Illinois, where I live, asked if I would compile a brief presentation on the early European settlement of the area. I am not a professional historian, but a trained psychiatrist and, as I probed the day to day lives of the early pioneers in that northeastern corner of Illinois, I came across the General. I asked about him, but no one, be they professional historian, public official or private citizen, could tell me much. James Shields, lost in the fullness of time, had become nothing more than a name on municipal ordinances and tax bills. I started digging to learn about Shields, and found myself drawn not only to his amazing story, but also to the magnetism of the man. I learned that Shields had started as a penniless immigrant from Ireland at the age of 16 or thereabouts, had risen to rub shoulders with the richest and most influential people in the land and, despite that, had died 50 years after stepping ashore in the new world almost as impoverished fiscally as when he first arrived. Yet, he left behind a rich legacy, a heritage of achievement unequaled to this day and probably for all days to come. General Shields became a United States Senator not just from one state, which would have been noteworthy in itself, but from three - Illinois, Minnesota and Missouri. He is the only person to have achieved such distinction. The fact that he, a Catholic immigrant from Ireland, did it in the face of Know-Nothing opposition to all immigrants, adds to his luster.

What an odyssey my research into the life of General Shields turned out to be. A voyage of discovery that took me from middle America, the part known in James

Shields' day by the vague and mysterious catch-all of "The Western Territories," across the Atlantic Ocean to the mists and squalls of Ireland, and then out to the "Far West" of our day, the foggy shores of San Francisco Bay. The venture took me south of the border to sunny Mexico, east again to our Nation's Capital, and north to Minnesota. It ended, finally, in the small town of Carrollton, Missouri, about 70 miles from Kansas City, where an enormous eighteen foot statue of the General presides over the main square.

The nomadic General Shields spent his final years in Carrollton but never lived in the Township of Shields Illinois, and, as far as I can ascertain, visited the area only twice. He did not dally either time. So, the first question that occurred to me was, how did the Township of Shields get its name? The answer, as to many questions, lies in its unique character and history.

Lake Forest today is a leafy suburb, less than an hour's drive from downtown Chicago. One hundred and fifty years ago the town did not exist; the region consisted mostly of bucolic farms and forestland situated on majestic bluffs overlooking Lake Michigan. The railroad had yet to be built, and the area was relatively isolated, the best part of a day's journey, either by road or lake steamer, from what would become the "Windy City." A majority of the settlers, then living in the area, hailed from Ireland. According to the United States census of 1850, of the 94 families inhabiting the region, 54 heads of household had been born in the Emerald Isle. Ten years later, urban development and an influx of newcomers changed the landscape irrevocably.

This came about when a group of Presbyterians rode the newly constructed railroad north in 1857, purchased 600 acres of land from the farmers, and carved the town of Lake Forest with its curvy streets from the pristine forests and farmland.[1] Later, Lake Forest's founding fathers were followed by famed meat barons, like the Armors and Swifts, from the Chicago stockyards. These wealthy individuals bought still more land and constructed magnificent mansions, which still stand today. Many Irish farmers were delighted to sell to the newcomers, especially at inflated prices. It made them wealthy beyond their dreams, but ended Irish dominance of the area. Though the Irish farmers were displaced, their influence would not vanish entirely. By the time they sold their holdings, they had titled newly platted Town 44, Range 12, the Township of Shields in honor of their illustrious fellow countryman.[2] Initially, the township stretched along the

Lake Michigan shore from Deerfield in the south almost to Waukegan (Little Fork) in the north, a distance of some 15 miles. Today, it has shrunk to about half its original size.

James Shields' first visit to the Township of Shields Illinois took place in September 1849. At that time, he was living in Springfield if he called any place home, and was stumping for the United States Senate.[3] He stopped at a local inn where he captivated the townsfolk with "his fine voice with just enough of the Irish brogue to give it flavor and richness of tone."[4] They were exhilarated by his "fluent, witty and eloquent speech."[5] Obviously proud of their garrulous fellow countryman, they discoursed on politics, the state of the economy, the future of their new country and of course, the Emerald Isle, the land they left behind. Shields and the settlers got along well, and according to an account "the General made such an impression on the gathering that Shields Township was named after him and two months later Shields Township became a taxing unit."[6] Shields second visit to his eponymous Township was in October 1852, when he was the incumbent Senator from Illinois. On that trip, he came to thank the populace for bestowing the honor of naming the township after him.

Newsletter from Shields Township, Illinois.

The Township of Shields in Illinois is not the only place that still has the Shields surname; another is Shieldsville, Minnesota, a village close to Faribault, that he helped create with his own hands. Nor are towns the only entities still bearing the Shields sobriquet. Others include a lake in Minnesota, an elementary school on the South side of Chicago, local chapters of fraternal organizations in Kansas, Missouri, Iowa and South Carolina, streets and boulevards, and militia in states as disparate as California and New York. All that begs a question: how could such a rolling stone have generated the moss of so much recognition and yet be so obscure today? I have attempted to answer that question in this book.

The saga of James Shields is not simply a story of one man's struggle for success; it is much more than that. It is the story of America even to this day, as more than one million immigrants, each with individual hopes and dreams, arrive from all over the globe annually. James Shields epitomizes the "great American experience," where an off-the-boat immigrant can step ashore in a new land without family connections or knowing anyone, find opportunity and acceptance, and accomplish much more than that person could have achieved in any other country in the world. America, in my view, still holds out that hope to native and immigrant alike. Compiling this material has been for me a labor of love for much of the past five years; I hope you enjoy the end result. This revised edition of the book by IrishQuill publishing contains some material not present in the first by 1st Books Library. There are additional illustrations and many are enlarged and in color.

J. P. Sean Callan, Lake Forest

Shields Township, IL 2004.
Email:irishquill@aol.com

Introduction

O Siaᴅail

Shields Coat of Arms. The old Irish name spelling O'Siadail is used for Shields. The legend of the red hand goes back to ancient times, when a Scottish king offered Ireland to one of his two sons, depending on whose hand touched the island first. The brothers set out in longboats across the North Channel and raced neck and neck until they neared the Antrim coast, when one brother pulled ahead. The other, seeing he would lose, cut off his own hand and threw it ashore ahead of his brother, and thereby inherited the land. In that way, the red hand became a symbol of Ulster and Ireland.

A brisk wind whipped the bunting and flags as Governor Elliot W. Major of Missouri, his staff, companies of the Third Regiment of the National Guard from Kansas City, dignitaries from Illinois and Minnesota, and hundreds of townspeople all marched through the town of Carrollton, Missouri on a crisp autumn morning before the unveiling of the statue of General James Shields on November 12, 1914. Shields' widow, Mary, was there too, from New York, and the massive crowd parted to permit her automobile to get through, since she was too feeble to walk. Spectators, who craned their necks to see her, nodded and commented that she had been married a great man. They reckoned that it had taken about 30 or 40 years to get a proper perspective on their locally buried national hero and were satisfied that Shields' reputation, like good wine, had improved with time.

"He showed his record as a lawmaker and judge, as a State and National administrator of important office; he saluted with the jeweled Palmetto sword and bared his breast, marked with the crimson scar of the bullet wound of Cerro Gordo; his arm bore the scar of Chapultepec and the wound of Winchester; his Senatorial toga from Illinois was unsullied,"[2] eulogized Francis O'Shaughnessy special commissioner representing Governor Dunne of Illinois, just before Dr. Daniel F. Shields son of the dead General, lifted the flags from the draped statue, to resounding cheers and applause.

That bronze likeness of General Shields in full military regalia, a sword strapped to his left side, now stands as it did then, nearly a century ago, on a rose granite pedestal in the east courtyard of the Carroll County Courthouse with the words "Patriot" and "Statesman" inscribed in golden letters on the side, above the heads of heroic semi-recumbent youths. One youth holds an outstretched flail, the other a burning torch. On the front of the plinth is a plaque bearing the words, "Erected by the State of Missouri in recognition of his distinguished public service and exemplary private virtues." Few in that large

General Shields National Monument, St. Mary's Cemetery, Carrollton, Missouri erected by the US Congress in 1910. The General, his wife, and four of their five children are buried there.

crowd would have disputed that "The life of General James Shields reads like a romance - lawyer, judge, senator, farmer, knight-errant and General"[3] as Lillian Buttre observed in her brief sketch of the General published in 1880, a year after the General's death. Nor

11

would they have objected to the words of another scribe who noted, that Shields was "a man of the fourteenth century who came into the world 500 years too late."[4]

For all that, no one, then or now, has a stock explanation about how James Shields achieved what he did and both his friends and foes were bemused by his success. Gustave Koerner an Illinois Lieutenant Governor and close friend of Shields, stated that Shields "did not seek to rise in his party and... even despised popularity."[5] Some critics say he should be dismissed as merely a 19th Century Irish opportunist and adventurer, albeit a colorful one. Others maintain that he was lucky, simply a man in the right place at the right time. That fair winds of fortune just blew his ship away from shoals onto a favorable shore. But that is selling him far short of his true value. A lot of people arrive in the right place only to find they have ended up in the wrong. That was seldom James Shields' destiny, even though he did not enjoy unmitigated success. He set his sails to achieve a worthy destination and, though

Shields National Monument in St. Mary's Cemetery, Carrollton, from the rear

he often sailed close to the wind, reached it more often than not. For that he, and he alone, must be credited, since he was his own helmsman. Inheriting no wealth, he had no family connections that could open doors and ease his way up the stairway of success and no one before him was pointing the way. Nor, as far as anyone knows, did he start out with a grand master plan; he apparently improvised, and did so masterfully, making the most of his abilities with each opportunity, as it came along.

In retrospect, General Shields' success lay in his innate intelligence, his energy and drive, his ability to forge friendships and his captivating yet capricious personality. The last named sometimes worked against his better interests. More than once his hot-headedness caused him to be unseated but, though unhorsed, General Shields was generally able to scramble to his feet and continue the fray as though nothing untoward had happened. His resoluteness saw him through where more fainted hearted would have faltered. Sometimes his risk taking proved too rash, even for the radical century in which he lived. For one thing, it got him unceremoniously booted out of the United States Senate, forcing him to vacate his hard earned seat, when he first arrived. But undaunted, he bounced back. His comeback was so effective that he was elected twice to that august body for the same session of Congress. Paul Simon, the former US Senator and Presidential candidate, believed that Shields was the only person to earn that distinction.

Design on rear of plinth consisting of three metal ovals resting on a palm frond. The Great Seal of Missouri with twin bears is in the center, flanked on one side by an agrarian scene and on the other by a heroic figure rising to the clouds.

Perhaps the most striking example of General Shields' mercurial make-up occurred when he and Abraham Lincoln later 16th President of the United States, met with swords in hand to fight a duel to the death on the banks of the Mississippi River. That brouhaha, over a woman, Miss Mary Todd who would become Lincoln's wife some six weeks afterward, appears to have impacted the future President's personal life more than any Lincoln scholar has ever acknowledged. At the very least it can be said, it catapulted Lincoln, who until then had been an apathetic suitor, into a precipitous marriage. Lincoln biographer John G. Nicolay noted that the face off with Shields "in the opinion of many had its influence in hastening that event (marriage.)"[6] How different American history would have been if the Shields-Lincoln duel had actually transpired, no matter the outcome. According to the *Kansas City Times* "the world might never have known what presidential timber there was in Lincoln or what a soldier and statesman was General Shields."[7]

After the dust up, historian Charles Spencer Hart aptly summed up the subsequent

course of events for both men "Lincoln, as all the world knows, lived to become one of the great immortals. Had he, in those earlier days in Illinois been of the same hot-tempered breed as his challenger, very probably a pistol-ball would then and there have terminated his career. Shields also lived on; not to reach the same pinnacle as his adversary, but to gather a list of achievements few men in our

Grave marker of General Shields in Carrollton. The May 18, 1810 birth date is most likely incorrect. The General was probably born in 1806. Some think that Shields deliberately misstated his age for personal reasons.

history have equaled."[8] Shields, it should be noted, also enjoyed a prominent place in the social and personal life of Lincoln's greatest political foil and rival, Stephen Arnold Douglas, serving as best man at his wedding to Adele Cutts in 1856.

The Carrollton courtyard figure is just one of three statues of the General in the town and one of five altogether on public display in the United States. The other two in Carrollton are busts. One sits on a staircase inside the court house; the other is atop the Shields family plot in St. Mary's Catholic Cemetery at the north end of town, where the General is buried. Above that quiet country graveyard, the Stars and Stripes wave proudly each day, since it has been designated a national monument by Congress. According to the Carrollton town directory, the Shields' memorial is the only national monument located inside a private cemetery anywhere in the country.

Introduction

The two remaining statues of General Shields are located in the rotunda of the Minnesota State Capitol in St. Paul, and the Hall of Columns in Washington DC.[9] The St. Paul Capitol is impressive; its walls are lined with ornamental marble and more than twenty other types of polished stone, gold leaf and rich decorative art, stretching all the way from the ground to the dome high overhead. On the second floor balcony, the statue of General Shields is one of four large detached bronzes that stand like the four cardinal virtues, Strength, Temperance, Prudence and Justice, at each corner. This is the "grand floor" of the Capitol, with the Minnesota chambers of the Senate, the House of Representatives and the Supreme Court all leading off it, and where much political action takes place. It is exactly where General Shields would have chosen to be, in the thick of things, had he been consulted about where he should be situated. In Washington, the statue of General Shields is similarly located, close the center of action on the House side of the building. His effigy was placed in the collection of statues less than thirty years after Statuary Hall was created and was the nineteenth. At its unveiling in 1893, Representative William Springer explained the reasons why the Illinois Legislature thought that James Shields deserved the honor of being the first of two renowned citizens of the "Prairie State" to be enshrined there.[10]

"The State of Illinois, which gave to the service of our country such illustrious statesmen and heroes as Lincoln, Douglas, Grant and Shields, was not wanting in citizens upon whom could be justly conferred the honor of erecting statues to their memory in Statuary Hall. A brief reference to the life, character and services of General Shields will prove conclusively that in honoring his memory by placing his statue in Statuary Hall at the Capital of his adopted country, the State of Illinois made no mistake," Springer proclaimed proudly.[11]

When the statue was uncovered later that day by the General's daughter, Katherine, the Parthenon was filled to capacity. As William Condon, a Chicago congressman, recalled, "Every inch of standing room was filled by congressmen, clergymen, presidents of colleges and others of note."[12]

A poem, *The Sword of Cerro Gordo* was recited:

> *That peerless sword in fight was seen*
> *To flash upon a foreign strand*

> *By mountain ford and forest green*
> *And here in freedom's holy land.*
> *At Winchester it gained the day—*
> *And vanquished Stonewall in the fray—*

Shields' record, in addition to Senate service, includes being a Brigadier General in two major American conflicts - the Mexican-American and Civil Wars, where he was nominated for promotion to Major General but did not make it either time.

General Shields was much more than a soldier and politician; he was a Supreme Court Judge in Illinois and State Representative in two States. He served as a railroad commissioner in Missouri and Military Governor of Tampico, Mexico. The list goes on. He was offered but rejected the Governorship of Oregon and was elected to the U.S. House of Representatives from Missouri, but denied his seat. His career was colorful; he embraced life with gusto, and participated actively in some of the most tumultuous events that shaped the history of America and influenced their outcome. In short, General Shields was a man of stature, of action, and a leader who was not afraid to grasp the nettle to his bosom no matter how sorely it stung.

For all that, James Shields remains a shadowy figure shrouded in the haziness of history. Henry A. Castle, who wrote an account of Shields' life for the Missouri Monument Commission believed it was because General Shields "left no memoranda by which even the number and consecutive order of his public employments can now be ascertained. He left his exploits to write their own history."[13] Clearly, they have not and, it seems as though he has been airbrushed from the canvas of history since so few now know about him.

James Shields, ever the Irish rover, died on-the-road in Ottumwa, Iowa on June 1, 1879, where he had gone to deliver a lecture. As news of his death spread, businesses in the town shuttered their doors as a mark of respect for a man they considered an American patriot and hero.[14] There was a tremendous outpouring of grief and, the St Louis, Kansas City and Nebraska Rail Road wasted no time in designating a special funeral car to transport his remains back to Missouri. A committee of leading Iowans representing military, ecclesiastic, business and civic organizations immediately dropped what they were doing to escort the General's body back for burial. At Moberly, Missouri, the Iowa cortege was joined by a similar group of mourners from the "Show Me" state. A

16

band played a slow dirge and people crowded the depot to pay their respects, as the General's remains were transferred to the Wabash line. When the body finally reached Carrollton, a detachment from the Nineteenth U.S. Infantry Regiment provided an honor guard, as hundreds filed past to view it lying in state at the courthouse. An estimated crowd of 10,000 turned out for the General's funeral on June 4th and, as in Ottumwa, the businesses closed. The town's little church, which Shields had helped construct, could not accommodate everyone and, the obsequies had to be held in the open air. When Shields' statue was unveiled in the Carrollton town square more than 30 years later, the crowd was even larger than at his funeral.

US Army parading through Carrollton prior to the unveiling of Shields' statue in 1910.

Many of the events in the life of James Shields are well documented, but others, especially his early years in Ireland, are shadowy. A comment by General Shields that "the early history of most nations is pure fable"[15] could just as easily apply to himself. According to Judge Kevin R. O'Shiel the General's grand-nephew who changed his own last name from "Shields" back to the Irish "O'Shiel," there are "no letters or documents bearing on or connected with the General's life while he was in Ireland."[16] The few details we have about the General's early years have come mostly from General Shields' comprehensive but largely uncritical biography by William H. Condon, whose book appeared in Chicago in 1900. After Condon's visit to Ireland, where he interviewed local people, he returned to America and published his recollection of their recollection of Shields' youth from some seventy years earlier. Clearly, there was room for error as time dimmed people's memories.

For example, Condon wrote that James' father, Charles, died in 1812 and was buried in 'Canaghmore.' Then, he added that news of the Battle of Waterloo reached the assembled mourners at Charles' wake.[17] If that is correct, it must have been some obsequy, even by Irish standards. Waterloo did not take place until 1815, some three years later. And what about 'Canaghmore?' There is no such town in County Tyrone where the Shields lived; it turns out that 'Canaghmore' was probably a 'typo' for Donaghmore, the location of the only Catholic cemetery in the area at that time.[18]

Additional difficulties confront a researcher attempting to catalogue the life of James Shields. One is finding original documents, since most have been destroyed or lost and, another is the absence of personal diaries. Shields was a prolific letter writer, but there is no single repository of what he wrote. One must comb through the personal collections of others for his lively but elusive correspondence. Clearly, James Shields was not thinking of posterity, nor his place in history, as he went his merry way.

Statue of General Shields in the Carrollton town square in front of the Court House. The statue was erected by the State of Missouri in 1914. (Courtesy Carrollton Democrat.)

There are a great many stories told about James Shields, some of which seem apocryphal. One does not need to travel far to find the first bone of contention: determining the day on which he was born. General Shields always maintained he first saw the light in May 1810 - on either the 17th or 18th. In his application to become a US citizen in 1840, he affirmed May 17th 1810.[19] Since 1810 is the birth year carved in white letters on rose-colored United States Government granite over the General's grave in Carrolton, Missouri, it seems reasonable to assume that 1810 was the year. But compelling evidence points elsewhere. Gustave Koerner, who himself came into the world in 1809, was Shields' law partner and, in his memoirs, Koerner wrote "Intimate as I was with him (Shields), I never learned anything about his age. "Appleton's Encyclopedia" has it that he was born in 1810. But he was certainly several years older than I was when I first met him ...in 1836."[20] We cannot be sure now, since there was no registration of his arrival into the world and no birth certificate from those days in County Tyrone.[21] Dr. Frank Shields, a dentist and great grand nephew of the General living in Ireland, recalls hearing as a boy that Shields deliberately misstated his age because he wanted to appear younger than he really was.

On his maternal side, General Shields was descended from Catholic Scots. His mother, Catherine was a direct descendant of one of the MacDonalds of Glencoe who escaped the massacre of 1692 at the hands of King William's soldiery. He had fled across the North Channel from Scotland and found refuge in Ireland. The MacDonalds took up residence at Shinahergina in the neighborhood of Cookstown, County Tyrone.[22]

James Shields' paternal ancestors also originated in Scotland; they had come to Ireland as gallowglass[23] warriors for the O'Neills of Tyrone nearly 300 years before he was born. Their presence was recorded under various name spellings such as *O'Siadhail, O'Sheale, O'Shiel, Sheill, Shiel* and *Shields*. Mercenary military service in Ireland by Scots was not unusual then, since the Land of Alba, at its closest point, is only thirteen miles from Ireland. The Highlands, over the years, had proved a ready recruiting ground for bellicose Irish chieftains. In fact, by 1522, the practice of the Irish raising armies in Scotland raised such red flags in England that warships were dispatched to blockade the narrow but treacherous North Channel crossing to Ireland.

Upon arrival, the first Shields had to defend the inner reaches of the O'Neill Clan while the keepe was being rebuilt following its destruction in 1532 by the English Lord Deputy William Skeffington. Subsequently, the Shields were deployed on a narrow pass on Altmore mountain about eight miles west of Dungannon Castle. There they proved their fighting mettle for Con 'Bacach' O'Neill, and later his son Shane the Proud against both Irish and English. When Hugh O'Neill, the London-educated 'Earl of Tyrone,' became "The O'Neill" in 1593, and took up arms against his former mentors, the Shields stood by his side, employing the land's spiny hills, bogs and bulrushes to their advantage. Invaders often learned, to their chagrin, that they could lose a lot and have little but wounds to lick in the natural fortress of County Tyrone. Shields forebears had participated in some of Ireland's greatest military triumphs, especially against Lord Devereux, Earl of Essex in the Elizabethan War at the end of the 16th Century.[24] For that, tradition states, the O'Neills granted to the Shields the honor of adopting a coat of arms similar to their own.[25]

The Shields coat of arms consists of an argent lion rampant between two dexter hands couped at the wrist. On the crest, out of a ducal coronet, is an arm erect holding a sword proper. This is the obverse of the O'Neills. The Shields crest carries the Latin motto "Omne Solum Forti Patria" which translates "Every land is a brave man's home." In other words - courage and country, the title of this book.

After following O'Neill's footsteps through seven years of war, General Shields' forebears were involved in an Irish calamity on Christmas Eve 1601. Spanish troops landed in Kinsale in the South of Ireland and, O'Neill's men marched the length of the country in appalling winter conditions to join them. Unfortunately for the Irish, waiting troops under England's Lord Mountjoy met and crushed them. The Battle of Kinsale broke the back of Irish resistance, and extinguished forever the power of the Old Irish clans. It was a bitter pill to swallow, since the Irish had thought that combined with the Spaniards, they would be invincible.

The seventeenth century in Ireland, much like the preceding one, was turbulent, bloody and bitter. The native Irish were marginalized and could do little about it. There were sporadic but unorganized risings, which were easily put down, and were followed by savage reprisals. For want of any other champion, the Irish supported King Charles I against Parliament in the English

Statue of General Shields in the Carrollton town square from side. It stands about eighteen feet high.

Civil War. Following the King's execution in 1649, Lord Oliver Cromwell hastened to settle scores with the King's supporters across the Irish Sea. The Lord Protector captured Drogheda and put everyone in the town to the sword. After that, he laid waste to Kilkenny, Wexford and Clonmel and Irish resistance crumpled; in little over a year the

Roundheads had completely routed the Irish.

Perhaps recognizing the futility of armed resistance, the Shields stayed out of that fray and swapped their swords for plough shares. They became farmers around Altmore, the mountain they once guarded for the O'Neills. The Shields reverted to type toward the end of the 17th Century when they took up arms on behalf of Catholic King James II against Protestant William of Orange, but that campaign proved just as futile for the Irish as the previous ones that century. The forces of the last Catholic monarch of England were no match for William and Irish Catholics were routed at the Battle of the Boyne in 1690. Two Shields boys survived the Williamite War and fled to serve in foreign armies

as the "Wild Geese," the name given to expatriate Irish soldiers. Those Shields that remained resumed farming and even came to an accommodation with their Protestant landlords by obtaining a long-term lease for their land. Thus, the Shields were still

Portion of the massive crowd in front of the Carrollton Court House at the unveiling of the Shields statue in November 1914.

farming more than a century later when James was born in the first decade of the 19th Century.[26] Young James spent the first twenty years or so of his life in Ireland and came to America around 1826. As shall be seen, he would spend the rest of his life in America and would make a not insignificant impact on his adopted country.

21

Chapter 1
From the Green Hills of Eireann
to the Purple Plains of Illinois

White bird of the tempest! oh, beautiful thing,
With the bosom of snow, and the motionless wing;
Now sweeping the billow, now floating on high,
Now bathing thy plumes in the light of the sky,
Now poising o'er ocean thy delicate form,
Now breasting the surge with thy bosom so warm
Now darting aloft with a heavenly scorn,
Now shooting along like a ray of the morn...
Lines addressed to a Seagull by Gerald Griffin (1803 - 1840.)

The shores of Lough Neagh, the largest lake in Ireland or Britain, are emerald green, low lying and marshy. Around the lough, the land teems with water hens, snipe, grebe and other amphibious fowl who find rich pickings in the alluvial soil. Close to the lough, their chattering and splashing fractures the stillness, while the sun, in an amazing feat of alchemy, transforms their droplets into shimmering diamonds whenever it shines. The water birds, for the most part, spend their whole lives in the vicinity of the lake, seldom venturing further afield. This was not the case for many of the people born in the vicinity of the lough over the centuries. Some, through want or want of adventure, left this secluded corner of Ireland and traveled to America in search of something new. Included was James Shields, an enterprising young Roman Catholic of Irish-Scottish extraction, who reached America in the early 19th Century. As Shields packed his string bag, few could have predicted that he was destined to become the best known Hibernian of his day.

Westward from the lough, the ground slopes upward toward the prosperous market town of Dungannon - not in one continuous sweep, but as an undulating succession of thickets, fertile fields and sturdy farm houses. Today, the holdings are well maintained and demarked by trim hedgerows, stone walls and stout fences. Such was not the case when young James Shields went barefoot across those broad hills nearly 200 years ago.

Beyond Dungannon the terrain becomes hillier with smaller fields, higher hedgerows, and twistier roads, and soil is harsh and less hospitable. For all that, the landscape is dotted with picturesque villages, irregular shaped parishes and town lands, many bearing names left over from Celtic antiquity. Musical names like Donaghmore, Kilnaslee, Altmore and Cappagh, whose origins are as long lost now as the majestic oaks that once dominated those hillsides.

Altmore House near Cappagh, Co. Tyrone, where General Shields was born. The house remained in the Shields family until 1962, when it was sold and turned into an hotel. It was destroyed in the recent North of Ireland "troubles" and not rebuilt.

Life for most in these outposts of Ireland two hundred years ago proved formidable, with poverty seldom far from the door. There was the constant fear of crop failure and famine and yet, the austere environment offered one benefit; if you could survive here, you could anywhere. The Parish of Pomeroy undoubtedly provided excellent training for the many Irish, including young James Shields who left the area to settle on the American frontier over the years. The migrants were well inured to endure the hardships and privations they would face in the new world.

According to Shields family genealogy, James Shields was born on May 6th, 1806 or some four years earlier than his Government gravestone in Carrollton, Missouri indicates.[i] James was the eldest of three; his brother Daniel was born in 1808, followed by Patrick in 1810.[2] While such a sequence does not jibe with an 1810 birth date for James, the will of General Shields' father, Charles, provides additional support for 1806. Drawn up on January 22, 1810, the will was entered into probate in Armagh by Charles' brother Daniel on October 22, 1816. It established that James had been born before it was prepared because Charles made provision for three children - James and Daniel by name and a third '*in ventre sa mere*,' indicating Mrs. Shields was expecting Patrick, who was born on March 17, 1810.

James was raised by his mother after his father died on March 14, 1812. She was well positioned to care for her brood, since she was 30 years younger than her husband and a capable woman. Catherine never remarried and managed family affairs until her death at 68, on February 13,

Altmore House as it appeared in 1966 just prior to the "troubles."

1847, the year of the great Irish Famine.[3] In the early 19th Century, Irish farms were doing well, providing food supplies for Britain's Continental Campaigns against Napoleon. The Act of Union enacted some eleven years earlier, merging Ireland with England facilitated such trade between the two islands.[4]

James Shields as a young man growing up in Ireland, had both a typical and an unusual upbringing. He was probably five when his father died and does not appear to have been compromised by his father's premature death. Surrogates were readily available, since five of Charles' seven siblings were married, and living in the area. Thus, James had advantages, even though being born into a Catholic family did not proffer many at the time. His family was one with land and relative prosperity, a rarity in that time and place, since most Catholics were landless and poor. There was an extended family to provide emotional support and in addition to farming, the family operated a retail drapery business in Dungannon.[5] Shop-keeping was one of the few means of livelihood then permitted to Catholics. So, from his earliest years, James was exposed to life on the land and to trade in the town, and he had a better than average education as well.

The ban on Catholic education had been lifted shortly before the future General Shields was born and he was educated as a Catholic. Initially, he attended an informal "hedge school" where itinerant teachers provided instruction in Gaelic, and for a while, was tutored by a priest relative of his mother. Since there was no higher education for Catholics in Tyrone, Catherine enrolled her son in Terman, a Protestant grammar school in Carrickmore, about four miles from home, as he got older. There, under rector Rev. John Stewart, James was taught Greek and Latin. He had a facility with languages and knew both Irish and English; he was intellectually curious and did well academically. By accounts, James was an avid book lover, but was not merely a brainy bookworm. He was a witty conversationalist who liked to discourse on battles and military strategy and spent hours listening to veterans of the Napoleonic Wars who lived in the region.

Most of the military pensioners were old soldiers who had embarked from the Cove of Cork for Iberia with the Duke of Wellington in the second week of July, 1808. They sailed in the flotilla that spread out behind the British cruiser *Donegall,* as part of Wellington's 8,000 strong task force headed for Corunna in northwest Spain.[6] Once there, they had slogged through mud and merciless heat on the Spanish Peninsula against the well-drilled forces of the French. From first-hand exposure, they were versed in military tactics, knew what worked and what did not, and were only too happy to share their experiences with the keen young James. As Oliver Goldsmith observed in *The Deserted Village:*

> **The broken soldier, kindly bade to stay**
> **Sat by the fire, and talked the night away**
> **Wept o'er his wounds or, tales of sorrow done**
> **Shouldered his crutch and showed how fields were won...**

Altmore Mountain, where James Shields grew up. Its rugged wildness prepared emigrants for the privations they would face on the American frontier.

James whiled away many hours with Bernard MacGuckian, a British pensioner, who had seen action at Waterloo.[7] From this old war horse, young Shields was exposed to the rudiments of fencing, military drill and strategy, which he would put to good use in the far off valleys of Mexico and Shenandoah years later.

MacGuckian even provided his young charge with well-thumbed tracts on military tactics. According to William Condon, James practiced what he perused and did it in "live-fire" fashion. He organized groups of boys into rival military factions and ordered them into action, where they employed tapered sally rods against each other. Shields' side emerged victorious through his superior stratagems and there is no mention of anyone suffering serious injury from the sharpened sticks.

No one can be sure exactly why James Shields left Ireland, and embarked for America, since he never provided any public or private explanations. Even if he had, his accounts might have varied over time, depending on whom he was talking to, since he tended to play to audiences. James apparently never regretted his trans-Atlantic move, but occasionally became wistful about the 'Old Sod' later in life, at least in letters to his brothers in Ireland. That was after he had a family of his own, and was struggling to settle down on a Missouri farm.

"Dear brother, you write in the loving spirit of your boyhood days, and this is heartily reciprocated by me. I hope God will spare us both to guide and encourage our families for many years. This perfect Union that exists between the family on this side and that on the other side of the ocean is very consoling. My little ones are taught to regard themselves as part of the family at home; you and Daniel are doing the same by us at Altmore. This will make them feel that they are all members of an old Irish Catholic family that has always lived without reproach,"[8] he wrote nostalgically to Patrick in 1874

Probably not a single force pulled or pushed James to the New World. Times were hard economically for farmers after Waterloo. According to Yale historian Linda Colley, "The economy had been geared for so long to war that the outbreak of peace precipitated a severe slump in agriculture."[9] Shields migration most likely came about through a combination of factors. According to William Condon, James' mother wanted him to remain in Ireland and become a lawyer but at an early age James would have recognized there were not many career opportunities for a talented Catholic in Ireland, even one with distant high placed Protestant connections. Catholics remained barred from Government

Altmore River. Author is standing on the spot where the potentially deadly confrontation between Shields and British Army veteran, Thomas Brackenridge, took place around 1820.

and parliament remained the exclusive province of Protestants.

One of James' paternal uncles, also named James, was a pivotal factor in Young James' decision to strike out on his own. Certainly his family thought so. Uncle James,

Charles' eldest brother, had migrated to Colonial America when it was still under the British flag and had settled in Charleston, South Carolina. Like other members of the Shields family, Uncle James altered the spelling of his surname. He dropped the "d" and signed himself, in official papers, as James Shiels. While still a young man, Uncle James had left Ireland to study for the priesthood in France, because in the 18th century, the repressive Penal Laws barred such pursuit in Ireland.[10]

Terman Church Hall, Carrickmore, Co. Tyrone, where James Shields attended school. The building, constructed in 1815, has all its windows on the opposite side. View is from rear.

Finding he had no vocation for holy orders, Uncle James dropped out of divinity school and went to America. Returning home to Ireland was not an option since such "spoiled priests" were considered the salt that lost its savor. As embarrassments to their family, they were not welcome back.[11]

After spending most of his life in America, Uncle James went back to Ireland in 1817 and stayed for three months. Apparently sufficient time had elapsed since he skipped from the seminary to blunt any lingering family animosities. At the old home site, Uncle James and Young James hit it off and spent a lot of time together. This started on the day following Uncle James' arrival at Altmore. The uncle summoned James and his two brothers Daniel and Patrick to give to each a small gift. Young James was carrying a book; the text turned out to be a French grammar and his uncle quizzed him on it. Uncle James was astonished that his nephew could answer his questions. In subsequent meetings, Uncle James spoke glowingly of America and promised to give his nephew his large gold watch if he should ever come there.[12] The Shields family afterward attributed Young James' resolve to go to America to his uncle's visit.

How young James Shields got to America or where he first made landfall are unfilled gaps in the story of his life. There is no verifiable information; nothing has been uncovered that links him to any ships or sailings.[13] There are several versions, some contradictory, about how James Shields actually arrived. James, for his part, may have muddied the waters by concocting some of them himself. This, he did in a vain attempt to salvage his United States Senate seat after he was unceremoniously ejected from Congress in 1849. Still other versions may have been spread by individuals working on Shields' behalf. One account of his arrival states that he landed first on the shores of Canada and then made his way south to the United States. Another

Kaskaskia road sign today showing a population of 18. The area, now open farmland, was separated from the rest of Illinois by the altered course of the Mississippi in the latter 19th Century. Today, there is almost no visible trace of what was the first Capital of Illinois.

asserts that he first arrived in New York and there is even a suggestion in an early Illinois history that he entered through the port of New Orleans and made his way up the Mississippi River to Illinois.[14] Judith Moran, a Shields biographer, combined some of the versions into a plausible account by advancing the theory that James arrived first in Montreal and then continued to New York. If nothing else, this version makes economic sense, especially if James, as a youth of slender means, was paying his own passage.[15] In those days, it was much cheaper to travel to Canada than to the United States, because, following the War of 1812, the British Government encouraged and subsidized Canadian settlement in an effort to bulwark Canada against another American incursion.

According to family historian Francis Shields, young James traveled first to Montreal, where he wrote to his uncle in Charleston announcing his arrival and was disappointed when he received no reply. James then concluded that it was due to indifference on the part of his uncle and never tried to contact him again. Young James did not know that, while he was on his transatlantic voyage, his uncle, stricken by yellow fever, had passed away.

Supposedly, after that setback, James abandoned the idea of going to South Carolina, and finding himself alone and without friends, took the first situation that presented itself and became a merchant seaman. In this capacity, he made a number of voyages both to the Caribbean and back to Europe. The ship was eventually wrecked on the rocky Scottish shore, with Shields, the captain and another seaman the only survivors. They were rescued by a laird who lived near the coast and the gentleman, impressed with Shields intelligence and scholarship, asked him to stay and teach his sons. James then tutored the boys for several months, until he received a letter from his former employer, the captain of the lost ship. He had a new command and the letter invited James to sign on as first mate. James bid the Scottish family good bye, rejoined his old comrade, and made several more transoceanic voyages.

One day, as the ship was entering New York harbor, James, while stowing a sail, was knocked off the yardarm by a sudden wind gust. He fell to the deck, broke several bones, lost consciousness and lingered between life and death for several days. When he came to, he found himself in hospital run by nuns. There, he remained for three months while his bones knit back together and, during this time, he decided to quit the sea and settle in America. As soon as he recovered, he anglicized his name from the Irish *O'Shiel* to Shields and made his way to Charleston.

Just exactly when all this happened is uncertain. In his application for citizenship on October 19, 1840, Shields declared he had migrated to the United States while still a minor and that he "continued to reside within the United States three years next preceding his arrival at the age of 21 years."[16] By that reckoning, using 1810, the year he wrote on the naturalization form as his year of birth, he would have arrived in America in 1828, when he was 18. Of course, if he had been born in 1806, as appears more likely, the year of his arrival would have been 1824.

Two sources attest to Shields' South Carolina sojourn: the memoirs of Shields' former law partner, Lieutenant Governor Koerner,[17] and the obituary of James' first cousin Mary Quinn Tally, also from Ireland.[18] Young James Shields probably traveled from

30

Charleston to Kaskaskia on the Illinois frontier sometime in 1829 when he was 23 years old and how or why he got there is not clear. Prior to the War of Independence, Kaskaskia had been the largest town in Illinois with a population of 7,000, mostly French speaking inhabitants. The town had been founded by explorer Louis La Salle in 1683 and French troops, on the orders of King Louis XV, garrisoned it in 1710. Following the French and Indian (Seven Years) War, the British took over and Kaskaskians then lived under the watchful eye of troops stationed a few miles upriver at Fort de Chartres renamed Fort Cavendish. As an active trading center, Kaskaskia conducted more business

Mississippi River flows where the town of Kaskaskia once stood. Indentation at the top right is mouth of Kaskaskia river.

proportionally at the time of the Revolution, than did Chicago a century later.

The town was located on a flat outcrop at an acute Mississippi River bend and its strategic location, which assured its prosperity initially, eventually proved its undoing, when it was flooded and washed away.[19] When Shields got to Kaskaskia, its star was already on the wane, having lost its status as the Capital of Illinois to Vandalia some ten years earlier. Still, it remained a vibrant river port and served as a springboard for pioneers crossing the Mississippi into what had been Spanish and later French territory prior to the Louisiana Purchase of 1803.

Just as it is not clear what drew Shields to America, it is equally uncertain what took him to Illinois, or if he had seriously considered other options. As a man of ability and ambition, Shields would have recognized that Charleston in the 1820s was no place for a migrant without important contacts or considerable wealth. That city, first settled by English and Irish colonists in 1670, was the largest port south of Philadelphia at the time of the Revolution. But by the late 1820s, it had slipped into an era of quietude and decay and grass was growing in its streets, so light was the commercial traffic.[20] People had been leaving the coastal region and striking inland as the interior of the nation opened up, following a trail blazed by Lewis and Clark. A contingent of Presbyterian Irish had moved from South Carolina to Randolph County, Illinois, not far from Kaskaskia, around the turn of the nineteenth century. Having planted roots at Plum Creek near the mouth of the Okaw River, in what became known as "Irish Settlement," they prospered. Shields, while living in Charleston and pondering his future, may have learned of the affluent Irish Settlement and been lured by that. The fact that he was Catholic and they Protestant would scarcely have bothered him; he had been raised around Protestants, had been educated for a while in a Protestant school, and was comfortable with them.[21]

From contemporary accounts, we can surmise that, when Shields got to Kaskaskia, he would have been wide-eyed with the sights he saw. His senses would have been assailed with strange scenes, smells and sounds, different from anything he had witnessed before. People's attire and demeanor would have been markedly different. According to Governor Ford whose memoirs Shields edited and published, men wore raccoon-skin caps with the tail of the animals dangling down behind, blue linsey hunting-shirts with red or white fringe, buckskin breeches and deer-skin moccasins. They strutted around town with belts around their waists and butcher knives and tomahawks dangling from them. Women were clothed in "old sort of cotton or woolen frocks, spun, wove and made with their own fair hands, and striped and cross-barred with blue dye and turkey red."[22] Such fashions, as Ford noted, were in transition in 1830, the year after Shields arrived. Men were tossing away their coonskin caps for hats of wool or fur and "the deer-skin moccasin, and the leather breeches strapped tight around the ankle had disappeared before unmentionables of more modern material." Women were making even greater alterations in dress. For them, "their feet, before in a state of nudity, now charmed in shoes of calfskin or slippers of kid; and the head formerly unbonnetted but covered with cotton handkerchief, now displayed the charms of the female face, under many forms of bonnets of straw, silk or leghorn. The young ladies, instead of walking a mile or two to church on Sunday, carrying their shoes and stockings in their hands to within a hundred yards of their place of worship as formerly, now came forth arrayed complete in all the pride of dress, mounted on fine horses and attended by their male admirers."[23] People walking shoeless to church and then putting on footwear before entering the building must have reminded Shields of his own boyhood back in Ireland. He had walked barefoot across fields to school in Carrickmore with his boots laced around his neck because he had not wanted to get them worn or muddy.[24] Such profound changes in fashion on the frontier, along with newcomers arriving in the state each day, facilitated Shields' plan for the future, if it had already gelled in his mind. It enabled him to fit right in from the get go, assume the mantle of leadership when it was cast his way, and appear polished in a rough cut society. In short, the confluence of East and West in Illinois in the 1830s provided James Shields with a tidal opportunity, which he rode to success.

This statue of President Andrew Jackson in Washington D.C. is based on a heroic lithographic of Jackson at the Battle of New Orleans in December 1814. General Shields' Uncle James, the man who inspired Shields to come to America, reportedly fought alongside Jackson and was wounded in the leg during that battle. This statue by Craig Mills was the first equestrian statue cast in the United States. Shields probably attended its dedication in 1853. At that time skeptics did not believe it could remain standing because of the way the horse is balanced on its hind legs. Mills proved the sturdiness of his design by climbing onto the sculpture during the ceremony and throwing his full weight onto the front legs to show it was secure. Behind the statue, the White House and Washington Monument can be seen.

To support himself, Shields opened a school for adults and children shortly after his arrival in Kaskaskia. He had not graduated from teacher's college or university, but a diploma or certificate of higher education was unnecessary. Even with only a grammar school education, Shields would have been amongst the better educated on the frontier, since many were illiterate. And, as we know from his subsequent career, he would have more than held his own with most university graduates of the day. James was well equipped to teach; his grasp of English literature was extensive, as was his knowledge of world history, both ancient and modern.[25]

But Shields was too ambitious to remain in an academic role for long. As his mother had desired, he set his sights on becoming a lawyer, and entered the law offices of Senator Elias Kent Kane as a law clerk. It was a good choice, since Kane, the most distinguished individual of the day in Illinois, had been an architect of the Illinois constitution in 1818, and a leader of the Illinois State Democratic Party. Being articled to Kane was a move that would open a lot of doors, both legally and legislatively, for Shields and it was a step he never would regret.

Recognizing that his future lay in his own hands, the industrious Shields applied himself diligently, in fact, more than most apprentice law students, and at the same time he continued to teach school.[26] He completed his studies within the short space of two years and was admitted to the Illinois bar in 1832. James, 26 at the time, with the world or at least Illinois as his oyster, then began looking around for fresh challenges worthy of his attention. He would find them further upstate in Illinois, where he would remain, more or less, for the next quarter century.

Chapter 2
From School House to State House:
Belleville and Beyond

They came from ports in Galway, from Cork and Baltimore
On the promise of more money, they had never known before
To carve a new beginning in a land of Liberty,
They said goodbye and sailed across the sea.
Bid farewell to famine, it's off to Amerikay
To work as a navigator for ninety cents a day
And hoped to dig a fortune by the time they reached LaSalle
On the Illinois and Michigan Canal.
The I & M Canal by Kevin O'Donnell
(courtesy of Tour Merle Music/BMI)

Recognizing that Kaskaskia's best days were already behind it, and that opportunity lay elsewhere, Shields, once he became a lawyer, closed the school he had created, and moved almost immediately to Belleville, St. Clair County some 50 miles to the north. The town was booming and offered fertile ground for a man of Shields' talent. The settlers were mostly German, but that would prove no barrier for James Shields, the newly minted lawyer from the Emerald Isle. Shields hung out his shingle in 1833, and as was the custom, his legal practice encompassed a *mélange* of cases, ranging all the way from land transfers and title registration to torts and capital crime. For his first three years, Shields practiced solo, riding the judicial circuit, working long hours, and making himself accessible to all. Prospective clients were often farmers who came to town to buy equipment and supplies, and transact other business all in a single day. When they sought legal services, they generally wanted them on the spot and, if an attorney was not there, the farmer went to one who was. Shields quickly recognized that he was losing business while out on circuit in the second judicial district and surmised that if he was in partnership he could do better. But before entering a partnership he knew he had to prove himself and eagerly awaited such an opportunity.

Belleville, established a mere fifteen years earlier, was growing rapidly and the

town was filled to the brim with newcomers. By 1835, Illinois had a population of 269,
974 and Belleville was one of its larger towns.[1] Buildings, mostly of brick, were
sprouting by the day, and were predominantly of German town house design. The
Germans, as a group, were thrifty, industrious and well educated and, by 1836, the town
had established a public library (now the oldest in Illinois.) In 1837, the population of
Belleville was 700, and three years later the population had risen to 1,207[2] while the
number of homes had doubled. Shields recognized that being able to provide these
immigrants with quality legal services would be profitable. But how to do it? Many of the
Germans spoke little or no English and Shields, despite his facility with languages, knew
no German. To gain their confidence, he needed an entrée and decided to affiliate with an
existing law practice serving the German community. Then, Shields came into contact
with the law partnership of Adam Snyder and Gustave Koerner and since Snyder was an
active politician, that was a plus in the eyes of the Irishman.

The three attorneys first met in 1836 while defending a man named Gannett
accused of murder in Clinton County. Koerner later described in his memoirs what
transpired.

"I opened the case" he wrote in his terse style. "Shields examined the witness
with skill. Snyder made a brief but very impressive speech. It was a tolerably bad case,
but we succeeded in clearing our client, a farmer living where Aviston now stands."[3]

Following that success, Snyder and Koerner liked what they saw in Shields and he
in them, and they decided to affiliate. The following year, Snyder became a member of
Congress and was the Democratic candidate for Governor of Illinois in 1842, when he
met a premature death. Synder and Koerner accepted the young Irishman gladly. When
Snyder bowed out to represent the State of Illinois in Washington in 1837, Koerner and
Shields commenced a profitable partnership that continued for three years, until Shields
moved to Springfield and became primarily a politician.[4]

Before joining Snyder and Koerner, Shields had striven to build up his law
practice, while, at the same time, his budding penchant for politics began to flower. He
started frequenting political meetings and soon it was obvious that the political process
was becoming an *idée fixe*. Still, by the mid 1830s, politics had not yet consumed him
and law was his main interest. He was readily sought after, especially for knotty

courtroom cases and faced off against some of the biggest and brightest at the Illinois Bar, including Lyman Trumbull and later Abraham Lincoln, both of whom were destined to lock political and personal horns with Shields over the years.

It was fortunate for all three men and their politics that the "Prairie State" welcomed newcomers, since they were from out of state. Six months residence and being a taxpayer was all that was required, either to vote or run for elected office in Illinois, no matter a person's place of origins. The state was growing rapidly and close to half its population had been in the state less than five years, which made Shields by 1835 one of the longer term residents.

Legal Notice section of the *Representative and Belleville News*, Nov 11, 1837, advertising the professional services of Gustave Koerner and James Shields. Subsequent notices advertise the legal services of Lyman Trumbull, Shields' *bete noire*, the transfer of business from Snyder and Koerner to Koerner and Shields, and the sale of timbered lots belonging to Judge Sydney Breese by Koerner. Breese, U.S. Senator from 1843 – 49, would be ousted by Shields, who in turn would be defeated by Trumbull in 1855.

According to Koerner, Shields "was well grounded in the principles of law - rather more so than most of his rivals. He argued closely and to the point."[5] Not all of Shields' cases involved settling estates, the transfer of land or defending murderers. Some involved the highest matters of commerce and Government. For instance, Shields was retained by St. Clair County in what, until then, was the biggest civil case in its history.

The County was pitted against the powerful Wiggins Ferry Company, a steamship line, and Shields against his future friend Stephen Arnold Douglas. It was definitely a convoluted scenario of litigation making strange bed-fellows. Douglas was the lead lawyer for Wiggins and Shields for the County was assisted by Lyman Trumbull. The case was about monopoly, and the fact that with no bridges across the Mississippi, everything had to be transported by boat. The shipping company maintained that it had been granted exclusive rights to ferry everything across, to the consternation of the County. The trade was highly lucrative and the County wanted to introduce ferry service of its own, contending that competition would lower prices and promote commerce to the benefit of everyone. The hard fought case ended with victory for Shields and the County; Wiggins lost its monopoly and Shields' won an enviable reputation.

Most agreed that James Shields owed his success at the Bar to his wit, winning ways and an uncanny ability to boil a case down to basics. As Koerner commented, he focused on the main issues and presented his arguments using a shrewd combination of logic and humor. He was able to influence juries by not beating about the bush, and relating to them on an emotional level.[6] This was in marked contrast with other litigants in court, who not infrequently found themselves lost for words and resorted to attacking opponents physically. They would try to maim them by gouging out their eyes or biting off a nose or an ear.[7] Early Illinois Governors often blasted the poor "class of men who had taken up the study of Blackstone."[8] Given such anemic opposition, it was perhaps inevitable that the red-blooded Shields should shine.

If law was Shields life, politics was his passion. Throwing himself into the political arena with all the gusto he could muster, he was attracted to the Democratic Party because of its egalitarian embrace of all comers. He approved its encouragement of territorial expansion, the extension of political rights to all free-men, whether American-born or adopted citizens, and its opposition to centralized policies, such as a general system of internal improvements, protective tariffs and particularly a national bank.

Of the Party he wrote, "But the cardinal principle of that (Democratic) party -the cherished principle of every liberal heart - is its sacred regard for the natural and political rights of individuals. The natural rights of man, the rights with which every human creature is endowed by his creator..., this glorious freedom which ennobles human

38

nature, has been secured to America by the triumph of the democratic principle."[9]

James Shields' admiration for the Democrats was reciprocated by their increasingly high regard for him. Acknowledging his obvious ability and talent, Party leaders soon gave him his chance. Shields attended the Democrats' Randolph County convention in 1835 and, to his delight, was invited to run for the Illinois General Assembly. Without hesitation, he accepted, took leave of his law practice and went on the stump.

Until that time, Illinois politics had been factious in nature, a place where individuals with strong personalities like Elias Kent Kane and Ninian Edwards, a former Governor, could attract followers, gain support and set the political agenda. In that process, the national political platform was generally subordinated to the aims of state politicians, but President Andrew Jackson's incumbency changed all that.[10] With "Old Hickory" in the White House, the Democratic Party crystallized into an organization where loyalty to the President was a preeminent qualification for national Party political support.

The Whigs were slow to respond and paid a high price. They did not become a national unity Party until some twenty years later, which gave the Democrats a distinct edge on the local and national scene for the next quarter century. This worked to Shields' advantage. As a candidate in his first campaign, James Shields did everything he needed to do: putting in long hours, paying homage to important constituencies and providing stirring speeches. He contributed generously to Party coffers, as was required. A candidate was expected, not only to support the Party but, to fund his own campaign as well. At the same time, while reaching for the heights, Shields did not lose touch with the lowly or common man. In keeping with convention, he plied the electorate with potent messages and liberal amounts of liquid refreshments, which resonated well with voters and, in return, they returned him for Randolph, a county that was largely Whig.

When Shields took his legislative seat in the lower house at a special session of the Illinois Assembly of 1836,[11] he sat with a talented class of lawmakers, the equal of which perhaps has never since existed in one assemblage in Illinois. Out of that Legislature there was one who became United States President, another, a viable candidate for the Presidency, a third, a candidate for the Vice Presidency; seven who became Senators for the United States; one attained the rank of Major General; another a Brevet Major General; there were a dozen Colonels; eight became United States Congressmen; three, Lieutenant Governors; two, Attorneys Generals; two, State Treasurers; three, State Auditors; two, Ministers Plenipotentiary and many became Judges of the Supreme and Superior Courts.[12] They included still well-remembered names like Whig leader Abraham Lincoln and his organ-voiced opponent, Stephen Arnold Douglas known as the "Little Giant" because he was only 5' 4" with a large head and broad shoulders. Their debates would rivet the nation, and define unmistakably the issues of the day for the country some twenty years later. Shields, both in debate and as a political strategist, was capable of holding his own with them all.

SENATOR FROM MISSOURI.

Signature of General Shields when he was Senator from Missouri. By then his handwriting was showing signs of coarseness associated with age.

The election of Shields was both a political and personal triumph; though not native born, he showed he was able to connect with and capture the hearts of the voters. This was no mean task, since there was no ethnic base of Irish support for him, and he had to reach out to the mainstream. Of course, he was not hurt by the fact that many of the voters in Illinois were immigrants themselves, and his foreign origins were less of a thorny issue than they would have been back East. The Gaels did not show up in Illinois in large numbers until the next decade and Shields never relied on the Irish to elect him to political office. When the Irish arrived, they were drawn mainly by construction of the Illinois and Michigan Canal.

The "I & M" Canal, as it became known, was the major public works project in Illinois for the following decade. It was poorly managed and lurched from one fiscal crisis to another, nearly bankrupting the State more than once. Designed to provide transportation from the eastern seaboard via the Erie Canal and Great Lakes to the Gulf of Mexico, it was destined to open up Northern Illinois to settlement and commerce. It was also destined to cause Shields innumerable fiscal headaches when he was State Auditor some six years later. The Irish who flocked to the state to construct the canal are now largely forgotten, but are remembered in a poignant folk song penned by Kevin O'Donnell and performed by the musical group Arranmore:

> *In the corner of a graveyard in the Parish of St. James*
> *Lies a noble Irish navvy who had pioneered these plains*
> *Who fled the great oppression just to build himself a home*
> *Now it's the only piece of sod he'll ever own...*
> (courtesy of Tour Merle Music/BMI)

By his election to the Illinois assembly, Shields demonstrated he was able to adapt and fit right in. He was accepted where other immigrants were not, at a time when nativism was raising its head to shut them out. Reasons for his success included his excellent education and well-honed verbal skills; his eloquent command of English, and his ability to establish rapport with any audience. Not infrequently, immigrants especially the Irish, were uneducated and spoke only their native tongue, at least when they first stepped ashore. When they eventually picked up English, they seldom mastered it fully, always sounded alien and were subjected to suspicion and ridicule. While Shields retained a touch of the brogue in his voice, he had other things going for him. He had flashing eyes that "shot fire" when he was crossed, a deep sense of commitment to his adopted land as strong as any native and an ability to develop and project a broad vision of America, beyond narrow ethnic and regional economic concerns. He was well able to communicate this vision and commitment in terms that did not talk down to audiences, who resonated to his tabor like tones.

William Condon the Chicago congressman who wrote Shields' biography, and had known Shields personally, had this to say "Shields was a man of medium height, five feet nine, slight in build, urbane witty, bright, intelligent, resolute and energetic. In dress he was scrupulously neat, in manner courteous, frank and manly. In speaking he was lucid, forcible and fearless and always master of his subject and well equipped for attack or defense. He was a well read lawyer, thoroughly versed in the principles of law and equity, and was warmly attached to his profession"[13]

Adam Snyder, son of Shields' law partner, though less partisan, was also complimentary. Snyder said that Shields was "raw boned, straight and soldier-like with ruddy complexion and dark hair, his face and manners were singularly pleasing and ingratiating. Large-hearted and generous to a fault, he was idiotic in all details of business and finances, and but for his pension would have died in abject poverty. He was a fluent, witty and eloquent speaker, and though not a profound scholar, no one ever made a better display of his natural and acquired abilities than he did. No one was ever more loyal to his country, to his friends, and to the loftiest conceptions of honor and justice than was Gen'l Shields."[14]

Others echoed the same remarks. Henry A. Castle in describing Shields in the Illinois Legislature, stated "Shields easily took his place on terms of equality in this distinguished company (the Illinois assembly.) His personal appearance and manners were engaging. He was five feet-nine inches tall, of fine figure and graceful bearing. His voice was well modulated, his speech frank, clear and resolute. He was prominent in debate and influential in council. It was a critical time in the affairs of Illinois, the inauguration of a policy of extensive public improvements, in which the youthful legislator bore a progressive part."[15]

Gustave Koerner, Shields' law partner, perhaps more analytic than anyone else of the man he called "my most intimate American friend," applauded the Irishman's personality and honesty, but rapped Shields as "vain" and occasionally "egotistical." "I knew all his weaknesses and his vanity amused me" said Koerner. "He was very ambitious, and, like most ambitious men, on occasions, quite egotistical."[16]

In his memoirs, written after Shields' death, Koerner noted "Shields was of medium height, very broad shouldered, and with rather long arms. His complexion was fair and healthy, his eyes gray and very sparkling. In a passion they seemed to shoot fire. His hair was dark brown and his features quite regular. In conversation he spoke rapidly and vivaciously showing very little trace of the Irish brogue. He was not an orator but a ready debater. His mind was discriminating. He succeeded better with the court than with the jury and on the stump. Indeed, he seldom addressed large crowds in election times. He was not given to intrigues, was careless about money, and, in spite of his many opportunities to enrich himself, never accumulated property. Upon the whole his ideas were lofty."[17]

On the other hand, the *History of Sangamon County* noted a much higher regard for Shields' oratorical prowess, stating "No more captivating speaker, for the masses, ever mounted the stump in Illinois unless it may have been the lamented Colonel Baker."[18] Shields retained a slight Irish lilt in his voice for all his days. Though times turned hard for him toward the end and his health was failing, he maintained an optimistic outlook. A reporter for the New York Times in 1877 observed that Shields was "genial and soft spoken" and he had "a keen eye and something like the "brogue" in his speech... He speaks without the least bitterness toward any of his contemporaries either in civil or military life and evinces the warmest interest in the prosperity and welfare of his adopted country."[19]

Despite those mostly flattering accolades, there is evidence suggesting that Shields, while undoubtedly warm hearted, was not one to pull his punches in a fight. He had his share of spats, could be mercurial and, at times, was quick to take offense but just as swift to make up again. Occasionally hot headed and headstrong, he was not one to bear a grudge, which was evident from early in life. According to William Condon Shields showed that characteristic as a lad in County Tyrone. At a gathering of locals, Thomas Brackenridge, a man of fiery temper and domineering character who was a retired sergeant-major of the Connaught Rangers, "was lauding the British soldiers to the skies for their valor." James, then a 15 year old stripling, protested the lavish praise being poured on the Tommies. The irascible veteran, angered at the interruption, called Shields a liar. This time Shields did not respond with words.

With lightening rapidity, he jumped forward and struck the ex-sergeant-major forcefully across the face. The old soldier spluttered an expletive and demanded that Shields apologize as the crowd reached back in alarm. James defiantly stood his ground. The veteran took a quick breath, narrowed his eyes and insisted on an apology or satisfaction - flintlock pistols by the Altmore River at dawn. Shields would not yield and the ex-soldier said he would supply the weapons. Though bystanders tried to intervene, neither Shields nor Brackenridge were prepared to back down, and insisted on going through with the deadly ritual.

Next morning, the two men stood shivering on the river bank in the gray light of a damp dawn. As they loaded and cocked their pistols in the mist, bystanders again tried to intervene, but to no avail. Counting out ten paces along the uneven riverbank, the two men turned, aimed and pulled their triggers. Onlookers winced, expecting the worst, but nothing happened. There was no sound other the continuously gurgling brook, the screech of a distant owl and droplets dripping from the trees. The two remained erect, looking puzzled first at each other and then at their guns. The moisture had dampened their powder and neither flintlock ignited and fired. As they struggled to get their guns into working order, bystanders again asked them not go through with the duel. This time wiser sentiment prevailed and both Shields and Brackenridge agreed that honor had been assuaged. They called off the duel and left the field as friends.[20]

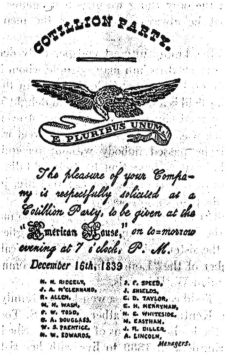

Invitation to the Grand Ball celebrating the relocation of the Illinois State Capital to Springfield in 1839. The Committee included: Shields, Lincoln, Douglas, Merryman, Whiteside and Lincoln's friend Joshua Speed.

James Shields had the necessary literary and editorial skills to write an autobiography if he had put his mind to it, but never did. Why not is anyone's guess. It is possible he was too active a man living too full a life to take the time. Because he was so involved with whatever was going on in the world each day, he did not permit himself to slow down and focus on either the past or future. It is axiomatic that adventurers seldom take time to write unless something unusual intervenes.[21] He was a prolific letter writer and corresponded widely, but most of his letters and other communications have been lost. Even contemporaneous secondary source material, such as newspaper accounts of his speeches and activities, is scarce and, like his career, strewn to the four winds. We are not totally bereft of firsthand Shields material and, a number of letters dashed off in his strong but scrawly hand remain and these provide a window into Shields' personality and make up.

There is an old saying that "every picture tells a story," and the opposite also is true; every story, be it written or oral, paints a picture. Graphologists believe that a great deal can be learned about individuals from examining the pictures generated by their handwriting and methods of expression. This can be deduced not only from reading the lines, but between and outside them as well. Handwriting, they contend, creates a "frozen moment," showing a person's mental make up at the point of putting pen on paper. This, so the theory goes, enables people to peer inside the mental make up of that person at a later time. Shakespeare certainly believed that when he wrote "Give me the handwriting of a woman, and I will tell you her character" as did French novelist Guy de Maupassant, who penned "Dark words on white paper bare the soul."[22] Thomas Carlyle, the English historian proffered a similar view when he said "In every man's writings, the character of the writer must lie recorded."[23] Today, graphologists claim to be able to go further, that analysts can conclude with reliability, who is at ease with the world, and who is anything but, from examining specimens of handwriting. How a man or woman forms and places words on the page makes a statement about them and their mental make up.[24]

Like fingerprints, each person's handwriting is unique which becomes apparent at an early age. Each pupil in a school may learn from the same teacher and the same cursive work book, but the end results, as everyone knows, are very different. Some students end up with writing that is symmetrical, legible and a joy to read, while others have penmanship that is erratic, jerky and difficult to decipher. But, though different from each other, an individual's writing pattern once it is established, continues, by and large, in the same format for life. Thus, handwriting becomes fixed and can tell us as much and possibly more than a photograph or even first hand statements about any given individual.

The first observation of the handwriting of James Shields is that almost everything is written in an unwavering angular script that is difficult to decipher. Shields has narrow page margins with text running close to the edges and also to the top and bottom of each sheet. There are strong bold strokes of consistent pressure throughout, and some rare flourishes, additional strokes to embellish a word. Shields' base lines - actual lines of text - and individual words are evenly spaced and the base lines themselves are as unwavering as if created by a compositor. They neither arch nor dip nor rise or tail off. Overall, there is a marked sense of orderliness, though there are sometimes extraneous ink drops or smudges. Individual letters themselves are slanted consistently to the right, at about the angle of a fada in Irish or a grave in French, and Shields does not avail of an up stroke at the start of any word.

Analyzing Shields' handwriting further reveals that his ovals, the letters "o" and "a," are a mixture of closed and slightly open loops on the top or right side, while his capitals are large in proportion to lower case letters. For the most part, except in his signature, there is an absence of flourish or ornateness. In fact, the only letter where there is some degree of flourish, that this author came across, was written to Judge Sidney Breese on October, 28th, 1843 as the judge was leaving to take up his seat in the Senate.[25] In that cordial letter from Edwardsville, Illinois, Shields uses about a half dozen extra loops and extensions apparently for emphasis.

Most of the letters in Shields' words are joined continuously with strokes that are neither narrow nor wide so there are almost no discordant spaces. His terminal "ds' are rounded backward on top, much like a "d" in Old Irish or Greek. His "t" crosses regularly begin across the down stroke of the "t" and are exaggerated to the right above the next three or four letters of a word. His "i" dots are never situated directly over the "i" but are displaced to the right of the following letter. Unlike his other terminal letters, Shields' ending "y" finishes with a down stroke and sometimes just the slightest trace of a hook at the bottom. His writing is notable in that it does not employ unusual punctuation or signs of emphasis, such as exclamation marks.

The one place where conventional or even inhibited individuals tend to let themselves go is in their signature. An autograph serves as an individual logo; it is a personal advertisement to the external world. Generally it is something people have practiced and is not infrequently more ornate and twice as large as their regular writing. A signature accentuates the dominant features of individuals and is a key to revealing the most about them.

In his signature, Shields is no different from most people. His letters lean to the right as in his regular script, are somewhat larger, and are penned with more flourish, especially the "J" of James and the "S" of Shields. These are embellished with curly "qs" at the bottom, and the signature is invariably flushed right and is never in the center of a page or on the left. When Shields was christened, he was not given a middle name and he never added one. He did, however, shorten his first name whenever he wrote. He never signed it in full on any document, be it personal or official. It was always abbreviated to "Jas" with a large "J," a smaller "a," about half the size of the "J" and an "s" about half the size again of the "a." All very orderly, in a 4:2:1 mathematical ratio. A striking characteristic is that the "s" in Jas is superimposed upon a period that is really beneath the stroke connecting the "a" to the "s."

What can be made of all this? The first observation is that Shields almost invariably wrote with a hasty hand. This indicates that he was generally in a rush and anxious to get to the next order of business, traits that had the potential to make him impatient and prove an irritant to others. To combat that, he would have had to consciously rein himself in. Others seldom found him irascible, which suggests that he was mostly successful in doing so. His angular, difficult to read handwriting suggests that he was not overly concerned with what others thought of him and it was not his custom go out of his way to woo others or create a favorable impression. If someone could not read his writing, that was their shortcoming, not his. This is consistent with Koerner's impression that he was not without a certain degree of egotism and arrogance, but at the same time, he would have come across as self-assured, confident and a leader to be followed.

Shields' evenly spaced words are consistent with a well-balanced and orderly mind. He would have been methodical, analytical and a problem solver. His right leaning letters denote optimism and self confidence and the even base lines indicate that he was level-headed and realistic. The fact that Shields' letters are generally connected indicates strong internal logic and powers of deduction. Shields post placed "i" dots indicate that he looked ahead with impatience and impulsiveness. The long "t" bar over other letters is suggestive of domination and authority.

Tall capitals are associated with pride, vanity and conceit. Shields had these traits to be sure, but his capitals were not disproportionately large, so none of these characteristics would have been extreme. The absence of beginning up strokes indicates directness and efficiency. The terminal "y" down stroke goes along with impatience and irascibility. The up-sloping "d" is associated with culture and discriminating literary taste while the tall looped "J" is associated with a love for intellectual work, for making speeches and organizational talent. Shields slightly open ovals indicate that he was mostly outgoing, an extrovert who would have been frank, sincere and assertive. He would have made friends easily and others would have gravitated to him, finding him pleasant and engaging. His use of the whole page without crowding the words suggests his basic nature was to be thrifty but not stingy; he would have cut his suit according to his cloth. He acknowledged that characteristic at least tangentially in himself. In a letter to his brother Patrick, he wrote, "Life has taught me the necessity of teaching the young habits of thrift… and to be provident."[26] From the accounts of others, it is known that he was generous to a fault, so he must have labored against his basic nature for that. In fact he also acknowledged that tangentially about himself as well. "Oh, I had to unlearn so much before I began to learn that the wonder is I am able to accomplish so much."[27] Conventional writers tend to sign letters in the center or on the left. Shields' signature, invariably on the right side, indicates that he had a tendency towards imprudence and the unconventional.

There is nothing in Shields handwriting to suggest that he was devious or possessed negative traits such as suspicion, paranoia, unfriendliness, hostility and dishonesty. Overall, his handwriting supports the observations that Shields had a logical mind, made friends easily, was gracious in manner and hampered by few liabilities. This would have made him a potent politician and a wise and learned professional no matter what field of endeavor he pursued

Copy of letter from Shields to unidentified Democratic County committeeman in 1844. The letter seeks support for Shields next time around for the Congressional seat of Robert Smith, the Alton businessman, who defeated Shields for Congress the previous year.

Written in Shields' typical scrawl, the words are evenly spaced using all of the page, but are not easily deciphered.

The letter contains some flourishes and dashes for periods at most of the sentence breaks. (For typescript see Appendix U)

Chapter 3
Trumped by Trickery:
Shields in Springfield

Cowslips, sweet lips, smelling of the summer
Coming with the cuckoo, bringing in the May,
Lifting heads in pastures, where the cattle spare you,
Waiting to be gathered when the children come to play
Daffodils were golden, nodding in the uplands,
Golden in the marshes flares the marigold:
Softer hued the cowslips, winsome and sweeter —
Sure the soul of flowers is the odor that they hold.
Cowslips by Stephen Lucius Gwynn (1864 - 1950.)

It is axiomatic that just about everyone has a hero, an idealized person, whom they find a source of inspiration and light. For some, it is a religious or political figure; for others, perhaps, a sports champion or poet. For James Shields, the hero he most wanted to emulate was Andrew Jackson, America's Seventh President. Like Shields, Jackson's forebears had traveled the route from Ulster, and Scotland before that to the United States. Throughout his life, Shields spoke glowingly of "Old Hickory," the man who placed his life on the line for America, and his hallmark stamp on the national Democratic Party. Shields and the "Hero of New Orleans" were endowed with many similar characteristics, which is the probable reason he identified so closely with Jackson. Jackson, a self made man, was a realist who harbored few pretensions. He showed himself to be a warrior, a son of the frontier and was less schooled formally than many of his political rivals. At the same time, he possessed an indomitable will and great moral courage and stamped himself indelibly on the national consciousness.[1] Shields too was carved from similar stock; he was a person of the people who emerged from humble circumstances, and through his own efforts scaled the steep stairway of success.

There were other similarities as well: the seventh President had fought a duel in 1806, which far from shrinking his stature, probably enhanced his standing in Shields' eyes. Jackson's deadly confrontation with Nashville lawyer, Charles Dickinson, was over what men often saw fit to duel about: a woman's honor. Dickinson had insulted Jackson's wife, Rachel, and paid for it dearly, in keeping the social convention of the time. To Shields way of thinking, such potentially fatal encounters were a legitimate means of settling scores and, Shields, himself, was involved in several such episodes, both as a principal and a second over the years. He came within a hairsbreadth of dueling to the death with Abraham Lincoln which will be discussed in detail later; was a second for William C. McKinney in his set to with Lyman Trumbull in 1839, and Shields was named second in 1852 for Democratic Congressman William H. Bissell in his dispute with Jefferson Davis, the future Confederate President.

State Capitol of Illinois, Vandalia (1819 - 39,) where James Shields took his seat as State Representative in 1836. Vandalia marked the end of the Cumberland Road, an overland route traversed by many early settlers.

As shall be seen, Shields could well have been talking of himself while paying public homage to Jackson in a presentation in Sacramento, California in 1860. There, Shields stated "Of all the men that ever lived, Jackson was the most fearless. There was on God's footstool neither man nor thing that, in pursuit of duty, could make that dauntless heart quail. Never was there courage like that since the days of Julius Caesar. The intellect of the time misconstrued his courage as lawless rashness, and yet he surpassed his contemporaries in wise prudence as much as in courage. He was able to employ all men and means for his own objects."[2]

To imply that Shields simply fashioned his style and manner on Jackson alone would be doing the Irish-American a disservice. Shields was his own man through and through, a person of unique strengths and sustenance, but also with his own peculiar quirks and shortcomings. For one thing, in an age not known for introspection, Shields was a keen student of people, showing unique insight into the duality of human nature. He recognized the bisexual balance of people's emotions, make up and motivation, long before the birth of psychoanalysis or psychiatry. For example, while speaking of President Jackson, at a time when Sigmund Freud was barely a toddler, Shields noted "His great distinguishing characteristic was his all achieving, all subduing will. In all past history, only Hannibal, the terror of Rome, was his equal in that respect. Yet his was a dual nature. Underlying all this strength of character - this great, strong, inflexible, masculine nature - was a tender, gentle, devoted feminine nature and this complexity of character was perhaps what puzzled the intellect of the time. The intellect of America rejected Andrew Jackson but the heart of America accepted him."[3] Such perceptive observations set Shields apart from his contemporaries; it showed him to be a sensitive and discerning individual, who was able to peer behind the mask of human veneer, in an era not especially known for it.

Thus, when Shields took his place in the Illinois assembly in Vandalia in 1836, he was well equipped intellectually and by inclination to hold his own. He demonstrated no sense of inferiority, was not cowed by the esteemed company he was keeping, and participated fully in the political process. Shields was convinced, like President Jackson, that the Democrats were truly the Party of the people, while the opposition Whigs were of and for the wealthy. This simplified things for Shields, even though it was not really accurate. In actuality, a majority on either side of the aisle were well to do; they had to be. Only a man of means could afford to run for political office, because candidates for either Party were expected to fund their own campaigns and contribute $250 to Party coffers. This was a considerable sum, since the average pay for even skilled work was only $1 per day or $300 annually.

In that Tenth Illinois General Assembly, half of the representatives were affluent farmers (46 out of 91) and a quarter, including Shields, were lawyers (21.) Each legislator received $4 daily per session and $4 for each 20 miles traveled from home to the Capital. Shields and his fellow members dealt with several pressing problems: state support for internal improvements (public works projects,) distribution of the school fund (to advance education,) salary increases for public officials, financially shaky banks, the election of a new United States Senator and transfer of the Capital to a more central site in the State.[4] The biggest potential expenditure by far was for the upstate construction of the Illinois and Michigan Canal which would open the Northern half of the State for development. The Democrats under Stephen A. Douglas supported the project, and Shields, pragmatically, was in favor of it too, with an eye to bringing home more political pork downstate.

The Illinois General Assembly, Vandalia where James Shields sat in 1836. Note the stoves at the back of the room and, on each desk, candles for light and inkwells.

James Shields and Stephen Douglas, who met in that august assembly, would subsequently become a potent political duo, and were generally inseparable. From the outset, Shields mostly saw eye to eye on political issues with the farsighted Douglas. But Shields was by no means a rubber stamp for his gifted colleague. For one thing, the future General was more favorably inclined toward business than Douglas and the anti-corporate stance of rank and file Democrats. Perhaps, from knowledge of the family linen store back in Dungannon he was more willing to accommodate trade and commerce. In other areas, Douglas opposed increasing state salaries for public officials while Shields was for it. When it came to terms of office, Douglas wanted short terms while Shields supported longer ones, though not as lengthy as the Whigs. Shields thought that county commissioners should serve for three years while Douglas wanted two. In this instance, Douglas prevailed. For finance and banking, Shields was his own man and had a better grasp of the problems than most on either side of the political aisle.

Apart from the I & M Canal, the biggest concern of the 10th Assembly was bank insolvency and failure. Financial houses, shaky institutions on the frontier at best, were often in trouble, and 1837 was a particularly bad year for banks. The nation was struggling with its first national depression and a state bank at Shawneetown was in danger of going bust. This created a political and financial furor. The bank had been established in 1816 by the territorial Government (before Illinois became a state) and still was considered the responsibility of the Government. For its part, the bank had a poor record all along and had been forced to close its doors temporarily in the financial scare of 1819. Now, it was ailing again and the Legislature decided to hold hearings into its problems.

No one knew what was causing the depression of 1837, but that did not stop politicians from pointing fingers and attributing blame. Some said it stemmed from President Andrew Jackson's Specie Circular Executive order of the previous year. Jackson's order required settlers purchasing Government lands to pay in gold or silver coins rather than bank notes or bills. Others maintained the down turn came from factors beyond America's borders, such as a Mexican debt default and Chinese acceptance of opium as payment for its goods, contending that when the English called in their investments, it deflated currency worldwide. Whatever the reason, the downturn ripped through mid-America like a tornado, felling the Shawneetown institution.

Following their investigation of the bank, the Legislature said the bank's problems were homegrown - due to mismanagement and foolhardy loans. Then, instead of reforming the bank, the Legislature simply authorized an increase of $2 million in its credit without any additional state oversight. The lack of teeth in the legislation did not sit well with Shields, nor depositors either. There was a run on the bank like never before. The redemption of bills for gold or silver had to be suspended and, there was a crisis of confidence in the system.

Douglas, like President Jackson, was militantly anti-bank and insisted that insolvent institutions should be closed altogether. Shields disagreed strongly and believed that bank liquidation would be counterproductive. He maintained that banks should be kept afloat, but with more regulatory oversight. This set him apart from most Democrats and Shields found himself at odds with his Party. However, when the Whigs drafted a motion condemning the banks but not asking them to modify their lending procedures, Shields was incensed. Forced to pick sides in an ensuing vote, Shields came home to the Democratic Party and supported the hard currency stance of Douglas.

That change of heart prompted the local Whig newspaper, the *Sangamo Journal*, to comment "Indeed, we cannot but regret that a gentleman (Shields) who promises to become of so much importance in our State should not have discovered the trap set for him by his political friend (Douglas.)"[5] In a dig at Douglas, the *Journal* went on to say that Shields could be forgiven, since he had not been long engaged in politics.

Shields feared that the financial fallout from forcing state banks into liquidation would close the State to commerce and stunt its economic growth indefinitely. Shields pleaded "Wretched as that system is, we cannot tear it up by the roots without prostrating our nation, and producing universal bankruptcy and beggary."[6] Recognizing that something had to be done, Shields decided a bipartisan approach would be best and approached opposition leader Abraham Lincoln and proposed a joint plan to bail out the banks. When word of the pair working together and their plan got out, there was mixed reaction. The ambitious Lyman Trumbull a fellow Democrat who disliked Shields, denounced it unequivocally. Nevertheless, Douglas thought it had merit. The Shields-Lincoln proposal made its tortuous way through the Legislature and eventually became law. The cobbled legislation permitted the bank to continue to suspend specie payment without being forced to shutter its doors. There were many sighs of relief around Vandalia and elsewhere, as the plan provided the necessary leeway for the continuation of statewide commerce.

The banking brouhaha had a fortuitous effect on the relationship of Shields and Douglas and brought them much closer together. It cemented a friendship that lasted, with some minor bumps, until Douglas' death in 1862. In a letter to Shields in 1841, Douglas affirmed his high regard for Shields by saying "Business aside, I have a few words to say on the score of friendship... You will excuse my neglect in writing to you and place it on the ground of great pressure of business, which could not be postponed... I remain truly your friend." [7] The depth of that friendship was underscored two decades later, when Douglas, the sitting Senator from Illinois, married Adele Cutts in Washington in 1856. Douglas asked Shields to be his best man. Shields was delighted to oblige and was even included in the honeymoon party that traveled to Baltimore.

The bench at the Supreme Court of the State of Illinois as it appeared in the 1840s, when James Shields served on it.

The contentious banking crisis had split the Democrats into rival factions, yet they mended fences sufficiently to get Circuit Court Judge Richard M. Young elected as the new United States Senator. The celebration that followed was some shindig. When the participants had been well oiled with "corn juice," Douglas and Shields, to the "intense merriment of the guests, climbed up on the table, at one end, encircled each other's waists, and to the time of a rollicking song, pirouetted down the whole length of the table, shouting, singing and kicking glasses, dishes and everything right and left, helter skelter."[8] After the party, Judge Young was singing a different song; he was out of pocket, for the combined costs of the bash and the breakages, to the tune of $600.

Though Shields had received positive reviews on both sides of the aisle for his efforts in the Tenth Assembly, he did not run for reelection in 1838. His reasons have not been documented and it was speculated that he did not want to compound the factionalism that split the Democratic Party in the wake of the banking controversy and wanted to give that time to heal. Or his decision could have been politically pragmatic, simply stepping aside because he thought he was vulnerable in the hands of a fickle electorate. He had supported an increase in state salaries for public officials, not a popular measure with the public, and his push for the internal improvement schemes for upstate were viewed with jaundiced eyes downstate, in his home base of St. Clair County, which was predominantly Whig. In addition, anti-Irish nativism was beginning to raise its spiteful head and, the Whigs were not above exploiting it. An example of doggerel beginning to make the rounds against politically active Irish immigrants was:

"Who thinks that freedom most consists
In proving points, with sticks and fists?"

Even though James Shields did not run for public office in 1838, he did not forsake politics. Remaining as active as ever, his law practice still took second place to politics, his passion. He spent much time at political meetings, sat in on strategy sessions late into the night, shared his opinions freely, and his commitment did not go unrewarded. Later in 1838, he was appointed secretary to the Board of Public Works, a state agency established to oversee state development or "internal improvements." It was an influential post, since it controlled a large amount of political patronage. Shields attended to his duties equitably, and there is no record of major complaints about his stewardship. In fact, as Koerner remarked, he developed a "reputation as an able and honest man."[9] Shields became secretary to Governor Kinney and, because of his integrity, was appointed by the Secretary of the Treasury of the United States to report on charges against the chief officer of the land office in the southern part of Illinois.[10]

There were significant changes in the demographics of Illinois in the late 1830s. By the end of the decade, almost all of the "Prairie State" had been settled and the fulcrum of political power was shifting northward. Chicago, fed by a continuous stream of new arrivals from the East via the Erie Canal and Great Lakes, was growing by leaps and bounds. The city, transformed from a fort and a few shacks on a marsh five years earlier, had been incorporated in 1837, and plans were afoot to shift the state Capital to a more central location. The energetic Shields took an active interest in this, and when the Legislature settled on Springfield he, as part of a bipartisan committee that included Stephen Douglas and Abraham Lincoln helped organize the move.[11]

Another view of the Supreme Court of the State of Illinois. The table was used by lawyers when they argued their cases in front of the Court.

By now, Shields' statewide influence had climbed as high as the corn on the surrounding prairie, and he wielded considerable political clout. He became a member of the nominating committee to select Party candidates and officers at the Democratic State Convention held in Springfield in December 1839. In that election, he inveigled his law partner Koerner into campaigning alongside him and they were successful for the Democrats in St. Clair County. Following that victory, Koerner was appointed electoral messenger to carry Illinois' electoral results to Washington. That was the first step of Koerner's highly successful political career.[12]

As occurs in so many political campaigns, the Democratic platform in 1839 resulted from a series of negotiated planks and compromises between rival factions. The Party had taken a stand against financial institutions, especially the Central Bank of the United States which was scapegoated for the recent financial crisis, even though the fiscal flood that engulfed the banks had ebbed. Shields supported the Party's stand against central government interference with "domestic institutions" (i.e. state's rights and slavery) and opposed state and federal financing of state development schemes. This platform, while it foundered nationally, enabled the Democrats to prevail in Illinois and Shields' star remained ascendant.

For the following year, Shields continued as a public face of the Party. He spoke at political gatherings, sat on committees and spent many hours meeting other officials around the state. For that he was rewarded, in March 1841, by becoming State Auditor of Public Accounts at a comfortable salary of $2,400 annually.[13] Shields was elected because he was affable and able, according to Koerner, who said "his election... by the legislation was owing to the fact that he knew most of the members personally, to his social qualities and to his reputation...(and)... tact."[14]

Shields must have been well pleased, as he reflected on his situation. For the first time in his life he was in a well paid job; he was a member of the state's Executive department and had friends in high places. The only cloud that marred his political sunshine was Lyman Trumbull who like Shields, was a teacher turned lawyer and legislator. A diehard 'ultra' or conservative, Trumbull's roots ran deep in America, though not in Illinois. He was descended from a politically-powerful family that had supported the Continental Army in the Revolutionary War, had moved to the "Prairie State" from Connecticut, and became the law partner of John Reynolds, the former Illinois Governor. The ascetic-looking Trumbull, had been appointed Secretary of State by Governor Carlin to replace Stephen Douglas, after Douglas had moved to the Illinois Supreme Court. Thus, the native of the "Nutmeg State" was in a favorable position to snipe at Shields, and seldom missed an opportunity. At that time, Adam Snyder, Shields' former law partner, was running for Governor and Shields strongly supported him. But Snyder died suddenly in May 1842, and the Democrats then turned to Judge Thomas Ford to replace him on the electoral ticket. Shields came out just as enthusiastically for

Ford as he had for Snyder, and following Ford's election, the pair became close.

As Ford lay dying eight years later, he handed Shields a copy of his memoirs, *A History of Illinois From Its Commencement as a State in 1818 to 1847,* asking that Shields edit and publish them. The impecunious Ford hoped that profits from the book would support his children after he was gone. Shields did as Ford bid, showing a capable editorial hand, but then found that getting the book published was altogether another matter. Shields had a difficult time finding a printer willing to take the risk.

The memoirs, a rollicking tell-all account of Ford's freewheeling career in Illinois politics, made a lot of people nervous. Several, who were depicted in less than flattering light, remained powerful in the State. Suppose they take umbrage, printers thought apprehensively - what then? They were concerned lest big political guns be brought to bear on anyone associated with bringing forth such an expose. But the loyal Shields had no such compunctions.

Illinois and Michigan Canal Lock XIV, La Salle. Largely built by Irish immigrants, the masonry, clearly visible in this winter scene, still stands as a tribute to their skill.

Displaying a moral courage that was his lifetime characteristic, and a strong dedication to his departed friend, Shields persisted. Eventually, he found a publisher willing to chance putting out the book. The memoirs finally hit the street in 1854, about four years after Ford's death. They attest to Shields considerable literary and editorial talents, and provide an entertaining insight into the rough and tumble of Illinois' early political and social life.

In his introduction to the work, Shields almost presciently noted that Governor Ford had died in 1850 "leaving his orphan children in a destitute condition." This foreshadowed a similar situation that would be reenacted with Shields' wife and children when James himself died, some thirty years later. And, as Shields exhorted that the Governor's children receive "a liberal percentage of the sales of the work," his own family had to depend on the largesse of friends for financial support after Shields was gone.

Shields, as can be seen from the foreword of the book, was aware of the risks he was taking. Anticipating negative reaction to Ford's no-holds-barred "opinions of men and measures very freely and unreservedly expressed," he tried to moderate the fall-out ahead of time. In a masterful spin, Shields interposed "I regret the severity of some of the author's judgments, and the censure with which he assails the character of some of our public men, who are both my personal and political friends; but I feel it to be incumbent upon me, by the very nature and circumstances of the trust, not only to have the work published according to this injunction, for the purpose intended by him, but also to abstain from making any alteration to the text. I thereby give it to the public just as I received it from the hands of the author, and with the sincere hope, for the sake of his destitute children, that it may meet with an indulgent and generous reception." Shields tactics worked; after all, what public figure could be against honesty and needy orphans? The book was a success and Ford's children received a modest income and no adverse political fallout or libel suits ensued.[15]

When Shields became State Auditor of Public Accounts in 1841, he displayed a vigor rarely associated with the position and, in his speeches, zeroed in on the Second Bank of the United States as a favorite foil, because "it gave too much control to too few."[16] Before long, this was too much for the Whigs who went after him with a vengeance. A week after Shields made that statement, the Whigs accused him of "blarney,"[17] marking the first public allusion to Shields non-American nativity.[18] This was calculated to foster an awareness and resentment on the part of the largely land owning Whigs against the continuing influx of foreigners, especially the Irish, and their expanding role in Illinois affairs. A year earlier in 1840, Springfield previously so accommodating of outsiders, began rolling up the welcome mat. The city charter of that year had limited the right to vote to naturalized citizens, even though the state constitution still permitted non-citizens to vote and hold office.[19] Resentment continued to fester, and the people of the state became so inflamed against outsiders that it culminated in the infamous mob lynching of Joseph and Hyrum Smith, two founders of the Mormon church, in Carthage, Illinois in 1844.

Despite Shields' stringent stewardship, the fiscal status of the state continued to teeter during his tenure and, it was not long before another state bank went bust, this time with $3m outstanding. With widespread ruin facing the people, Shields, as State Auditor had to act forcefully. But, the medicine he provided was so bitter, that he became embroiled in political and personal conflict with Whigs and Democrats alike. Ultimately, the bank crisis led Shields to a weapons-in-hand face off with Abraham Lincoln, the nation's future President. On the Democratic side, Shields was ensnared into a vendetta by Lyman Trumbull who, as before, objected to any measures Shields proposed, to ensure the integrity of the money supply. Shields tried to forge one solution after another to keep the bank functional but Trumbull would have none of them. Trumbull joined forces with the Attorney General of the State to sue the bank on behalf of the citizens. Shields found himself in the unenviable position of having to defend the bank, even though he knew it to be mismanaged. Shields put up a good fight, insisting that the bank's money be considered at face value even though the bank once again had suspended payment and its money was worthless. Things continued in that vein until Thomas Ford was elected Governor and, the situation was finally resolved.

Though Ford was not an active politician, he was elected by a majority of more than 8,000 over Whig candidate Joseph Duncan in August 1842. As soon as that happened, Shields proposed to the Governor a long term plan to bail out the state banking system once and for all. Shields suggested, that in exchange for bank liquidation, the state would replace $2 million in bank stock with the same amount in state bonds. Once again Lyman Trumbull dug in his heels and would have none of it. The bank's situation continued to deteriorate by the day and Shields by law was forced to enforce an unpopular measure, that he disallow paper money to pay taxes. Ford thought that Trumbull's opposition was due more to dislike of Shields than the merits of the auditor's plan and supported the Auditor. The measure was implemented and worked but, the process earned Shields the undying enmity of Trumbull, if it was not there before, and a near brush with death with Lincoln, which will be discussed later.

Lyman Trumbull, a Connecticut Yankee, fought Shields tooth and nail throughout Shields' career in Illinois politics. Highly conservative, Trumbull objected to the fiscal remedy Shields and Abraham Lincoln crafted for the state in 1837. He ensured that Shields was not elected to Congress in 1843 and defeated Shields for the Senate in 1855. His wife, Julia Jayne, coauthored anonymous antiShields Rebecca letters in 1842. Trumbull authored the 13th Amendment to the Constitution outlawing slavery.

As another state banking crisis waxed and waned, so did Shields' interest in the position of State Auditor and, he wanted to turn his hand to something else. As he demonstrated repeatedly, the restless Shields became bored with beaten paths. He craved novelty, looked constantly for fresh mountains to climb, and sought new challenges. Not for him the routine of an everyday rut, once he had mastered a position. Shields made it known that he wanted to move on, and campaigning for national office appeared to be just the ticket.

Because of its growing population, by 1843, Illinois was entitled to a new Congressional seat and, Shields had his eye on it. So had John Reynolds, Governor of Illinois during the Black Hawk War whose roots ran deeper than Shields' in the state. Reynolds was the influential owner-editor of the Belleville *Advocate* and had been elected to the state's highest office before Shields had even run for his first political post. In addition, he enjoyed considerable support especially among conservatives in St. Clair and the surrounding counties. Shields, on the other hand, was a 'blow-in,' but, as he had demonstrated, had a winning way when it came to the hearts and minds of the voters and the election promised to be close.

In addition to the political prize, Reynolds had a personal score to settle with Shields, which went back some three years to the Presidential campaign of 1840. At that time, Shields had been in favor of Presidential candidate Martin Van Buren, while Reynolds supported the former Vice-President Richard M. Johnson.[20] Shields had swayed the delegation away from Johnson and Reynolds had not forgiven him. He wanted his revenge and the stage was set for him to get it.

Both Shields and Reynolds rolled up their sleeves and went after the new Congressional seat hammer and tongs. Shields, the more able campaigner, was the early favorite; he quickly locked in the support of the Springfield Democrats where he was strong, and then traveled downstate to Belleville nearly 100 miles away. Belleville in St. Clair County was Reynolds' country and, since Shields had not lived there for five years, he faced an uphill fight. Reynolds pulled out his political IOUs, contending that his long affiliation with the Party entitled him to first dibs on the decision. Shields disputed that, saying that ability and merit should be decisive and, that the election should be about the future, not the past. When Shields took credit for pulling the state's fiscal feet from the financial fire, the outraged Trumbull, who was supporting his law partner Reynolds yelled "Humbug."[21] Trumbull contended that Shields had done nothing to save the state's financial bacon and insisted that Reynolds should get the nod.[22] Despite such formidable forces lined up against him, Shields still managed to hold a slight edge when the delegates went into caucus. A majority was tilting toward him and, it looked like he would prevail. But Shields' opponents were not prepared to concede defeat as they racked their brains against the Irish-American. Then, Trumbull saw an opportunity in Robert Smith, a prosperous businessman from Alton, in Madison County. Smith, a loyal Democrat, was not an official delegate, but he happened to be present at the convention. Working feverishly behind the scenes, Trumbull arranged for Smith to be credentialed and included in the Madison County delegation, even though this was highly irregular. Shields did not object because, in the interest of Party harmony, the Auditor saw no harm in granting Smith a "courtesy" vote, and agreed that he should be seated. In so doing, Shields unwittingly played into his wily opponent's hands. Smith, now an official delegate, was not only entitled to vote but, according to the rules, could become a candidate for the Congressional seat as well. This gave the crafty Trumbull the opening

he had been waiting for and, he arranged for Smith's name to go forward on the ballot. Smith acquiesced and Shields shrugged, still thinking he had nothing to fear. It was widely believed that Smith was not a serious contender and, any support he might get would be at the expense of Reynolds, rather than Shields. But the shrewd Trumbull had anticipated that. He prevailed on Reynolds to step aside and on the nonaligned delegates to throw their support behind Smith. That strategy was a success. When the final tally was announced, Smith had 14 votes, Shields 11 and Reynolds 2; Smith had won by one. It was clear that Shields had been outmaneuvered and, Mr. Smith was going to Washington instead of him.[22]

Stephen Arnold Douglas, U.S. Senator and close friend of James Shields. Shields was best man for Douglas when he married Adele Cutts in 1856.

Shields, being a loyal Party man, accepted his fate, and did not contest the result even though he must have been galled.

Though James Shields was down, he was not out. Shortly after that Machiavellian maneuvering by Trumbull, Shields again bounced back. On August 22, 1843, he was appointed by Governor Ford to fill a vacancy on the Illinois Supreme Court, which occurred when Stephen Douglas stepped up to the United States Senate. Appointing Shields to the Supreme Court was not simply a case of political cronyism; Shields was well qualified for position. He had ridden the second circuit, which included the Southwest Illinois counties of Madison, St. Clair, Monroe, Randolph, Washington, Clinton, Bond, Fayette, Montgomery and Selby, had proven himself in a wide variety of criminal and civil cases, and had even been victorious in the most prominent civil case up to that time: St. Clair County against the Wiggins Ferry Company. Thus, when Shields donned the ermine, he richly deserved that honor and was happy following the footsteps of Douglas, his friend and mentor. Shields went on to be elected to a full term of the Court in Feb, 1845. The position paid $1,500 a year and, while important, it was considered a stepping stone to higher political office. As shall be seen, even then, Shields had his sights set on that.

Adele Cutts, a grand-niece of President James Madison, whose ancestors hailed from Ulster. This picture of Cutts was taken around the time of her marriage to Douglas.

Chapter 4
Showdown in the Shadows:
Springfield and Alton

Through the purple dusk on this pathless heath
Wanders a horse with its rider, Death.
The steed like its master is old and grim,
And the flame in his eye is burning dim.
The crown of the rider is red with gold
For he is lord of the lea and the wold,
A-tween his ribs, against the sky
Glimmers the stars as he rideth by.
A hungry scythe, o'er his shoulder bare
Glints afar through the darkening air....
The Heath by Thomas Boyd (1867 - 1927.)

To all appearances, James Shields was striding tall in the Summer of 1842, since, as State Auditor of Public Accounts, he moved in circles of power and carried considerable clout. He was well paid, single, and could come and go as he pleased. On the surface, he should not have had a care in the world but, in the turbulent world of prairie politics where a tornado could level a house in a few seconds, there was stormy build up ahead. It would involve the temperamental Miss Mary Todd and, her husband to be, Abraham Lincoln, the redoubtable Whig leader. Before the dust finally settled in late September, a chain of events had culminated into a situation where not only was Shields' political life imperiled but his mortality as well. By the same token, Lincoln's survival was in jeopardy too and, in retrospect, had the scenario played out differently, someone else would have been the sixteenth President of the United States; there might not have been a civil war, and the whole map of America might be different.

As Shields settled into Springfield the asset side of his ledger had shown him to be strong willed, capable and confident, with an impressive record of legal and political success. His liabilities encompassed similar features, but to a fault; he could be cocky, vain and hot headed, and he had an Irish pride that could be pricked. Though he had not acquired much wealth, he had accumulated a large reservoir of political capital, that could be drawn on as needed. He was obviously a man to be reckoned with, and had standing socially, and in the affairs of state.

Shields played his part well, blending in easily with the Springfield social and political elite, and doing nothing to jeopardize his position. He did not emphasize his immigrant origins, and ensured his position in the mainstream by joining the influential Freemasons. Frequenting lodge meetings, he moved rapidly through the ranks, and became the Grand Orator of the Grand Lodge of Illinois.[1] He addressed the state convention of Masons in October 1842, and maintained his ties through the next decade, attending the Grand Lodge in Chicago in 1849.[2] Shields did not associate with Roman Catholics at that time and, as far as his law partner Gustave Koerner knew, never attended church. He was socially active and, like Abraham Lincoln became a regular at Elizabeth Todd Edward's dinner parties.

Elizabeth, a leader of the Springfield smart set, was married to Ninian W. Edwards of a politically well-pedigreed family; Elizabeth's father-in-law had been territorial Governor of Illinois and her husband was a lawyer and later a legislator. Though Governor Edwards had died in the Belleville cholera outbreak of 1833, the family dynasty continued to flourish. Elizabeth enjoyed hosting soirees for young Turks from the Legislature, men such as the cosmopolitan Shields, and the gawky Abraham Lincoln whose social skills were considered suspect by Springfield high society. Elizabeth introduced them all to her nubile sister, Mary Todd then 21.

Mary lived with the Edwards, having moved to Springfield in 1839, from Lexington, Kentucky, where she and her sister had both been born and raised in well-to-do circumstances. If Elizabeth reveled in socializing with the legislators, the prospect was even more to Mary's taste; she loved bantering and exchanging pleasantries with them. No shrinking violet, she was their intellectual equal, and was delighted both to debate and coquette as circumstances permitted.

In Elizabeth's gatherings, Shields was sought as a highly desirable dinner guest, since he was a wit and a bachelor to boot. Mary Todd acknowledged that she found Shields attractive and, in describing her "little coterie of Lincoln, Douglas, Trumbull, and Shields" stated, "Such choice spirits were the habitués of our drawing room. Gen. Shields, a kind hearted, impulsive Irishman was always creating a sensation and mirth, by his drolleries."[3,4]

Shields and Mary socialized frequently, and had ample opportunity to vet each other as potential marriage partners. But at the end of the night, the free spirited Shields would scarcely have cared for Mary's Patrician temperament and tart tongue. He demonstrated repeatedly, that he preferred girls of the "old fashioned" type, like Fraulein Knoebel, who did not try to boss him about. She was the dimpled daughter of his German landlord and that relationship went nowhere, because her father cried "verboten." He forbade her to have anything to do with Shields. Herr Knoebel, a sound judge of horseflesh, considered the Irish-American too flighty, and did not see Shields ever settling down.[5]

Besides his active social life, Shields was busy with affairs of state and, in the summer of 1842, the two realms would become intertwined into a latticework of intrigue, that involved Shields, Lincoln and the scheming Mary Todd. The seeds of the dispute, that would escalate into a near fatal encounter between Lincoln and Shields, had been sown many years previously. In fact, they had been planted long before Shields, or Lincoln, or Mary ever set foot in Illinois. They originated in faulty legislation, when the state bank of Illinois at Springfield was first chartered and, the Legislature passed an act stating that, in the event of bank failure, the State's Governor, Auditor and Treasurer were "authorized and required" to notify the public through the press, that the currency of that bank would not be received for taxes after a specific date. Since there was just such a fiscal emergency facing the state that summer, the three designated state officers, in accordance with the law, issued a proclamation prohibiting tax collectors from receiving the bank's paper after September 12 of that year. To further protect the state, collectors were admonished to receive such notes for no more than their "current value," then about ten cents on the dollar. Beside that, they were requested to suspend additional tax collection until after the Legislature next met. *(Appendix A.)*

A second document, addressed to the tax collectors of the state, was issued by Shields, as State Auditor. Although signed by Shields alone, this document was, as declared by Governor Carlin the expression of the judgment of the three state officers as required by law. *(Appendix B.)* This was not unreasonable, given the threadbare nature of state coffers. But, as might be expected, the situation did not sit well with the citizenry burdened by such draconian measures. Furious, the Whig Party set out to exploit the people's discontent and whipped up discord for political purposes. For them, and Lincoln their leader, the financial crisis offered a priceless opportunity to make mischief; they could, through political alchemy, transform base currency into electoral gold. Using a common technique of the time, various writers sharpened their quills into darts, and generated poison pen letters about the State Auditor to the *Sangamo Journal.* That newspaper, widely regarded as a Whig organ, since its editor, Simeon Francis gave the Whigs free rein, published the anonymous discourses lambasting the State Auditor.

One letter went on, not without humor, about the financial travails of the Illinois farmers. The lengthy piece, purporting to be the work of a farmer's down-to-earth wife named Rebecca was really by Lincoln. Using rural dialect and colloquialisms, Rebecca described her visit and conversation with a neighboring farmer, Jeff, who was lamenting the sorry state of the economy, and fretting that he would not be able to meet his financial obligations because of the state fiat. The letter, calculated to rile the Democrats in general and Shields in particular, stated vindictively "Shields is a fool as well as a liar, with him truth is out of the question." Then, it accused the young auditor of being a vacuous ballroom dandy "floatin about on the air, without heft or earthly substance, just like a lock of cat-fur where cats had been fightin." It also said that he was seen frittering away state money at a gathering of fast women, and quoted him purportedly saying, "Dear Girls it is distressing but I cannot marry you all… it is not my fault that I am so handsome and so interesting." *(Appendix C.)* The letter caused intense merriment among the general public and annoyed Shields to the same degree, but he did not react publicly, since neither he, nor anyone else, knew whom had penned the piece.

If Shields hoped the attacks would blow over, he was wrong. Another letter signed "Rebecca of the Lost Townships" followed, but it lacked the deft hand and ribald humor of the first. *(Appendix D.)* According to historian Hart, the second letter flatly "misrepresented" both the language and motives of Shields,[6] accusing Shields of theft of state funds, even though there was no substance to the charges, and the Whigs knew it. The letter ended with an appeal to the editor to repudiate Shields and what he stood for.

As Rebecca had advocated, the editor himself then took up a cudgel to bludgeon Shields. Simeon Francis published a belittling editorial, which must have deeply wounded the auditor, since it included insulting allusions to Shields' Irish nativity and immigrant origins. It stated "Who authorized you to dictate to the people when they shall

pay their taxes and in what kind of money. You certainly forget you have been translated to a land of freemen where we claim the right of thinking and acting for ourselves and are not in want of a Dictator to instruct us in the discharge of our duty." This was not the first attack on Shields because he was foreign born. A year earlier, an anonymous letter, which accused Shields of being ignorant and a liar, advised him to "Go back to the place from whence you came. Perhaps there you can succeed; but here you cannot." Though his patience was wearing thin, Shields was prepared to let the political attacks run off his back, like water off the

Abraham Lincoln. This is the earliest known photograph of the Sixteenth President of the United States. Shields and Lincoln were political and personal rivals for twenty years, 1835 - 55. This picture was taken about three years after their near duel.

proverbial duck, but this was going too far, even in the raw dog-eat-dog world of frontier politics. The letters had gone beyond the political Pale in assailing his character and personality and, in the face of such persistent attacks, a goaded Shields had to respond or lose all face.

The first step for Shields was to learn who had instigated the letters and, he asked his friend Gen. John D. Whiteside to find out. Whiteside approached Simeon Francis the editor of the *Sangamo Journal* and Francis, after some prevarication, revealed Lincoln to be the author. Shields was stunned because, he knew Lincoln socially, as a colleague in court, and as a collaborator and capable adversary in the Legislature, but could scarcely credit him capable of such perfidy. As far as the perplexed Shields was aware, there was no personal rancor between them, nor grounds for it. Nor could he think of anything else that would account for such a barbarous character assassination. As Shields stewed on the situation, he had no way of knowing that the malicious letters involved not only Lincoln, but Mary Todd as well. There was an obvious irony in Lincoln ridiculing Shields' dress and manner, since until then Lincoln had done little to improve his own backwoods appearance and indelicate language. In fact, Shields, at that time, was the more polished of the two. Following the second letter, Shields had to go to Quincy on state business, a round trip of 240 miles on dusty roads. The drought of summer had lingered into mid-September and, the fields were brown and heat merciless all the way there and back. Judging from subsequent events, Shields' thoughts were even hotter than the sun beating down throughout the trip. His preoccupied mind ignored the long stemmed prairie grasses and abundant asters and other wild flowers rippling in the blustery wind as far as the eye could see.

When Shields returned to Springfield on Friday September 16, 1842, another anonymous salvo struck him; this time a sarcastic rhyme signed "Cathleen" appeared in the *Sangamo Journal* saying he and the widow Becky had wed. *(Appendix E.)* This was too much for the enraged Shields and he asked Whiteside to locate Lincoln for an immediate retraction and apology. But Lincoln was nowhere to be found; it turned out that he was on circuit in Tremont about 50 miles away and would be gone a long time. When Shields learned that, he could not contain himself. Too hot under the collar to await the Whig leader's return to Springfield, he decided to travel to Tremont and confront the Whig leader there. Wasting no time, Shields and Whiteside jumped into a buggy and set off.

The duo's departure was not exactly a secret, and by this time, all Springfield was abuzz. People everywhere were chuckling at the brazenness of the letters and at Shields' obvious discomfort. The townspeople, unaware of who had authored the letters but knowing the two politicians involved, anticipated a dramatic turn of events. They would not be disappointed. A pair of Lincoln stalwarts, William Butler[7] clerk of the Sangamon County Court, and Dr. Elias Merriman, a Springfield physician, not knowing if the irate Shields was about to shoot Lincoln out of hand, dropped what they were doing and raced north after the two to warn Lincoln.

Traveling through the night, Butler and Merriman passed Shields and Whiteside on the road, and arrived in Tremont next morning before them. Butler told Lincoln what was afoot, and Lincoln, forewarned, was forearmed, when General Whiteside walked up to him next day and handed him a letter from Shields. Under the impression that all the anonymous correspondence had been generated by Lincoln, Shields said he was perplexed by Lincoln's "secret hostility" in relation to his "private character and standing as a man." He finished by asking Lincoln to retract the insults so that it "may prevent consequences which no one may regret more than myself." *(Appendix F.)*

Clearly, Shields was incensed, but very much in control of his emotions. The tenor of the letter was measured, indicating that Shields, bewildered at the ferocity of Lincoln's personal attacks, was offering Lincoln an olive branch, if they were retracted. But Lincoln demurred; he could not, or would not, bring himself to apologize. Moreover, since he had not written all the offensive letters, he was not about to accept complete blame. One of the letters, as it turned out, had been penned by Mary Todd and the other by herself and her friend Julia Jayne and, Lincoln, as far as is known, had nothing to do with either of them. (Jayne would later become the wife of Shields' *bete noir,* Lyman Trumbull.)

Lincoln decided to turn his non-authorship of all the letters into a defense. He and his two friends, Butler and Dr. Merriman huddled most of the day composing, drafting and rewriting a suitable response. Finally, they were satisfied and, toward evening, a reply was delivered to Shields. The response did little to assuage Shields' anger, since the answer was really an evasion, and Shields naturally rejected it. *(Appendix G.)*

The reply sidestepped the basis for Shields' righteous indignation, and suggested disingenuously, that since Shields had not pointed out what was "offensive in them" and was making "so much assumption of facts," and that his letter had "so much of menace" that Lincoln could not possibly respond to it. Lincoln finished by trying to turn the tables on Shields, suggesting, that any consequences could be just as bad for Shields as for himself. That observation certainly was true, but it did not deter Shields.

A response from Shields was not long in coming, and arrived an hour later. In his second letter, Shields backtracked to ask Lincoln if the information he had received from the editor of the *Sangamo Journal* was true? If it was, Shields requested that Lincoln provide a retraction of "offensive allusion.. to my private character and standing." Shields was playing by the rules - where political attacks were sanctioned, but personal assaults were suspect. If Lincoln had not written the articles, all he had to do was say so, and Shields indicated he would be satisfied. "If you are not the author of any of the articles your denial will be sufficient" he wrote in a measured hand. *(Appendix H.)*

Then Butler butted in, and spurned the Shields note when it was delivered.

"It cannot be presented to Lincoln unless the first note is retracted" he said haughtily. "On the withdrawal of the first note and a proper and gentlemanly request for an explanation, I have no doubt one will be given." Butler's response was calculated to wound Shields, since it intimated that the latter was less than a gentleman. The Irish-American remained irate; the impasse continued and, the Butler rebuff ended communications for that day. Next day, Sunday, both parties remained holed up in Tremont and did not communicate at all. Each had drawn a line in the sand, daring the other to cross, and neither was willing to budge. On Monday, Whiteside again presented the "unacceptable" note to Butler and, this time he passed it to the Whig leader who read it, but refused to respond. He said he thought it "not consistent with my honor to negotiate for peace with Mr. Shields unless Mr. Shields will withdraw his former offensive letter."

This was not good enough for Shields, who insisted on nothing short of a complete retraction and, he let Lincoln know that the situation had gravitated into a full blown affair of honor. He threw down the gauntlet, and Lincoln, much to everyone's surprise, picked it up and ran with it. How exactly this transpired is not known, since there is no extant correspondence to explain it. What is known is there was going to be a price to pay and the currency was blood; there was no other honorable way out. All that remained was to pick the time, the place and the weapons.

In accord with dueling protocol, each of the principles had to select seconds and, Shields named Gen. Whiteside as his "friend," while the future President opted for Dr. Merriman who was experienced in the rubric of the duel. Whiteside and Merriman rode back to Springfield together that afternoon, discussing the terms and conditions of the duel, but came to no agreement. According to various historians, there were no better, or possibly worse, men for the job. The bellicose Whiteside, Adjutant of the State Militia, loved listening to and telling war stories and, according to Lincoln biographers, Nicolay and Hay, his opposite number, Merriman, was "one of those combative medical men who have almost disappeared from the scene." Davidson, another historian, noted "Dr. Merriman, said to have been an old rover of the high seas, was mixed up in nearly all the "affairs" of that period." And Koerner later added that Shields' man Whiteside "had seen some service in the Black Hawk War and was a good Indian-fighter. But he was no better qualified to manage an "affair of honor" than Black Hawk himself. Whatever the pretensions of Dr. Merryman might have been, he certainly was equally ignorant of the "code of honor, the first and foremost rule of which is that the combatants should, as much as possible, meet on an equal footing. Air and sun must be equally divided."[8]

Merriman for his part was less than impressed with General Whiteside, and afterwards sniffed, "The valorous General beguiled the tedium of the journey by recounting his exploits in many a well fought battle, dangers by flood and field, doubtless with a view to produce a salutary effect on his nerves and impress him with the proper notion of his fire-eating propensities."[9] What Whiteside thought of Merriman is not recorded but clearly, the seconds thought no better of each other than, seemingly, either of the principals at the time.

By the time Whiteside and Merriman reached Springfield news of the impending clash had preceded them, and the town was agog. Dueling had been outlawed in Illinois more than twenty years previously, and the Sheriff was threatening to arrest the potential combatants, regardless of their status. Illinois was serious about suppressing the deadly practice of dueling and, in 1821, the state had hung Timothy Bennett, in a public execution, for killing Alphonso Stuart in such an encounter over a horse.[10] After that, insulted Illinoisans thought it prudent to transport themselves and their compromised honor across the Mississippi River to Missouri, whenever they sought satisfaction. There, Bloody Island, a scrubby piece of land at the river's edge, had earned its infamous reputation as "the convenient and safe battle ground resorted to by... belligerents for the settlement of their personal difficulties by barbarous rules of the bloody code... and this is said to have given origin to the horrid name by which the island was known."[11] The site continually attracted both the morbid and the curious and, earlier in 1842, English author Charles Dickens, after visiting the island as a tourist, noted it was a popular spot for settling scores.

There was precedent for Shields and Lincoln to go to Bloody Island since altercations there often involved politicians. In 1823, U.S. District Attorney Joshua Barton and General Thomas Rector exchanged gunfire on the isle, after Barton accused Rector of corruption in political office. Barton died in that duel. Eight years later, Congressman Spencer Pettis and Thomas Biddle, the Army Paymaster in St. Louis, also slung lead there, after Pettis made disparaging remarks about the Second National Bank of the U.S. and Biddle's brother, Nicholas, who ran it. Because Biddle was nearsighted, the combatants agreed to fire from only five feet. Not withstanding Biddle's myopia, neither man missed the mark and, both subsequently succumbed from their wounds. Thus, there was nothing exceptional, or incongruous, about Lincoln and Shields, as just another two local politicians, facing off there, in a macabre dance of death.

Weapon selected by Abraham Lincoln for his duel with James Shields in 1842. Measuring 42 inches from handle to blade point, this weapon bestowed an unfair advantage on the taller and longer-armed Lincoln. Picture is from a display at Cowboy Hall of Fame, Oklahoma City.

Both Lincoln and Shields knew of the risks they were taking from weapons and the law in defending their honor. To evade the law's long arm, Lincoln made arrangements to be gone from Springfield early on Tuesday, in case the sheriff should try to nab him. Prior to his departure, he went to his office on North Fifth Street, and penned a two part note stating his terms for the duel, which he handed to Merriman. *(Appendix I.)*

"Use the first part if Shields withdraws his notes and the second if he does not" instructed Lincoln. "Any preliminary details coming within the above rules you are at liberty to make at your discretion; but you are in no case to swerve from these rules, or to pass beyond their limits" Lincoln continued.

Merriman noted Lincoln's carefully considered conditions and saw that they included "Cavalry broad swords of the largest size" and "a plank ten feet long to be firmly fixed on edge, on the ground, as the line between us which neither is to pass his foot over upon forfeit of his life. Next a line drawn on the ground on either side of said plank and parallel to it, each at the distance of the whole length of the sword and three feet additional from the plank; and the passing of his own such line by either party during the fight shall be deemed a surrender of the contest."

Lincoln, as permitted by the rules of the *Code Duello* was exercising his right to choose the weapons and, historian Nicolay stated, Lincoln "certainly made no grudging use of his privilege."[12] At the same time, the Whig leader was dictating the dimensions of the arena, and attaching additional conditions without any discussion or agreement with Shields, which was suspect. Lincoln was stretching the rules in his favor, since choice of venue and thus the duel's format, by tradition, should revert to the challenger, after the challenged party has named weapons and time. What Lincoln had done was assume both choices, calling heads and tails together, to ensure an extra edge for himself.

At first glance, cavalry broadswords seemed an unusual selection, since Lincoln was better known for using an axe. The slightly curved cavalry sabers, the blades about three and a half feet in length, razor sharp on one side and blunt on the other, had been devised for hacking enemies to death from above, especially from the back of a horse. Such weapons were unequal, since Lincoln, being seven or eight inches taller than Shields, had an advantage in height and reach, which he maximized by defining the dimensions of the arena. He knew he could retreat beyond Shields reach, if he wished, while Shields could not get away from him. As James E. Myers observed, the choice of weapon was no accident; Lincoln had "carefully calculated the weapon and carefully figured the position so that his own 6'4" height will present to Shields, who was of only average height, an insuperable advantage."[13] Of Lincoln forgoing ethics to establish the edge for himself, Joseph Wallace wrote "this was contrary to the established code of honor and gave to Lincoln who was much the taller and larger armed man of the two a decided advantage."[14]

Later, when asked by Usher F. Linden a legal colleague and state legislator, why he had selected broadswords as weapons, Lincoln did not acknowledge that it was to gain unfair leverage over Shields. Rather, he ventured a politically expeditious response, "I did not want to kill Shields and felt sure I could disarm him, having had but a month to learn the broadsword exercise; and furthermore, I did not want the d—d fellow to kill me, which I rather think he would have done if we had selected pistols."

If Lincoln thought that the preemptive conditions he had stipulated and his obvious advantage in reach would deter Shields, he underestimated the character of the man he was dealing with. Shields was a tenacious terrier, who would neither flee nor flinch in the face of a fight, even to the death. Time and again, he demonstrated courage and determination when facing similar situations. With all due ceremony, Merriman visited Whiteside and presented Lincoln's first note, saying that Shields first note should be withdrawn. As soon as he read it, Whiteside threw up his hands and rejected the offer out of hand.

"I would as soon ask Shields to butt his brains out against a brick wall as to withdraw that paper" he chaffed.

Lincoln must have anticipated such a response, because he had already gone to Jacksonville, thirty miles away, to procure the broadswords and practice his swordsmanship. On Tuesday afternoon, the law stepped in to prevent the deadly contest from taking place, and affidavits were sworn out in Springfield for the arrest of both Lincoln and Shields, to preserve the peace. But neither could be found. Shields had not yet returned to the State Capital and, Lincoln had already left. Shields had been delayed by his lame horse, and was still making his way slowly back from Tremont.

As soon as Whiteside heard of the affidavits, he rushed to meet Shields, to warn him that the sheriff was lying in wait. They met about 20 miles from Springfield and, Whiteside squired the Irish-American safely to town via side roads. Once they reached Springfield, they learned that Merriman was already on his way to Alton, Illinois, which was directly across the river from the proposed dueling spot on the Missouri riverbank. If Shields had any objection to any of the conditions, it was now too late. He had not been given a chance to negotiate and was boxed in by Lincoln's preemptive terms.

Though, by this time, it was 11 o'clock Tuesday night, Shields and Whiteside wasted no additional time. They knew that delay could mean arrest, incarceration and inability for Shields to obtain personal satisfaction. That would scarcely do and, they set out for Alton right away. En route, they passed through Hillsborough, where Shields asked the powerful Democratic leader, Gen. W.D. Ewing to join his team. Ewing, a former acting Governor of Illinois, would serve as his second "friend." Ewing joined the party and they pushed on, making good time to arrive in Alton on Thursday morning. There, they added a third second, Dr. Thomas M. Hope since doctors were indispensable members of a dueling team. Surgeons could make the difference between life and death by staunching the blood and binding the wounds of a downed duelist.

When Shields reached Alton, he found Lincoln already waiting with the weapons. The Auditor registered no objection to anything - neither the weapons, the dueling site nor conditions, and both parties agreed to proceed as planned later that day. As arranged, the two would be combatants and their seconds crossed the Mississippi River, by horse ferry later, on a warm afternoon. The river was at its lowest point for the year and, they crossed without difficulty, followed by large group of spectators. A giddy excitement pervaded the air and, like a Roman holiday at the Coliseum, the people were looking forward to the spectacle of blood. It was not every afternoon they got a chance to see two of the leading political lights of the state commit mayhem and, it was an event they would talk about for a long time to come.

Bloody Island, their destination, was set on a swampy inlet close to the Missouri shore. Upon reaching dry land, the rival parties stepped onto the bank, and strode through a thicket of scrubby trees, whose leaves had yet to change color. They walked until they reached a clearing. There, gnarled boughs and broken branches attested to the fact that the site had been used before for such nefarious purpose as they had in mind. The two duelists pulled their swords from their scabbards and checked weight and balance. They moved them up and down with deft flicks of their wrists, like fly fishermen teasing a salmon. Speckled sunlight angling through the trees flashed off the razor sharp blades as they were brandished. Then, the men noted that the contrasting light and shadow would make it difficult to judge depth and distance and that conditions would influence the outcome; whomever faced the setting sun would almost surely face death as well.

As Lincoln and Shields practiced their cutting strokes, their seconds haggled over the layout of the dueling ground. A sharp whoosh echoing through the trees each time a quivering saber slashed through the air made onlookers wince. Clearly, a single well aimed blow could maim or kill an opponent and, at the same time, the duelists learned that broadswords were not easy to handle since they were heavy and unwieldy. As time progressed, the seconds continued to argue in a more desultory fashion, hoping for a last minute settlement. None was forthcoming, since neither party was prepared to budge. Shields had been deeply wounded by the insults, and wanted nothing short of full satisfaction. The only way Lincoln was prepared to give it to him was with a sword blade. Neither was going to back down. Shields was dressed in a formal three piece suit, while the lanky Lincoln was clad in slacks and an open neck shirt, its sleeves rolled up showing off his sinewy arms. Shields, if he was going to die, was determined to go out in style, meeting his maker in gentleman's attire. But, of course, in his mind, he anticipated that it was Lincoln who would pay the price

Bloody Island as it looks today. It was used as a federal prison during the Civil War and now is a park known as Lincoln-Shields Recreation Area.

After a while, the ground had been prepared to Lincoln's exacting specifications, the boundaries marked off and a ten foot plank placed in the middle, but still the delay dragged on. Shields, his patience becoming thin, strutted and scowled and, growing warm from his exertions, removed his jacket and hung it on a small branch. Finally everything was ready. Lincoln, towering over everyone, nodded his acquiescence and the two prepared to face off. They positioned themselves *en gard* and, as their seconds prepared to give the starting signal, there was a sudden commotion; two men burst into the clearing, interrupting the action. Shields and Lincoln blinked to see General John J. Hardin, a relative of Mary Todd and Dr. Revel W. English, a Springfield physician standing between them. Dr. English, founder of the Sangamo County Medical Association, was the most highly respected physician in Springfield, while Hardin was a well regarded military General.[15] Both English and Hardin were friends of Lincoln and Shields and were grieved to think that either, or both would be killed, or even if the outcome was less serious than that, that both men's promising political careers would be shattered. Thus, Hardin and English were on a mission to prevent any such outcome, and had raced furiously across the state to forestall the fray. Neither of the duelists was especially happy to see the two newcomers, but agreed to hear them out.

Throwing dueling protocol to the wind, Hardin approached Shields directly and said that the issues between Shields and Lincoln, instead of going to the sword, should go before a panel of four responsible citizens to be adjudicated. A postponement at this juncture did not sit well with Shields and, he shook his head. Not that Shields was especially blood-thirsty, but having prepared mentally for the fight, he was unprepared to call it off at this juncture and referred Hardin back to his seconds. Still English and Hardin persisted, and dashed off notes presenting their proposition to each set of seconds. *(Appendix J.)*

As the seconds weighed the proposal, Hardin and English said that it was fortuitous that they had arrived in time because, when they had reached Alton, they thought that they were too late. No boats remained at the town, since they had been deployed to transport spectators across the river. But Hardin and English found a canoe, paddled across as fast as their arms could take them, and were glad to have arrived in time. Theirs was a desperate last minute attempt at resolving the dispute and, no one was sure it would work. The arguing and posturing resumed and what exactly transpired, at each step, has given rise to countless arguments and heated discussions ever since. No one now can ever know exactly what happened, since everyone present had their own version of events and there must have been more than a hundred different accounts, each with more spin than a gyroscope.

Most versions indicate that, when the notion of a neutral panel was proposed to Shields, he rejected it out of hand. Then, acting behind Shields back, his seconds submitted a note to Merriman, offering to rescind all previous notes, if Lincoln would provide a mitigating explanation for the acrimonious Rebecca letters. Merriman, with

Lincoln's acquiescence, then pulled out the second half of Lincoln's note, which the future President had penned in Springfield and handed it to Shields' seconds. They in turn gave it to Shields, but to no avail; Shields' dander was up and, he would be danged if he would come to any accommodation.

"My seconds are overstepping their authority and I am amiss at Hardin and English. They've no right butting in" he reportedly yelled.

Obviously distraught, it was not clear with whom Shields was most vexed: his own seconds, the newcomers, the intransigent Lincoln or everyone's blatant disregard for the rules of the *Code Duello.* He told Hardin and English in no uncertain terms to mind their business, which Hardin and English refused to do. They insisted what was going on was indeed their business, and continued pouring oil on turbulent waters. Meanwhile, Lincoln stood languidly by, or practiced his swordsmanship, depending on which account one reads. Most agree that both men looked ready to go through with the duel, if that is what it took.

How long the stalemate lasted or was resolved is not really clear. One version states that, while negotiations were going on, Lincoln reached incredibly high above his head and lopped off a willow branch, which made Shields shiver. *(Appendix K.)* Another, uncorroborated account, says Shields' seconds abandoned him, because of his pig headedness and failure to compromise and, he could not proceed without them. General Whiteside's version of events, written ten days afterward, appeared in the *Sangamo Journal* and is generally accepted as the most reliable rendition of the episode. *(Appendix L.)* Whiteside said that he and Ewing accepted the second half of Lincoln's letter as an "apology" and deemed Shields' honor "satisfied." "This was all done without the knowledge or consent of Mr. Shields; and he refused to accept it until Dr. Hope, Gen Ewing and myself declared the apology sufficient and that we could not sustain him in going any further." According to Henry Castle, in the official record of the Missouri Monument Commission, "No material part of (Whiteside's account) has ever been contraverted."

Whatever transpired, the duel did not take place and neither struck a blow in anger. Hardin reportedly took possession of the swords and both men patched things up. They left Bloody Island together on Mr. Chapman's horse ferry, apparently on amicable terms. Seemingly, the only casualty of the afternoon was lanky Jake Smith, the Alton city marshal who was overcome on the trip back by heat and excitement. Years later, an apparently disappointed eyewitness gave this account of the episode "I notice an account of a "historic spot" on the island on which Abraham Lincoln and General Shields met to fight a duel. I was there and saw everything that took place, which was not much."[16]

Dickering over the duel was apparently thirsty work, because no sooner had the ferryboat reached the Illinois side than "The Springfield party hurried to Charlie Uber's saloon and amidst general rejoicing soon consumed what champagne he had on hand." *(Appendix M.)*

As can be gleaned from those and other descriptions, ink flowed copiously in place of blood. Most accounts, especially after Lincoln's assassination, tended to present the episode in a bright light for Lincoln, and a dim one for Shields. Some Lincoln supporters, even contended that the episode was all done in jest. If that was the case, it showed a peculiar sense of humor, since there is little that is potentially funny about the business side of a saber.

A notable exception to the version offered by sympathetic Lincoln biographers was a harsher judgment by historian John T. Morse Jr., who compiled a two volume biography of Lincoln in 1892, at a time when many eyewitnesses to the confrontation were still living, and could have disputed his statements. Apparently, no one did. Morse wrote:

"It is fair to say that my view of the "duel" is not that of other writers. Lamon says that "the scene is one of transcendent interest." Herendon calls it a "serio-comic affair." Holland gives a brief deprecatory account of what he calls "certainly a boyish affair." Arnold treats it simply enough but puts the whole load of the ridicule upon Shields. Nicolay and Hay deal with it gravely in the same way in which they deal with (Lincoln's reluctant) marriage; that is they eschew the production of original documents and, by their own gloss, make a good story for Lincoln and a very bad one for Shields; they speak lightly of the "ludicrousness" of the affair. To my mind the opinion which Lincoln himself held (that all the parties concerned were placed in a most humiliating light) is far more correct than that expressed by any of his biographers."[17]

Koerner, who knew most, if not all there was to know, about the duel, concluded that Shields and the whole episode had been treated most unfairly by Lincoln biographers. He stated "Messrs. Hay and Nicolay, in their monumental history of Abraham Lincoln which ran for years in the *Century Magazine* did Shields great injustice. And it was with great pleasure that I vindicated his memory in the same review in a manner that gave great satisfaction all over the country."[18] *(Appendix P.)*

Regardless of the partisan accounts about how the matter ended, the official correspondence, between the two sets of seconds terminating the matter, is documented in the appendix of this book. *(Appendices N and O.)* Shields' seconds withdrew Shields' original letter and, in response, the friends of Lincoln submitted Lincoln's letter expressing his regret for his part in the poison pen campaign. Shields' seconds accepted the Lincoln regret, and declared Shields honor satisfied, even though the truculent Shields was reluctant to accept it himself. He knew he could not proceed without his handlers, or an opponent, and had to acquiesce. The letters demonstrate that the intervention of General Hardin and Dr. English was the paramount reason that Lincoln and Shields did not end up locked in mortal combat.

Neither Lincoln nor Shields ever talked much about the incident afterward, and in fact, both men appeared embarrassed by it. Lincoln's biographer Herndon wrote, that in 1858 when he asked Lincoln about the near duel, the future President replied "If all the good things I have ever done are remembered as well as my scrape with Shields, it is plain I shall not be forgotten." Shields also avoided the subject and, later in life, Shields would acknowledge only Lincoln's statesmanship, saying that he "knew President Lincoln well [and] had lived as a neighbor in the same town."[19]

Sign leading to Lincoln-Shields Recreation Area.

Many have speculated on how the duel would have turned out had it taken place. Not surprisingly, Lincoln stalwarts maintained that Lincoln's longer reach and physical strength would have ensured his success. Lincoln was quoted as saying "If it had been necessary I could have split him from the crown of his head to the end of his backbone."[20] On the other hand, Shields was a trained swordsman, who

84

throughout his life displayed such fearless indifference to bullet and bayonet that he survived life threatening wounds in two wars. His dexterity and determination could well have offset their great disparity in size. As for the role of Mary Todd and Julia Jayne, neither publicly admitted their involvement at the time. It was only after Lincoln's assassination, when the incident was being scrutinized by Lincoln biographers, that the President's widow acknowledged being involved at all. She said that the *Cathleen* doggerel had come to life in the Jayne parlor and was the joint work of herself and Julia Jayne. Mrs. Lincoln minimized her role in its publication, claiming it was all done in jest and that she had not intended that the poem should be published. Still, as she made excuses for her wayward behavior nearly a quarter century earlier, the President's widow, for her own reasons, took a swipe at Shields. "The Genl (Shields) was very impulsive & on the occasion referred to, had placed himself before us, in so ridiculous a light, that the love of the ludicrous, had been excited, within me & I presume, I gave vent to it in some *very silly* lines."[21] She contended, in other words, that Shields had asked for and deserved what he got. How that might have happened, and the reasons underlying Mary's disaffection with Shields, will be discussed in the next chapter. A few days after her first comment, Mrs. Lincoln embellished her defense, when she wrote to Mary Jane Welles "On one occasion he (Shields) amused me exceedingly, so much so, that I committed his follies, to rhyme, and very silly verses they were, only, they were said to abound in sarcasm causing them to be very offensive to the Genl. A gentleman friend, carried them off and persevered in not returning to them (sic), when one day, I saw them, strangely enough, in the daily paper."[22] Mary said nothing about writing the second offensive letter, even though many researchers, as shall be seen, believe it came from her invidious hand.

Gustave Koerner, in the context of the times and in contrast with Mrs. Lincoln, had a very different opinion about the sequence of events. "No man of the least spirit could have taken those insults without seeking satisfaction, even by arms, if necessary. The provocation was of the strongest, and no blame attached to Shields at the time. It is no proof of Shields's irascibility. He was a young man who had his reputation for honesty at stake; and to have in addition his personal features and peculiar habits ridiculed in a small but select society in which he daily moved was more than even a saint could have borne" he stated. *(See appendix P.)*

Chapter 5
Decoding the Code Duello:
Understanding the Unconscious

When Pat came over the hill, his colleen fair to see,
His whistle low, but shrill, the signal was to be.
"Mary" the mother said, "Someone is whistling sure;"
Says Mary, "Tis only the wind, is whistling through the door."
"I've lived a long time, Mary, in this wide world, my dear,
But a door to whistle like that, I never yet did hear."
"But, mother, you know the fiddle, hangs close beside the chink,
And the wind upon the strings, is playing the tune I think."
"I'm not such a fool as you think, I know very well it is Pat:
Shut your mouth, you whistling' thief, and go along home out of that!"
"And you be off to your bed. Don't play upon me your jeers;
For though I have lost my eyes, I haven't lost my ears."
The Whistlin' Thief by Samuel Lover (1797 - 1868.)

Following the near duel between James Shields and Abraham Lincoln in 1842, it is scarcely surprising that authorship of the anonymous anti-Shields letters remained in dispute, since, according to Lincoln biographer John T. Morse Jr., "all the parties concerned were placed in a most humiliating light" and, Abraham Lincoln (at least) was "heartily ashamed of the affair."[1] No one rushed forward to claim credit for the disparaging correspondence and, even today, no one can say for sure who really generated it. Most authorities, but not all, accept that Abraham Lincoln and his future wife Mary Todd were in fact the authors or major instigators of those derogatory pieces. James Meyers, a writer, who delved as deeply into the matter as existing evidence permits, summarized prevailing opinion:

"It is no means certain that Mr. Lincoln wrote any of the Rebecca letters. Mr. Benjamin Thomas scholar and author of the best single volume on Lincoln, believes that Mary Todd wrote the offending letter (the first) and that Mr. Lincoln was shielding her. Roy Basler also a great Lincoln scholar, is quite certain that Mr. Lincoln did write the letter because he said he did and because no one else has his mastery of dialect and colloquialism. Mr. Albert Beveridge another fine Lincoln biographer, confuses the letters but thinks that Mr. Lincoln wrote the first and third ones, which Mr. Roy Basler is certain that Simeon Francis [editor of the *Sangamo Journal*] wrote. An anonymous letter published in Alton at the time of the duel, states that William Butler wrote two letters and Mary Todd wrote one. No one truly knows."[2] *(Appendix Q.)*

An analysis of the content and writing styles of the various correspondence supports Mr. Lincoln's contention: that he wrote the initial letter, but not the others. He was an accomplished writer, as he demonstrated repeatedly when he became President. The subsequent Shields letters lack the satiric touch and even whimsy of the first, and are increasingly ham handed, heavy, and offensive. While not devoid of a certain compositional proficiency, the later letter and poem obviously were generated by a less fluid hand. Their content would not be out of character for a person with "a sharp tongue, a sarcastic wit, and a shrewish temper, over which perilous traits she had no control"[3] as Morse described Mary Todd. The circumstantial evidence lends credence to the notion that Mary not only wrote the third piece, as she admitted, but the second as well. The second letter appearing in the newspaper on September 8th, included a spurious offer of Aunt 'Becca's hand to Shields in marriage. The letter stated (in part):

> *"Dear Mr. Printer:*
>
> *…You say that Mr. S. is offended at being compared to cat's fur, and is as mad as a March hare, (that aint fur) because I told him about the squeezin. Now, I want to tell Mr. S. that rather than fight I'll make any apology, and if he wants personal satisfaction, let him only come here and he may squeeze my hand as I squeeze the butter, and if that ain't personal satisfaction, I can only say he is the fust man that was not satisfied with squeezin my hand… I have all along expected to die a widow, but as Mr. S. is rather good looking than otherwise, I must say I don't care if we compromise the matter by-really Mr. Printer, I can't help blushing-but-I-it must come out-I-but widowed modestly well if I must, I must wouldn't he-may-be-sorter, let the old grudge drap if I were to consent to be-be-h-i-s-w-i-f-e? I know he's a fighting man and would rather fight than eat; but isn't marrying better than fightin though it does sometimes run into it?…*

Maybe I'm counting my chickens before they're hatched - and dreamin' of matrimonial bliss when the only alternative reserved for me is to take a lickin... I never fights with anything but broom-sticks or hot water, or a shovel full of coals, or some such thing; the former of which being somewhat like a shillalah may not be very objectionable to him.

    Yours & c, Rebecca.

    P.S. Jist say to your friend if he concludes to marry, rather than fight, I shall inforce one condition, that is, if he should ever happen to gallant any young galls home of nights from our house, he must not squeeze their hands.

Several questions arise, because of the content of this letter, as well as by the whole episode. Why would Mary Todd have gone out of her way to write and publish a letter, albeit a mocking one, to Shields pretending to propose marriage? Was it done in jest, a "wish fulfillment" or, could she be settling a score? A second question: why would Lincoln have acted so out of character as to place his life on the line in his dispute with Shields, when he had other options? Normally so careful and canny, it was odd that the future President would have permitted himself to be drawn into an illicit dueling episode, that could have put paid not only to his political aspirations but his life as well. And why would Lincoln direct a barrage of sarcasm at Shields for imagining he was handsome and thinking women were striving for his hand in marriage? The overriding question is, perhaps, the most intriguing - what about the role of interpersonal rivalries? Did they influence events more than meets the eye or, were ever discussed in public? In other words, was Shields more than a mere political foil? If the episode was simply politics as usual, why was Lincoln so perturbed about it afterward? For the remainder of his life, Lincoln was deeply troubled by the episode to a degree that politics alone can scarcely account for. He hushed the affair up, forbade anyone to discuss it in his presence, and swept it under the rug like it had never happened. As Mary acknowledged after her husband's death, "My husband was always so ashamed of it we mutually agreed - never to speak of it ourselves."[4] And shortly afterwards she wrote "This affair always annoyed my husband's peaceful nerves... he said he felt he could do no less than be my champion."[5] Being Mary's champion certainly implies a personal motivation going way beyond politics.

Over the years, historians and commentators alike have not ventured beyond politics to explain the event. They contend that the Whigs simply wanted to make hay at the expense of the Democrats and, Shields provided them with the implement. That was all there was to it and, they can point to Lincoln's statement that the Rebecca "article was written solely for political effect." *(Appendix I.)* Perhaps so, since there is little in the way of concrete evidence to the contrary.

But several puzzling elements remain. Lincoln, as he demonstrated previously, did not have to let the situation progress to a swords-in-hand face off with Shields, on a bleak mud bank some eighty miles from where he lived. He could, as he did in 1840 after a similar challenge from W. G. Anderson following another political flap, have fenced with shrewd words instead of fighting swords. So, why not this time? Myers raised, and tried to answer, that very question "Mr. Lincoln could get out of a scrape when he wanted to. With Anderson he removed himself with dignity and honor from a fight; why not with Shields? The obvious reason was that he did not want to."[6] But Myers falls short of answering "the why not" and that, along with other elements that remain entangled, has defied straightening ever since. These elements include Mary's supposed collaboration with Lincoln, when the two were estranged and had not spoken to one another in the preceding eighteen months.[7] Then, there was their sudden reconciliation, followed by their mad dash to the altar six weeks after the near duel. Many citizens of Springfield believed those three events were all interconnected. Writing forty five years later, John G. Nicolay summed up the situation under the heading "The Shields Duel," when he wrote "An incident which occurred during the summer preceding Mr. Lincoln's marriage, and which in the opinion of many had its influence in hastening that event, deserves some attention, if only from its incongruity with the rest of his history."[8] That is certainly true; it was incongruous since people usually act in character and human behavior does not take place in a vacuum. Individuals respond not only to the external world around them, but internally to their hearts and heads as well. Sometimes inner reasons are more compelling than outer, and defy logic. To place this episode in perspective psychologically, one must back up three years before the near duel, to the time when Abraham Lincoln and Mary Todd first met and began a relationship that ran anything but smooth. In fact, Lincoln biographer Morse described it as an "almost grotesque courtship."[9] A reason was that the "proud and high tempered" Mary in "point of social position and acquirements" stood much above Lincoln and many, including Mary's sister Elizabeth, thought their relationship ill advised."[10]

Morse went on to summarize, "Upon Lincoln's part it was a peculiar wooing, a series of morbid misgivings as to the force of his affections, of alternate ardor and coldness, advances and withdrawals, and every variety of strange language and freakish behavior." He noted that Mary for her part was "jealous and exacting" and "after many months of this queer uncertain zigzag progress, it was arranged that the marriage should take place on January 1, 1841."[11]

Then Lincoln got cold feet; he backed out at the last minute and failed to show at the altar, leaving Mary devastated. According to a wedding guest, Mary, "bedecked in veil and silken gown, and nervously toying with flowers in her hair, sat (waiting for Lincoln.) Nothing was lacking but the groom."[12] The episode

Mary Todd Lincoln circa 1846. She admitted involvement, along with her friend Julia Jayne, in writing two of the offensive Rebecca letters. A woman of strong temperament, Mary had several well-publicized feuds during her life.

caused Mary great pique, but she was not one to take it lying down. She started a gossip mill, saying it was she who had abandoned Lincoln, not vice versa. Personal rejection did not sit well with Mary and, she was paying him back for the insult.

At the time of her broken engagement, marriage would have been very much on Mary's mind. At 23, she was old for marriage by contemporary frontier standards. Her sister Elizabeth, engaged at 14, had tied the nuptial knot two years later at 16. Another sister, Francis, had wedded a prosperous druggist and physician, Dr. William Wallace the previous year, after traveling to Springfield to catch him and, Mary had hoped to reap a similar harvest from the same field. Yet, she was forced to remain sitting on the shelf, a guest in her sister's home, to the consternation of both herself and her sister, Lizzie. If Lincoln did not want her, her actions demonstrated that she was not going to sit around waiting for him and was determined to find another. Thus, began a frantic odyssey in search of a spouse that stretched far and wide.

Less than a month after Mary's let down at the altar, a letter dated Jan 27, 1841 written by a Springfield socialite commented that Miss Todd "has a great many beaus."[13] Another observed that Mary moved "gayly and serenely" through the Springfield social whirl, that she "danced with other men and had her name linked with suitors in marriage."[14] There were rumors that Mary was "seriously interested" in Edwin B. Webb, a wealthy widower, supposedly the richest man in Illinois.[15] According to Ida Tarbell, "She went with Mr. Douglas or some other escort who offered."[16] It appears that James Shields was included among the "some other escort." The Guide of Carrollton Missouri noted that Shields and Lincoln had "a squabble which arose while they, as well as Stephen Douglas, were courting Mary Todd in Springfield, Illinois."[17] It is scarcely surprising that Mary would have become involved with Shields or Douglas after being so unceremoniously left in the lurch by Lincoln. Logically, her first stop for a Lincoln replacement would have been the men closest to hand, the "little coterie" who frequented her sister's parlor.[18]

In the late Summer of 1842, it was no means certain that Lincoln and Mary would ever wed and, in fact, the odds were against it. They had had nothing to do with each other for a year and a half and Mary was seeing others. Everyone knew it and, as already mentioned, Lincoln and Mary's reconciliation was not effected until after the near duel.[19]

The Todd family had not approved of Lincoln, and expected Mary to marry Stephen Douglas. One of Mary's relatives later remarked "I used to think Mr. Douglas would be your first choice."[20] But perhaps Mary had a different idea. It is plausible that another member of the "little coterie" one James Shields was more to her liking, at least, for a while. Since she was considering all comers why not him? Then, Mary might have discovered Shields' interest in his landlord's daughter, Fraulein Knoebel. Her temperament would not have taken that well and, as she demonstrated with Lincoln, she would have wanted to turn the tables. That could explain her underlying motive for the spurious marriage proposal letter to the newspaper. In the guise of Aunt 'Becca, she censured Shields, because he was "not satisfied with squeezin my hand." Then, she admonished him, that if he really wanted her he must be careful about "other galls" and "must not squeeze their hands."

That there was hand squeezing going on is clear enough. But who was doing it to whom is not. William Butler who lost no love for Shields, later accused Shields of squeezing not Mary's, but Julia Jayne's hand. He said Julia wrote the Rebecca letters to get back at him. "They had a party at Edwards' and Shields squeezed Miss [Julia Jayne's] hand. Miss [Jayne] took her revenge by writing the letters from the 'Lost Townships' and probably with Mary Todd's connivance sent them to the editor of the Journal by Mr. Lincoln" Butler told Lincoln biographer John G. Nicolay[21] So who knows what really happened? One is forced to make assumptions to try to make sense of the situation. Shields may well have squeezed Julia's hand which annoyed Mary, when Mary thought he should have been squeezing hers. Then Mary, her feelings incensed, wrote the letters out of spite? But we will never know. All one can surmise is emotions and raw feelings had to be part, if not all of the picture. So much for Mary's possible motivation in writing the letters, what about Lincoln? Could passion more than politics have influenced his judgment? Lincoln dodged that very question when it was put to him by "a high up General" in the White House in February 1864. According to Mary Todd Lincoln, when the General "playfully" asked after dinner "Mr. President, is it true, as I have heard that you, once went out to fight a duel and all for the sake of the lady by your side? Mr. Lincoln with a flushed face replied, "I do not deny it, but if you desire my friendship, you will never mention it again."[22] Mary had already noted that Lincoln had been her champion in the episode. If so, how?

The first record of a duel in Illinois was between two young military officers at

Fort de Chartres shortly after the British took possession in 1765. "This quarrel arose as did the war of the Greeks against the Trojans, on account of a lady. These officers fought with small swords early on a Sunday morning, near the fort, and in the combat one was killed."[23] As we have seen, in 1806, the future President Andrew Jackson killed Charles Dickinson a fellow Nashville lawyer, in a duel, because he had cast aspersions on Jackson's wife Rachel. By the same token, the Lincoln - Shields encounter could have progressed as far as it did because they were romantic rivals. A review of the psychological dynamics, based on known evidence, suggests not only that possibility, but also its probability.

Shields' deadly challenge to Lincoln, when he could not obtain personal satisfaction, was not out of character for him. As he demonstrated repeatedly, he was a warrior, a knight errant "of the 14th Century" as much at home with a gun as a gavel. Lincoln, on the other hand, while quick-thinking, was more phlegmatic. He did not shrink from adversity, but was anything but impetuous. Time and again, he vacillated long and hard before making critical decisions. For example, one need look no farther than his hesitation in changing ineffectual commanders during the Civil War. But here, in a situation that could have cost him his life, he displayed practically no hesitation, and rushed right in. Something was very different. A reasonable interpretation suggests that his impulsivity was due more to hot passion than cold politics. But was it passion about Shields alone or, did it encompass Stephen Douglas as well? The evidence is less clear on that. Elizabeth Edwards, Mary's sister, told Lincoln biographer Herndon that Stephen Douglas was the cause of Lincoln and Mary not getting married the first time round. Without additional explanation, Herndon's notes state "Lincoln's & Mary's engagement &c. were broken off by her flirtations with Douglas."[24] Now Shields was part of the picture. The *menage-a-trios* had become *menage-a-quatre*. After Lincoln left Mary standing at the altar, she wasted no time paying attention to other beaus. Some of her actions were undoubtedly out of antipathy to Lincoln, the man who had betrayed her. Others were likely generated by romantic interest. After all, she was still single and free to choose whom she liked. Lincoln knew what Mary was up to, since Springfield was small and, it would have been hard for him to avoid hearing about her and her amorous activities.

During this period, Lincoln did not stay home all the time either and dated at least one woman, Sarah Rickard. But like all faint hearts, he would have agonized that he had lost the real Fair Lady. His dilemma was; should he try to patch things up with Mary, or leave them be, to wither and vanish like fallen leaves before the wind? Then the Shields opportunity cropped up with its political and personal ramifications. After vacillating about Mary for twenty months, it came as a relief. He could take a decisive action that might seem based in politics, but would also resolve his personal dilemma - his war with himself.

Julia Jayne who was Mary Todd's bridesmaid when she married Lincoln two months after Lincoln's near duel in 1842. Thirteen years later, Mary and Julia fell out irreconcilably following another episode that involved James Shields. When Julia's husband, Lyman Trumbull defeated Lincoln for Shields' Senate seat in 1855, Mary was furious. Lincoln biographer William Lee Miller stated, "A year later, according to Mrs. Trumbull, when the two almost met outside church, Julia came over to speak to her old friend Mary, but "she turned her head the other way and pretended not to see me." They never made up.

In this context, it is consistent that Lincoln's sarcastic salvo at Shields in the first letter included a reference to marriage being on Shields mind "Dear girls, it is distressing, but I cannot marry you all" (the implication being that Shields intended to marry one) and irritation at the Auditor for squeezing a girl's (possibly Mary's) hand. The letter stated that Shields "seized hold of one of their hands and squeezed, and held onto it about a quarter of an hour. O, my good fellow, says I to myself, if that was one of our democratic galls in the Lost Township, the way you'd get a brass pin let into you, would be about up to the head."

It is possible that the psychological underpinnings of Lincoln's dilemma may not have been about Shields alone, but embraced Stephen Douglas as well. While the evidence is strong that Douglas had called on Mary seriously, it is less so for Shields. But this may have made no difference to Lincoln's jumbled mind at the time. In Lincoln's subconscious, the two could have been one and the same. After all, Shields and Douglas politically and socially were Siamese twins and, the unconscious does not always discriminate. For many years before and after, a blow against one was a strike at the other. Then Shields presented Lincoln with his opening. Shields, either as himself or a surrogate for Douglas, was Lincoln's romantic rival and, in Lincoln's mind, Shields became the dragon Lincoln had to slay, if he were to cut through his fetters and be free to marry Mary.

In the struggle with Shields, Lincoln's pent up emotions made him throw caution to the winds. By accepting and being prepared to duel, he demonstrated to himself, and to Mary, that he was prepared to give his life for her, that his love for her was real and, it would prevent her reaching for the hand of someone else, such as Douglas or Shields.

Shields' motivations, as far as can be gleaned, appear not to have been influenced by any affair of the heart, since he did not know of Mary's involvement in the letter-writing at the outset, nor when he asked Lincoln for personal satisfaction. This only came to light later, but one can never know for sure. Shields could have shone more light on what really had happened, if he had wanted to, when the Lincoln biographies began to appear after the President's death. But he chose not to do so and, one may speculate that the reason was by then he was married to his own Mary and, did not wish to revisit old battlegrounds lest he create new ones. Certainly, he responded cautiously to a question about the matter when it was posed by his biographer Condon.

"No. Lincoln's dead. I'll not discredit his honor (by discussing it)"[25] said Shields, who never made much of the incident. This was confirmed by Shields' wife and son more than eighty years later. "Mother says father considered it (the near duel) a trivial affair and never spoke much of it" wrote Dr. Daniel Shields to Joseph Gurn in 1928.[26]

Psychological theory suggests that the near duel with Shields was the lynchpin in resolving Lincoln's marital ambivalence, his war with himself, and strengthened his resolve about marrying Mary. The pair got together five days after the near duel at the wedding of Martinette Hardin, a relative of Mary, in Jacksonville, and made up again after their twenty one month estrangement. Sarah Rickard, the young woman who had gone out with Lincoln, when he was on the outs with Mary, was a guest at the wedding. Sarah told a reporter "I sat next to Mr. Lincoln at the wedding dinner. He was going with me quite a good deal then. Mary Todd sat just across. Of course, rather than bring constraint upon the company, they spoke to each other, and that was the beginning of the reconciliation."[27] Apparently, Shields was at the wedding too, but no one knows what role, if any, he directly played in cracking the ice between Honest Abe and Mary. The sequel was that Lincoln and Mary, at short notice, rushed into what Lincoln described as "getting hitched" six weeks later, on Nov 4, 1842. According to anecdotes, mostly apocryphal, Lincoln remained a reluctant bridegroom to the end. "It was asserted that Lincoln at last came to the altar almost reluctantly. He was pale and trembling as if being driven to slaughter;… the little son of a friend, noticing that his toilet had been more carefully made than usual, asked him where he was going, and that he gloomily responded: 'To hell I suppose.'[28] The boy was Speed, the son of William Butler who had been Lincoln's second in the near duel. Douglas L. Wilson, in *Honors Voice,* a perceptive study of Lincoln's early years, concluded that Lincoln's marriage to Mary was "the culmination of a long and severe inner struggle,"[29] an interpersonal conflict that included the indomitable Irish-American, James Shields.

The outcome of the near duel and its attendant notoriety had no adverse effect on either Shield's or Lincoln's subsequent political careers. In fact, it may have enhanced them, since dueling was considered a sign of virility. On the other hand, the *Alton Telegraph and Review* the following week tut-tutted and called for their arrest and criminal prosecution. The paper made no bones about damning the "two distinguished gentlemen of the city of Springfield for violating the laws of the state. Because they had agreed to duel while in Illinois they were guilty of a crime, asserted the anonymous editorial writer. The newspaper stated "We consider that these gentlemen have both violated the laws of the country and insist that neither their influence, their respectability nor their private worth should save them from being made amenable to those laws they have violated. Both of them are lawyers - both have been legislators of the State and aided in the construction of laws for the protection of society - both exercise no small influence in community - all of which, in our estimation aggravates instead of mitigating their offence...."[30]

The newspaper did not spare the people of Alton either. It censured them because, "large numbers of our citizens crossed the river to witness the scene of cold-blooded assassination between two of their fellow human beings." *(Appendix R.)* No one else publicly called for their criminal prosecution and, Lincoln and Shields crossed swords only rhetorically after that. Though they continued on opposite sides of the political aisle, they remained amicable and both went on to higher offices and accomplishments.

Not everyone was happy that the affair had ended the way it did. William Butler, Lincoln's second, really wanted the duel to take place and was disappointed that blood had not been shed. Dissatisfied with his own man as much as with Shields, about a week later he wrote "a not very complimentary account" of the conduct of the belligerents to the *Sangamo Journal.* In that he "bore fully as severely upon his principal as his adversary."[31] What Lincoln's reaction was to that

Sketch of James Shields during his middle years.

is unknown, but the stout-hearted Shields was not about to let Butler get away with it. Dispatching a curt note to Butler, through the hand of Gen. Whiteside on Oct 3rd, 1842, he wanted satisfaction. Butler called once again on the services of the redoubtable Dr. Merriman and they stalled for a whole day before responding with their "terms" which were:

Time - Sunrise the following morning
Place - Col. Robert Allen's farm - (in Springfield about 1 mile
north of the State House.)
Weapons - Rifles.

Distance - 100 yards.

Butler further stipulated that the parties were to stand with their right sides toward each other - their rifles to be held in both hands horizontally and cocked, arms extended downwards. Neither party to move his person or his rifle, after being placed, before the word fire. The signal to be "Are you ready? Fire! one - two – three!" about a second of time intervening between each word. Neither party to fire before the word fire, nor after the word three.

These terms were indignantly refused by Whiteside. He and Shields had waited all day for Butler's answer, which now came at 9 p.m. after Shields had left to attend a social function. Whiteside said that while the terms were satisfactory, the place and time were not. Moreover, as state officer, Shields should not violate the laws of the state by dueling within its limits and, Whiteside claimed the challenged party had no exclusive right to dictate time and place. In "curt and abrupt" language, Whiteside insisted the terms should be a matter of agreement. The conditions were further unfair in the position assigned to the combatants. The left-handed Butler would have a distinct advantage over the right handed Shields, if their right sides only were turned toward each other.

Later that night, Gen. Whiteside sought Dr. Merriman at his lodgings to deliver his objection, but could not find him. No meeting took place on the morning of Oct 4th, since neither second could be found. Shields, by now back from the previous night's party, took matters into his own hand. He addressed another note to Butler, which explained that because of the absent seconds, he proposed that he and Butler make preliminary arrangements themselves. He offered to go out to a lonely place on the prairie to fight, where there would be no danger of interruption. Or if that did not suit, he would meet Butler on his own conditions, when and where he pleased. The note was declined by Butler, who claimed that the affair was closed. Neither of them pursued the matter any further.

But it was not the end of Shields' involvement with duels. He was to become entangled in another episode nearly a decade after his own, when he was serving in the US Senate. Shields was named second for Illinois Democratic Congressman William H. Bissell in his heated dispute with Jefferson Davis, the future Confederate President, over which regiments had been the most valiant at Buena Vista in the Mexican War. Davis accused Bissell of insulting the Mississippi Rifles and issued his challenge – army muskets loaded with ball and buckshot. The note was presented to Shields who accepted on behalf of Bissell. Shields immediately set about trying to resolve the affair peacefully and succeeded. Despite his involvement in several near duels, Shields colleagues continued to see him as "genial" and easy to get along with,[32] "a man of great ability,"[33] and someone whose judgment they respected.

After his imbroglio with Lincoln, Shields blossoming political career continued to flourish. He remained State Auditor and, eleven months to the day of his near duel, was appointed to fill a vacancy on the State Supreme Court. When he completed his first term on the bench, he was elected to a full period by the state Legislature on February 17, 1845. During his first term, Shields had received an annual salary of $1,500, which delighted him. At last he was making real money, but it was not to last. No sooner was he elected to a second term, than the Legislature decided to cut the salaries of judges in half to $800 annually. That infuriated Shields and he wrote an angry letter to Senator Breese, with whom he was then on good terms. Shields stated "There is a perfect furor here on the subject of retrenchment… [Judicial] salaries have also been reduced to a miserable pittance. There never was a Legislature so little governed by sound policy and temperate policy."[34] His relationship with Breese was to change four years later in dramatic fashion, which will be discussed later.

Shields' career on the wool sack received mixed reviews and, according to one source, "no cases of national importance came before the Illinois Supreme Court while Justice Shields sat on the supreme bench."[35] That might not have been surprising given that when Shields, "was admitted to the bar the practice of law was in a very crude condition in Illinois. General principles gathered from a few text books formed the simple basis upon which lawyers tried cases and framed arguments in improvised court-rooms."[36] Even Lincoln thought that reading Blackstone once or twice was all that sufficed! Nevertheless, Shields' legal judgment was sound and his most controversial decision was upholding a $400 judgment regarding a fugitive slave against Dr. Richard Eells, president of the antislavery society and later Liberty Party candidate for the US Presidency. According to Condon, Shields was well regarded and was honest, and ranked high as a justice and he "wore the ermine without stain."[37] Shields biographer Henry A. Castle stated "An eminent Minnesota lawyer of a later generation has carefully studied the decisions of Judge Shields as recorded in the Illinois Supreme Court reports, and testifies that they bear conclusive evidence of a legal erudition and discrimination rare in that period." That research was presented by Judge Martin M. Shields at a meeting of the Rice County, (Minnesota) Historical Society in Feb.1932.[38] Eight years earlier, Judge Martin Shields had voiced a similar opinion of his illustrious namesake, stating, "His decisions found in the Supreme Court reports evince a thorough knowledge of jurisprudence."[39] Gustave Koerner held the same view and stated "the few opinions he wrote during his short stay on the bench are lucid and forcible."[40]

One of the rulings, that Shields handed down while he was on the high court, was arguably the most progressive judgment advancing the rights of women in Illinois, or elsewhere on the frontier, until then. It was a case of *Dorman et ux V. Lane,* which aroused considerable interest, because it pitted Lincoln (for William and Nancy Dorman) against Trumbull, (for Nancy's stepfather John Lane) in a high profile case that was socially controversial.[41] The case hinged on a woman's right to inherit her father's land, at a time when women had little legal standing anywhere in the country. It began when Nancy Robinson's father, Charles, who had considerable land holdings, died without making a will. Charles' widow, Mary, took over the land, and subsequently married John Lane, while Nancy was still a young girl. Mary then died and John Lane administered the land, and was guardian to his stepdaughter Nancy, who was still a minor. When Nancy turned 18, she married William Dorman and let her stepfather know that she wanted her father's nearly 500 acres turned over to her. Lane refused and, Nancy and her husband sued to get it. The case wound its way through the Illinois courts and eventually ended up in front of Judge Shields.

William Blackstone's oft-quoted description of a wife's lowly legal status applied in Illinois: "The very being or legal existence of the woman is suspended during the marriage, or at least is … consolidated into that of the husband: under whose wing, protection, and cover, she performs everything." For Nancy Dorman to gain possession of her inheritance, her husband had to file the suit on her behalf, which he did. Lincoln became involved when he was contacted by the Dorman's attorney, Samuel Marshall and Lincoln agreed to take the case on a contingency fee basis. The future President stated "I will do my best for the 'biggest kind of a fee' as you say, if we succeed, and nothing if we fail."[42] After listening to the arguments, Shields ruled for the Dormans. In handing down his decision for the court, Shields said, that since Lane had allowed fifteen years to pass before applying to sell the land to pay his expenses for administering (and profiting) from it, that "it would be extremely hazardous for this court to sanction such gross negligence, and particularly in a case where the same person was both administrator and creditor." Shields added that John Lane "permitted the order to lie dormant for the space of fifteen years, to continue a lien upon the real estate, and after such an extraordinary lapse of time, he applies to the circuit court, and without offering any excuse for this unreasonable delay." With this case, the Illinois Supreme Court established a new rule in the law of estate administration and considerably advanced the rights of women.

After the Supreme Court pay cut, Shields hoped to get off the bench and into a better paying, possibly federal position. He was not disappointed, when his friend, Senator Stephen Douglas, recommended him to President Polk who appointed him Federal Commissioner of Public Lands at a salary of $3,000. It was a desirable post, one that Abraham Lincoln would seek later, but fail to get, when his first term in Congress ended in 1849.[43] Shields could scarcely contain his glee at his Washington

Washington in the mid-1840s around the time James Shields first arrived. This view is looking south east along Pennsylvania Avenue from Washington Circle towards the White House in the background.

appointment; he quickly packed his bags and headed for the nation's Capital to take up his post on April 16, 1845. In his mind, he was following the nation's river of power upstream to its source, where he hoped to influence its course subsequently.

Chapter 6
Courage in Combat:
A Brush with Death

From the halls of Montezuma, to the shores of Tripoli,
We fight our country's battles on the land, as on the sea,
First to fight for right and freedom and to keep our honor clean,
We are proud to claim the title of United States marines.
Marine Hymn Author Unknown.

When James Shields made his way across the country to Washington in the Spring of 1845, he traveled by horse, stage and steamboat, since railroads were still in their infancy. There was less than 5,000 miles of track in the country at the time. The Irish-American set out with a happy heart, for he was on his way to take up the position of Commissioner of Public Lands where he hoped to make his mark. He was qualified for the post since he had overseen public works projects and negotiated contracts for internal improvements in Illinois. He would be doing the same on a national basis.

The countryside through which Shields passed was mostly rural, but for all that, it was a hive of industry. There was movement everywhere and, restless energy was changing the nature of the landscape. Crude cabins in the near wilderness of Indiana and Ohio were giving way to booming towns, with buildings springing up as though overnight. As he progressed, Shields could see great blue herons and red tailed hawks soaring overhead, while below, smoking chimneys from new factories belched black smoke into the once pristine sky. Shields encountered a steady stream of settlers heading in his opposite direction: men in baggy pants with determined looks on their faces, accompanied by women in calico dresses and shaker bonnets and lots of chattering children. They sat quietly on the decks of steamers, strode purposefully alongside heavily laden wagons pulled by straining teams of oxen and crowded the railroad depots. All had one thing in common; seeking the potential bounty that the young country of America would disgorge. Shields, as he sat inside jolting stagecoaches, had good reason for satisfaction; he had arrived in Illinois 15 years earlier, a penniless immigrant from Ireland and, in that relatively short time span, he, without family connections or formal introductions, had become a successful attorney, state senator, United States citizen and had vaulted up the rungs of the political ladder until he was close to as far as a nonnative could go. He had been a state Supreme Court judge, a viable candidate for Congress, was well regarded, and had shown himself to be capable and effective even in the face of adversity. His many successes outweighed his few setbacks and, his biggest defeat by far was being out maneuvered by Lyman Trumbull for the new Illinois Congressional seat in 1843.

As James Shields entered the Washington's graveled streets, he passed beneath newly strung copper wiring shimmering in the sun. Samuel B. Morse, the previous year, had sent a coded message "What God had wrought" between Washington and Baltimore via the newfangled telegraph. To many it seemed an apt augury for the changes occurring in the country as a whole and, they were convinced that the Almighty had indeed deigned it for good.

Shields quickly made his presence felt in the nation's Capital. Taking over a ninety person department administering public lands, he imposed a sense of direction and leadership. Washington was ripe for him and there was the political will to expand the frontier, to acquire more western territory and develop it. Shields, convinced that this was the right course, was determined to make it happen. From his dealings in Illinois, Shields had a good grasp of the required resources and handled his position well. He did his best to bring integrity to his office by resisting the special deals congressmen not infrequently sought for themselves and their friends. His appointment to the land office was political and he remained politically involved. Cultivating relationships with leading Democrats, he became James Buchanan's liaison with President James K. Polk and, when Buchanan sought a vacant Supreme Court position, Shields lobbied hard but unsuccessfully for him. Undeterred by this setback, Shields, not totally impartial to political pork, strengthened his political base by recommending friends from Illinois to the Administration for Government positions.

To encourage western migration, the Government acquired land in great tracts from Native Americans and sold it off in 640 acre sections, or fractions thereof, to individual pioneers for settlement. Shields administered this process, and soon realized that many settlers were poor and could not afford large tracts. To facilitate them, and assist the Government, Shields called for graduated land pricing. He proposed that lots, not bought by the settlers when they first came on the market, should be marked down over time; the longer the Land Office held the land, the lower the price. This was not new, but had never been pushed so hard by anyone else before. Despite his efforts, the measure failed with the Legislature. It got lost in a crowded Congressional calendar that included the Oregon 54'40 boundary dispute with Britain, the Texas to the Rio Grande push with Mexico, and the harbors internal improvement bill. So, settlers in states such as Illinois still had to buy larger lots and pay more than the Government's land acquisition costs, which were in the region of a dollar and a quarter an acre.

Another Shields initiative was more successful and would change how mineral rights were awarded by the Government. Instead of leasing lands with mineral deposits, Shields suggested that the lands be sold outright to mining concerns at an appropriate price. This proposal passed and was signed into law by President Polk in 1846. Mineral land then became available at $5 an acre in forty acre lots. That measure and other incentives proved a boon to the mining industry.[1] Though the Shields recommendation applied only to lead mining in the mid-west, his initiative set a precedent for all subsequent mineral land acts.

In the Spring of 1846, the resourceful Shields was following closely developments on the nation's southwestern frontier far away from Washington. Like most of his political party, he favored annexation of Texas, and was not unduly concerned about any ensuing fall out with *Los Senores*, south of the Rio. The stage had been set for confrontation with Mexico earlier, when President John Tyler in one of the last acts of his Administration, had invited Texas to join the Union. Texas accepted and, the Lone Star State had become the nation's 28th state on Dec 29, 1845. A state Government was formally installed at Austin on Feb 19, 1846. The annexation of Texas did not sit well with *La Republica* and the Mexicans withdrew their ambassador to Washington and began making bellicose moves. Though the Mexicans talked of war, the Administration dismissed their threats as mere saber rattling without substance, and in this case, the Administration guessed wrong. President Polk, who had made settlement of the Oregon boundary dispute and acquisition of California and the Southwest cornerstones for his Presidential campaign, did not especially want war, preferring peaceful acquisition of the Mexican territory. At the same time, the President was not prepared to go out of his way to avoid conflict, if the Mexicans insisted on it. Still, President Polk made a conciliatory gesture, by offering to buy Alta (Upper) California, the territory north of San Diego, and the adjacent western territory, and to settle the disputed boundary line between the United States and Mexico. By the same token, he wanted the Mexican Government to redress the grievances American citizens had against it. The United States claimed that Mexico owed Americans $3 million for lives and property lost since Mexican independence from Spain in 1821.

Feelings ran high below the border and Mexico, refusing to negotiate with *Los Gringos*, railed against them. The National Assembly even went so far as to pass a law saying that to bargain with the *Nordamericos* would be tantamount to treason. Against this backdrop, President Polk, on Jan 13, 1846, ordered Gen. Zachary Taylor to the Rio Grande, to enforce that river as the southern boundary of the United States. The Mexicans were outraged and protested all the more, claiming that the demarcation between the two nations should be the Nueces River 100 miles to the northeast and that General Taylor had made an illegitimate incursion

Shields in uniform following his return from the Mexican War. His left arm is partially immobilized from his battlefield injuries.

onto Mexican soil. He should withdraw, they threatened, or remain at his peril.

Four months later, on April 26, 1846, the first blood of the Mexican-American War was spilled. General Pedro de Ampudia commander of Mexican troops at Matamoros had admonished General Taylor to retire beyond the Nueces or "arms and arms alone must decide the question."[2] When Taylor refused, General Mariano Arista, who had relieved Ampudia two days earlier, notified Taylor that he considered hostilities to have already begun. The nonplussed Taylor replied that "the responsibility must be

105

with them who actually commence them."[3] With that, Ariana dispatched a force of 1,600 cavalry under Gen. Torrejon across the Rio Grande. After crossing, they encountered a US reconnoitering party of 65 dragoons under Capt. Seth Thornton whom they attacked, killing 11, wounding 5 and capturing the remainder. Taylor immediately sent a dispatch to Washington stating that "hostilities may now be considered as commenced."[4] Two weeks later, on May 11, 1846, President Polk called for war saying "Mexico has… shed American blood upon American soil."[5]

Even though what the Administration considered American territory had been violated, Congress was not of one mind on what to do. The Whigs were adamantly opposed to war and 67 voted against it, foreshadowing the opposition that would increase as the war progressed. Some representatives believed that President Polk was making false statements as to both the facts and the merits of the quarrel, and accused him of forcing the fight upon a weak and reluctant nation. Garrett Davis, an outspoken Whig from Kentucky, asserted "It is our own President who began this War" while Thomas Corwin of Ohio admonished "If I were a Mexican I would tell you, 'Have you not room in your own country to bury your dead men?' If you come into mine we will greet you with bloody hands, and welcome you to hospital graves."[6] The Democrats, including Shields, had no compunction about the rights of the matter; they wanted war and embraced it eagerly, as an excellent opportunity to implement the "manifest destiny" of the United States.

Like many in Washington, James Shields became infected with war fever and saw the situation as an opportunity for personal advancement. Shields, anticipating that the war would be short, longed to see action before there was none left to see. He immediately, requested permission from President Polk to be relieved of his federal lands post, for an assignment "in the field." He told the President that he planned to return to Illinois, raise an army of volunteers and march south against Mexico. The President, who regarded Shields highly, was reluctant to let him go. He noted that Shields was serving his country perfectly well where he was. Polk wrote in his diary on May 25, 1846,[7] "I told Judge Shields that there was no propriety in his leaving his office, and that he could be of no possible use to the Government in bringing out or organizing the volunteers. I told him plainly that I thought all public officers in Washington ought to remain at their posts and do their duty, especially during the session of Congress."[8]

But Shields was not to be dissuaded. Over the objections of the President and the Illinois Congressional delegation, which also wanted him to remain in Washington, he was commissioned Brigadier-General and confirmed by the Senate on July 1, 1846. Even though President Polk was disappointed to see Shields leave his Government post, he was not altogether unhappy for pragmatic political reasons. The President thought the military was becoming too eastern-establishment and too Whig based for the good of the Democrats. West Point Military Academy had been established some 40 years earlier, and the officer cult was beginning to make its presence felt in the offices of state. Polk hoped that the war, and the associated expansion of the army, would permit him to appoint Democrats and Westerners to it to achieve some degree of balance and, "to break up the monopoly of the officer corps that West Point graduates had begun to develop."[9] Polk's strategy was unsuccessful, largely because most politically appointed generals and volunteers were inept and not up to the job. The few exceptions worth their stars were, according to historian Winders, William Butler, James Shields and Stirling Price.

Throughout the war, Regular Army officers looked with askance at the non-regulars and carped constantly about them. A young Lieutenant, George Gordon Meade, later a distinguished general in the Civil War, derided the nonprofessionals as "one costly mass of ignorance."[10] There was particular resentment about politically appointed generals with no previous military experience, such as Shields, and his commission was criticized both in Washington and Illinois. According to Koerner "His appointment to so high a rank created considerable dissatisfaction at the time in this state and criticisms of his military qualifications were freely indulged in."[11]

Even though Shields claimed to have had military experience in the Seminole War which had spluttered on and off for 20 years, and to have learned military tactics back in Ireland, he had no experience in a war of this magnitude. Shields' aide-de-camp Lt. Francis Collins said that Shields was so new to military matters that he (Collins) felt "no oppressive sense of his superior rank when thrown in contact with him."[12] But Collins, a butter-barred West Point graduate of the previous year, infused with the brashness of youth, might have felt that way about any superior, even one with formal military credentials. Despite Collins' misgivings, Shields adapted and performed well, in a war where 4,811 Irish-born served on the American side.

Once commissioned, Shields returned to Illinois and wasted no time recruiting a twelve month volunteer force, for a war not expected to last even that long. After raising the third and fourth Illinois volunteer regiments, Shields headed south at their head to join Taylor's forces on the Rio Grande, and arrived at Brazos Island on August 4.1846. Shields and his Illinois volunteers were assigned to Taylor's Central Division under the command of General John E. Wool who already had a large contingent of Illinois recruits serving under him. They were proving a handful because Wool, a strict disciplinarian, did not know how to manage such men. The troops maintained they had come to fight and took a dim view of merely lounging around. Because of that, there was a constant series of infractions and

American army bivouacs in the interior of Mexico as it prepares for the Battle of Cerro Gordo.

disciplinary problems and Shields proved himself invaluable in sorting them out. As one historian noted "The addition of the energetic and able politician-soldier did much to ease the strain on Wool, for he served as a buffer between the stiff professional soldier and his fun-loving, ill-disciplined volunteers." One of the latter later commented: 'All the Illinoisans were glad to meet him (Shields) as it gave them the 2nd officer in command, who was in a position sufficient to represent their rights."[13]

The Central Division under Wool, with Shields in command of the infantry, began its assault on the interior of Mexico on Oct 16. By early November, they occupied Monoclava, where they awaited further orders from General Taylor. A week earlier, on Oct 27, the Mexican garrison had evacuated Tampico half way down the Mexican Gulf Coast and General Taylor decided to secure the city for further advances. He ordered Brigadier General Shields to proceed there and upon arrival to assume command, which the Irishman did.

Overall, the US military strategy for the war was sound, and well executed. The plan was to capture California in the West, occupy the northern states of Mexico as far south as Monterey, take Tampico on the Coast, and sit and wait. The expectation in Washington was that no further military advances would be required, because the Mexicans, then realizing their position was hopeless, would want to negotiate a peace settlement. They would be forced to relinquish California and the Southwest territories in exchange for withdrawal of the American army from the remainder of their territory. Once that ensued, President Polk would have achieved his fourth major political goal. But like so many actions in love and war, things did not go completely according to plan. Though the US achieved all its military objectives, Santa Fe occupied on Aug 18, 1846; Monterey falling on Sept 24 after a gallant four day resistance, and California by the end of the year, the political objectives proved elusive. Just as it takes two to tango, it takes two to negotiate, and Gen. Santa Anna, the "Napoleon of the West," was not about to become President Polk's dance partner. The descendants of the Aztecs stubbornly refused to parley and continued to fight, leaving the President frustrated, since he wanted a quick end to the war. The longer wars go on, the less popular they become and, this was proving no exception; time was not on President Polk's side. Casualties could start to mount and though their numbers thus far had not been excessive, he knew that they had the potential to climb. The death rate was 110 per 1000 and the majority, as in many wars of the time, was not from combat but disease, mostly yellow fever and dysentery. In addition, there was a political threat to the President. Because of his military success, General Taylor was now a popular war hero and Polk recognized that Taylor, a Whig, could parlay his military success into a move to unseat him. For that matter, so could General Winfield Scott, if he ever got into the fray.

Scott, who had been chafing to see action, had been held back in Washington under the plea that the Administration needed his military council at home. Scott, no newcomer to politics, had already been a Whig candidate for the Presidency, and likely would be again; but to assure future success, he needed to move to the sound of guns before they stopped booming. The charge was made in newspapers that Scott was being kept from the front by the Administration because military success would make him a more formidable candidate for the Presidency in 1848. Stung by that allegation, President Polk released Scott to the war in January 1847. The President hoped to dim the luster of

Taylor's victories or at least to divide popular support between the two generals to compromise the political prospects of both. Polk thought that both Taylor and Scott were incompetent and that given a big enough pot, would stew in their own juice. Another reason Polk released Scott was Whig gains in mid-term State and Congressional elections, indicating slipping support for the Administration and the war.

Shields, far from the intrigue of Washington, saw the situation differently. He was eager for a war of larger dimensions and thought the US should assimilate most, if not all, of Mexico. He wrote to his friend, Secretary of State James Buchanan, "The whole country needs Government and protection. I have already written my views to the President on the subject. Had I the power I could as soon arrange affairs on this side of the Sierra Madre... A sudden peace will accomplish nothing. This is the first war of invasion waged by our country. It had been conducted thus far with the strictest regard for the rights of the people... but thus far it has been a war of preparation... if it terminates now we will have the legacy of heavy debt and neither territory or glory."[14] Shields would get his wish, which would reap him rich rewards.

Today, Tampico is about a day's drive south of Brownsville Texas, and sits in a low lying region where the Panuco River meets the Gulf of Mexico. Warm in winter and cooled by the Gulf in summer, the area blends a mixture of Spanish colonial and Indian heritage. It was similar in the Fall of 1846, when James Shields moved there and garrisoned the city on Nov 18.[15] As military commander of Tampico, General Shields was responsible for maintaining good order and discipline, which presented a challenge, both from restive Mexicans and unruly Americans. Because of that, Shields was ordered by General Scott to introduce Martial Law to keep the peace after Scott arrived.[16] The order set up a system of dealing with transgressions not defined in the Articles of War and when Shields enforced that measure, it was for the first time by an American army abroad. Shields conducted court-martials, trying individuals for offenses committed by and against the occupying American forces. The lull in the war during Shields' Tampico Governorship brought other benefits; it gave him and his troops an opportunity to savor some fruits of victory: haute cuisine from a gourmet French cook, imported fine wines from Europe, military balls, splendor and pageantry.

Despite the facile victories by the *Nordamericanos*, Shields thought well of the people south of the border, both as a race and as fighting soldiers. He faulted poor training, deficient leadership and inferior equipment for their defeats, not any lack of courage. He stated "In scenery, soil and climate, Mexico is certainly a wonderful country, and the history of its people is as singular as the country. I think they would make the best light troops in the world, if well disciplined and well officered. The American victories over the Mexicans are not to be ascribed to their cowardice. Their losses in battle were often tremendous, a proof that they were not deficient in some of the attributes of soldiers; but it is singular and something without parallel, that in no single battle or encounter were they found able to withstand the shock of the Americans."[17]

Shields was well ensconced when General "Old Fuss and Feathers" Scott arrived and established his headquarters at Tampico in February 1847. Scott immediately began to prepare for an expanded war and, calling on his experience in the War of 1812, proposed an amphibious assault on the southern port city of Vera Cruz about 250 miles away. Following its capture, he would use the city as a springboard to Mexico City some 250 miles inland. He anticipated total victory, if the war should continue long enough. Shields worked closely with Scott as he made plans and built up his forces for the largest sea-based operation of the conflict.

Within a month of Scott's arrival, his plans for the second phase of the war were complete. As he prepared to embark, he suffered a temporary setback, an outbreak of smallpox among the troops. This did not deter him nor Shields either. Determined not to be left behind, Shields insisted that he too be deployed with Scott down the coast. Initially, the Americans had planned a marine assault alone, but that changed to a combined land and sea operation after Scott surveyed the port. He realized the city could best be attacked from several sides, not just the sea. American troops then landed unopposed close to Vera Cruz and began digging trenches toward its stone walls. The defenses were formidable and included San Juan d'Ulloa, a large Gibraltar-like castle fortress which overlooked the city. As the soldiers excavated into position, the American fleet, under Commodore Matthew Perry laid off offshore. Finally all was in place, and on March 18, General Scott formally called on General Morales, the commandant of both city and castle to surrender. Morales returned a polite note stating that he meant to defend himself to the last extremity.[18]

General Scott saluted and ordered mortar batteries to open fire at a quarter past four that afternoon and this was done "with much spirit and effect." The Navy then sailed to within a mile of the city and commenced fire; as the navy poured it on, the Mexican batteries replied. The castle, armed with some heavy mortars, now and then "threw a shell of immense size and destructive force." Despite being massively outgunned, the Mexican garrison resisted stubbornly for more than a week. After 10 days of pounding, the castle lay in ruins and United States forces breached the city walls, and occupied the city in what came to be known as "the bloodless victory of Vera Cruz." It was not exactly bloodless, at least for the defenders, whose dead numbered more than a thousand. American losses, however, were light, with only nineteen killed.

Things had been going favorably for Americans in the North as well. A month earlier, an attacking force of 20,000 Mexicans had been defeated by a quarter their number under General Zachary Taylor at Buena Vista. After intercepting a communiqué from Scott in the south, requesting the dispatch of 9 regiments for the assault on Vera Cruz. Santa Anna had massed his forces and struck in the north, expecting success. The battle took place on Feb 22-23, and the outcome hung in the balance for most of the fight. But the skill of "Old Rough and Ready" Taylor, the persistence of his men, and the fact that the Americans were entrenched along deep gullies and ravines gave the US troops a resounding victory. Taylor became the hero of the hour, and Buena Vista was to make him an irresistible Presidential candidate the following year. Of course, that lay far in the future. Taylor's Presidential campaign would be enhanced by some jingoistic doggerel subsequently making the rounds:

Old Zack's at Monterey,
Bring out your Santa Anner.
For every time we raise a gun,
Down goes a Mexicaner.

In the south, General Scott began his push inland a mere two weeks after taking Vera Cruz. He rushed because he wanted to remove his troops from the low lying coastal region to reduce their exposure to yellow fever and *la vomita,* which could decimate them. In addition, he was in a foot race not only for Mexico City but with Taylor for the White House as well. Scott's brigade generals were Patterson, Twigg, Pillow and Shields, and the last named was destined to play a pivotal role in a victory at Cerro Gordo ten

112

days later.

Today, a toll road whisks traffic from Vera Cruz up through the Sierra Madre del Sur mountains to Mexico City in a few hours. The scenery is spectacular with snow capped peaks towering above the highway, the tallest mountain being the 18,406 foot Pico de Orizaba. During the Mexican-American War, the route was similar, since even then, the national highway of Mexico snaked across the same difficult and treacherous terrain, but the going was slower. As the route wound upward from the lowlands, it ran between the commanding "Devil's Jaw" heights at Cerro Gordo, at an altitude of 8,000 feet where men, unused to the height, gasp for breath. Santa Ana knew that Scott's forces must traverse the towering *el paso del Diablo*, on the way to Mexico City. He also knew that the pass, about four miles wide at its narrowest, would provide his forces with their most formidable defense, the place

American troops hauling cannons up the sheer cliffs of La Atalaya in the Sierra Madre Oriental during the Battle of Cerro Gordo.

where he stood his single best chance of turning back the Americans, if he was ever going to do so. He also realized that if Scott was not stopped there, there would be no stopping him at all. Santa Anna mobilized all the men he could get, even going so far as to marshal the National Guard defending the Capital, and fortified his position with heavy guns along the mountain ridges. As he entrenched, he determined to make the pass his Thermopyle and, like that ancient Greek battle, the odds at the "Devil's Jaw" overwhelmingly favored the defenders.[19] Santa Anna positioned his troops well and as Scott approached, the pass appeared impregnable. Scouts reported that Americans advancing over open ground would be exposed to withering fire and would sustain enormous casualties. Yet the pass had to be captured and the challenge was to do it without incurring heavy American losses.

General Scott discussed tactics with his command generals, not knowing that history was about to repeat itself, that what happened at Thermopyle 2000 years previously would recur again. As the generals conferred, a young Captain, Robert E. Lee, later Commander in Chief of the forces of the Confederacy in the Civil War, jumped from his froth flecked mount, saluted crisply, and reported that an old disused path entered a deep ravine flanking the sheer cliffs on one side. Though dense undergrowth had all but obliterated the trail and Lee did not know how far it went, the young Captain thought it presented an opportunity. Rather than risk his troops in an all out frontal attack, Scott ordered Generals Twigg and Shields to advance along the unused path in a night assault, thinking that his forces might outflank the Mexicans. If nothing else, the move could prove divisionary, and force the Mexicans to relocate previously entrenched troops from the ridge line.

The Mexicans, as it turned out, knew of the trail, but had deemed it impassible. It was steep as a mule's face and little more than a goat track; a man might traverse it they surmised, but certainly not an army with the impedimenta of war. That was the reason the trail was lightly guarded.

Shortly after nightfall, Shields, at the head of the Third and Fourth Illinois and the Second New York regiments, entered the ravine along with Twigg's brigade. The two forces advanced only a short way before coming under fire and Shields and Twigg devised a strategy: Twigg would stay to engage the enemy, while Shields would advance as far as possible along the track. Neither knew if the path would provide an outlet, or if it would turn into a deadly deathtrap. Battling through the darkness, Shields forces moved along the crooked, rocky and narrow ledge that, at times, was barely wider than a man's shoulders. At one point, Shields forces were blocked by a steep gorge. Displaying considerable ingenuity, Shields advanced his heavy guns by jerry rigging a harness to swing them across the ravine. His brigade made it all the way through the mountain and emerged at dawn behind enemy lines, throwing the Mexicans into confusion. Quick to press his advantage, Shields ordered an immediate advance and charged at the head of his men. The defenders, scrambling to cover an attack from this unexpected quarter, swung their guns around, opened fire at close range, and struck Shields in the chest with a one and a half inch piece of grape shot. It tore through his right lung before exiting close to the center of his back near his spine and Shields fell to the ground, a bloody mess. Though medics carried him to safety and worked feverishly, they were unable to staunch his internal hemorrhage, or stop his sucking chest wound. Shields' injury was pronounced "mortal" by the army field surgeons and the "Devil's Jaws" had become jaws of death for the Irishman.

Battle of Chapultepec a massive painting, by James Walker from a photograph by Louis Daguerre. The blouseless Shields, on foot after his horse had been shot from under him, is in the center foreground. This picture hung for many years in the U.S. Capitol. It is currently in the Historical Center/Marine Museum, Washington, D.C. Navy Yard.

The medics could only stand idly by and watch as Shields slowly deteriorated and died. The General, recognizing he was about to breathe his last, summoned his remaining strength, and said to Richard J. Oglesby, an officer in one of the Illinois regiments: "I am no further use to my country. You are. Lay me down and let me die. I may as well die here as to be taken off the field to die. You are all strong able-bodied men, able to do your country some service. For God's sake lay me down and go do your duty."[20]

There was not much left to do, because the Mexicans, thrown into turmoil by the Americans at their rear, had already panicked and fled.[21] At that point, it seemed that Shields, like Patrick Sarsfield and so many of the Irish "Wild Geese" before him, was destined to die on a foreign battlefield, a long way from his native shores. Surrounded by gloomy men, Shields was awaiting his own demise when help arrived from an unexpected quarter: a Mexican battalion surgeon with the surprising name of Dr. McMillan. At that time, McMillan was a prisoner of war, having been captured by the Americans. It turned out that McMillan had been trained as a doctor in Ireland, had previously been a surgeon in the French army, had moved to Mexico and was now serving Santa Anna. Most importantly, he was skilled in the treatment of war trauma and sucking chest wounds. McMillan asked leave to examine Shields and the US Army

115

surgeons shrugged their shoulders, thinking there was nothing to lose. McMillan, after examining the downed General, removed a silk handkerchief from his satchel, wrapped it around a ramrod and gently but firmly pressed the rod and handkerchief through Shields' chest, along the shrapnel track, into his lung. He then delicately removed the ramrod, leaving the silk cloth in place, inside the chest cavity. By passing the silk entirely through Shields' body, McMillan was able to seal the wound.

Once inside the chest, the silk expanded acting both as a matrix and compress to congeal the blood oozing from the lacerated lung. Meanwhile, General Winfield Scott informed of the severity of Shields' wound, sent a missive to Washington stating "Our loss, though comparatively small in numbers has been serious. Brigadier General Shields, a commander of activity, zeal and talent, is, I fear if not dead, mortally wounded... Shields' brigade, bravely assaulting the left carried the rear battery on the Jalapa Road and added materially to the rout of the enemy." When the dispatch reached the United States, people lamented Shields premature passing. Funeral bells tolled and his obituary and a full sketch of his life were published in newspapers.[22]

But Shields, though close to Valhalla, had not yet stepped across the line and McMillan's improvised surgical treatment began to take effect. The General was carried from the field in a gray twilight and remained for some days in a desperate "struggle between life and death." Reflecting the concerns of his brigade, Capt. Robert E. Lee, wrote "I have heard contradictory reports that he (Shields) was doing well and that he was dead. I hope the former."[23] It turned out to be the former indeed, because Shields' constitution was sound. After an up and down week of spiking temperatures and icy chills, his crisis broke and the General began to show signs of recuperation. Two weeks later, though weak and shaky, he was back again on his feet and began to assume duties. But he suffered a relapse by attempting to do too much too soon and, it was six more weeks before he recovered to the point where he could again assume command. By then, his troops had been reassigned and he was placed in charge of the Palmettos of South Carolina and the New York Volunteers.[24] At that point Shields did not forget the surgeon who had saved his life and rewarded McMillan with a horse and bridle.

Detail from Battle of Chapultepec by James Walker, The storming of Chapultepec Castle on the outskirts of Mexico City occurred on Sept 13, 1847. This detail from the larger painting shows General Shields without his horse in the thick of the fight. Minus his military blouse, he stands out against the dark blue uniforms of the surrounding marines in his white shirt and golden pants.

Shields actions at Cerro Gordo were later eulogized in *"The Sword of Cerro Gordo,"* a poem by Charles J. Beattie, a Chicago attorney.

> *For Shields, the statesman, pure and true,*
> *For Shields, the hero of two wars,*
> *Who led the gallant boys in blue*
> *To victory 'neath the stripes and stars*
> *Whose sword flashed in the hottest fight*
> *For home and country - truth and right*
> *The Sword of Cerro Gordo!*

As he recuperated, General Shields inquisitive mind, much like that of a botanist or explorer, took note of the country of the Aztecs. Later, he described what he saw in eloquent terms *"The region on the coast, which is called the tierra caliente, or torrid country is low hot and unhealthy. It abounds in every variety of tropical productions found in the torrid zone, the most valuable of which are coffee, chocolate, cotton, indigo, tobacco and sugar. The coffee and chocolate, if carefully cultivated would be equal to any in the world, and the sugar cane is, in many parts richer and more productive than any that grows on the island of Cuba...*

About seven or eight thousand feet above the level of the sea, we reach the summit of the Cordilleras. The summit of that mountain range is an immense plain, about one thousand miles long, and from two to six hundred miles wide. This, properly speaking, is Mexico. Here is the mass of the Mexican population. Here are the principal cities of the Republic, including the capital. Here the soil is rich and productive. The region is called the tierra fria, or cold country - not because it is cold, which it is not, but generally pleasant - but because it is cold in comparison with the country between the summit level and the coast. The year in all these regions has but two seasons - the wet and dry seasons."[25]

Shields pushed any thoughts of academic exploration from his mind as the war built up like a symphony to its crescendo: the final advance on Mexico City. However, there was a lull in the fighting due to dispatches from home, which gave Shields additional time to recuperate. North of the border, the presidential campaign season was approaching and President Polk, his popularity fading faster than autumn flowers on a frosty morning, still sought a quick end to the war. He could no longer wait for a military victory and to truncate the war, he and James Buchanan devised a scheme to bring it to a speedy end. The President dispatched Nicholas P. Trist, Chief Clerk of the State Department, as a peace commissioner to Mexico on a secret mission "to enter into arrangements with the Government of Mexico for the suspension of hostilities,"[26] and specifically to offer Santa Anna $10,000 for doing that.

To achieve the President's goal, Trist needed the concurrence of General Scott and, Old Fuss and Feathers, as a military man, was dubious about Trist's activities. He saw it undermining the military mission, but rather than make a unilateral decision, Scott thought it wiser to seek the advice of his senior officers and held an informal council with Generals Shields, Quitman, Pillow and Cadwalader. Pillow was the only one of the group to support the Trist plan, which was seen by the others as an indecorous attempt to grease Santa Anna's palm. The others, including Shields, strongly opposed the move and the anemic peace effort initiated by the Administration fizzled out. But that was not the end of the matter; it proved embarrassing to both Polk and Pillow when news of Trist's activities leaked out later via the American press.

On August 7, 1847, the Americans resumed their move toward Mexico City and captured the town of Contreras where Shields, again in command of his brigade, was reinforced by Palmetto regiments from South Carolina. There, under dark masses of clouds drifting across an angry sky or gloomily capping the distant mountains Shields proved his mettle once again. According to the Semmes Campaign of General Scott, "General Shields brigade, under his skillful management, not only protected in a great measure the movements of (General) Smith, but intercepted in great numbers of the fugitives, who were either cut down under the sure fire of the South Carolina rifles or were made prisoners. Several hundred of the enemy were killed in this battle and fifteen hundred made prisoners and the road opened to the capital."[27]

Semmes also noted that Shields was a courteous officer, not one to stand on gratuitous protocol, when there was an urgent job to be done. He observed how Shields did not argue when General Smith usurped his authority stating "General Smith, in command on the preceding evening, made his plans for the attack the next morning. Upon the arrival of Shields shortly thereafter, Smith, mistakenly thinking that he was the senior officer of the two, gave Shields orders as to the part he was to play in the engagement. Shields, knowing that he outranked Smith, but sensing that the latter was acting in good faith, did not wish to deprive him of credit for his able and carefully worked out plan, and proceeded to carry out his assignment without a word to challenge Smith's right to retain command."

At one point during the Battle of Contreras, Shields and his troops were cut off from the main American force and surrounded by Mexican cavalry and infantry. Believing it was certain death to remain where they were, Shields summoned his officers and ordered them to fight their way out at any cost. The General mounted his horse and led a swift charge catching the Mexicans off guard. Fighting was intense and Shields, as usual, was where it was heaviest. The American colors were carried away three times,

119

two of the color bearers being killed. Bullets had pierced Shields' clothing at the shoulder and through his hat and Shields' horse was bleeding from flank wounds. The American losses at Contreras were 137 killed, 879 wounded and 40 missing.

Churubusco on August 20, 1847 was another stepping stone on the way to Mexico City and once again, the Shields brigade was in the van. Critics subsequently questioned the wisdom of the battle, because the objective was a tough nut to crack, caused significant casualties and, it could have been bypassed on the road to Mexican Capital. Taking a leaf out of the Texan Alamo book, the Mexicans had converted a church and adjoining convent into a fortress and, the Shields brigade, consisting largely of Palmettos, was assigned to capture a well defended bridgehead, the *tete de point,* linking the two. The capable Capt. Robert E. Lee was by Shields' side, helping to improvise strategy during the assault since the American batteries "were too light to make an impression on the works" and "the only manner of carrying the convent and the *tete-de-pont* was by *coup-de-main,* or severe hand to hand conflict."[28] The *tete-de-pont* was the "key" to capturing the citadel, and Scott "sent Shields on the prominent mission of the day" with 273 men to take it.[29] The other American divisions had critical objectives as well "but the grand one of the entire field, which united and combined in itself the requisites to induce upon it an overwhelming force was the point that Shields assailed... It was the strategic (objective) because, of vital importance, its possession would insure the abandonment of the works and decide the combat."[30]

During the attack, the defenders put up a fierce fight and Shields narrowly avoided serious injury when Gen. John A. Quitman, Shields' divisional commander, ordered Shields down from an exposed ridge. Just as Shields was leaving, the area was raked by Mexican shellfire narrowly missing the Irish-American. Quitman was heard to yell "Shields, you owe me one.[31] Despite the resistance and against long odds, Shields' troops stormed the citadel. According to a report "Shields's command was too small, as to numbers, and their practice with the enemy too limited, to accomplish promptly the object of the movement. The wonder is that they succeeded at all, for the Palmetto regiment, as a body, was the only one that, from first to last stood bravely up to their work. And they counted but hundreds, against *more than twice as many thousands!*"[32] The defenders exacted a high toll from Shields and his troops for his victory; out of the

273 men who started the day under the Irishman, 137, or exactly 50%, were lost. Nevertheless, Shields was ecstatic, and Col Ward B. Burnett of New York complimented his leadership saying, "I am proud to say for my gallant regiment that this was the third occasion in which we served under [Shields] with equal success.[33]

Further Detail from Battle of Chapultepec by James Walker showing General Shields on foot holding a converted flintlock musket with bayonet affixed. The shirt-sleeved Shields, appears to be coolly selecting a target while the battle blazes all around. He has removed his military blouse but still is wearing insignia of rank, his tie and golden officer hat.

A side note of the battle of Churubusco was that two hundred defenders, who stiffened the ranks of Mexican resistance, were Irish born members of St. Patrick's Brigade. Some had served previously in the American army and had switched sides after being promised "rich fields and large tracts of land." by Santa Anna.[34] Following their capture, the *"San Patricios"* underwent summary court martial and fifty were executed on the spot.

Chapultepec, a fortified hill, on the outskirts of Mexico City was the last major battle of the war. Its defenses included a military academy which was defended by 5,000 troops including young cadets, *Los Ninos*. Like their elders, they proved no match for the Americans either.[35] At this battle Shields' arm was shattered, yet he stayed in the fray until the city wall was breached and the Capital fell. Shields was among the first to burst into the beleaguered city, even though he had been instructed to play a secondary role. He was supposed to make a diversionary move and the city was to be attacked by the main bulk of forces under Gen. Worth. But in the confusion of battle, things did not work out that way.

With his own words, Shields recounted what happened "I had been ordered by General Scott to make a demonstration on the city of Mexico from the Chapultepec side. I gathered up the magnificent Palmetto regiment, Colonel Butler, the Mounted Rifles, the New York Volunteers and O'Brien's battery, and led a sudden dash along the aqueduct toward the city. The enemy gave way, and seeing that, we pressed them all the harder to prevent re-forming. General Scott, who intended that General Worth should take the city by the San Cosme route, instead of the Belen route, saw from the heights I was making rather rapid progress, and immediately detached two aides-de-camp to stop me. I saw them coming and suspected their errand. I didn't want any message from General Scott at that precise moment, and when the aide de-camp got within speaking range and said "General Scott

Captain (later General) Robert E. Lee, as he looked when he fought alongside Shields, during the Mexican-American War. Lee became commander in chief of the forces of the confederacy in the Civil War. His confiscated estate in Virginia was turned into Arlington National Cemetery. One report stated that Gen. Shields' son Charles was buried at Arlington. The Arlington authorities were not able to confirm that.

sends his compliments to General Shields, 'I hollered out, All right, but I haven't time to talk with you now; wait a bit.'

General Scott seeing that we were still pushing ahead at a breakneck speed sent General Quitman to me, and my horse having been shot under me, I was on foot, explaining to Gen. Quitman it would be madness for us to desist from our advantage, and that he General Scott would never have ordered it if he knew how gloriously we were advancing. Oh! But he was a gallant soldier, that General Quitman, and a generous one, and instead of ordering me back, he told me to go ahead. So, on we went, and in less than twenty minutes we entered the garita, or city gate, and unfurled the first American flag in the city of Mexico - the flag that was borne by the gallant Palmetto regiment."[36] Thus, it was Shields "that led the advance troops into Mexico City and planted the Stars and Stripes on the halls of Montezumas."[37] That action has become legend and is immortalized in the words of the marine hymn, *Halls of Montezumza* which is sung whenever marines meet in official ceremony.

Shields role in the battle of Chapultepec was immortalized in a painting of the battlefield by James Walker that hung on the walls of Congress for many years.[38] In that picture Shields, in the foreground in shirtsleeves can be seen brandishing a long barreled musket in the middle of the men, while General Quitman on horseback is conferring with another officer. Years afterwards, Shields was asked if that painting was a "fancy sketch?"

"No. We were taken just as we stood by a photographer who followed the army to take sketches. He got his cameo in focus" laughed Shields. According to Francis O'Shaughnessy the painting was a copy of a daguerreotype made on the battlefield by Daguerre, the father of photography.[39] Following the capture of Mexico City the wounded Shields was breveted Major General by General Scott, but the rank was not confirmed by the Senate in Washington and he reverted to Brigadier General. Even though General Shields was not promoted by his superiors, he could scarcely have been better regarded by rank and file troops, or, for that matter, by noncombatants according to anecdotes going the rounds. One tale claimed that during the battle for Mexico City a lady of "unchallengeable virtue" fell into the hands of the "soulless" Mexicans and, General Shields personally facilitated her rescue. A "sweet singer" of the period celebrated this crowning act of heroism in a long, long ballad which concluded with the stanza:

> *But not a braver deed was done,*
> *The conquering siege will show,*
> *Than General Shields for woman wrought*
> *Defying Mexico"*[40]

Shields in dress uniform. This portrait reportedly was created by Currier and Ives.

Shields did not remain long in Mexico following cessation of hostilities, and soon was furloughed home on convalescent leave. His orders, signed by General Scott, stated "Brigadier General Shields, so much distinguished for gallant and efficient services, will for the recovery of his general health, impaired by repeated wounds, return to the United

States to report in person, or by letter to the Department of War. Overall, Brigadier General James Shields had shown that he was an able and audacious commander who sought glory for himself, but not at the expense of his men. He never asked them to do something he would not do himself and, as a result, they willingly followed him into the thickest fray. He demonstrated a determination on the battlefield that would stand him in good stead in his many political battles looming ahead.

Chapter 7
Senator from the "Prairie State":
Twice Elected for Same Session

If sadly thinking, with spirits sinking,
Could, more than drinking, my cares compose
A cure for sorrow from sighs I'd borrow,
And hope tomorrow would end my woes.
But as in wailing, there's nought availing,
And Death unfailing, will strike the blow,
Then for that reason, and for a season,
Let us be merry before we go!
Let Us Be Merry Before We Go by John Philpot Curran (1750-1817.)

James Shields, if he had wanted adulation, could scarcely have wished for a better reception when he arrived home from the Mexican War. Everywhere he went he was feted, famed, and fussed over as a conquering hero. Flags were flown in his honor and, nothing seemed too good for a man who had given so much for the young U.S. Republic. There were rapturous receptions, speeches and glorious galas in his honor. Senator Stephen A. Douglas organized an enormous testimonial dinner for him in Washington and, the State of South Carolina, because sons of the Palmetto State had served under his command, bestowed on him an ornate commemorative sword, at a cost of $5000. It was embellished with gold, emeralds and garnets, plus engravings of his successes at Vera Cruz, Cerro Gordo and Chapultec.[1] Shields own state of Illinois also awarded him a ceremonial sword, but was less generous, laying out a mere $3000.[2]

With such widespread acclaim from a grateful nation, Shields, no doubt, expected recognition from the Polk Administration as well. He had supported the President politically during the conflict, had kept Polk and Buchanan well informed with private correspondence about what was going on behind the scenes in the field, and had laid his life on the line for one of President Polk's political cornerstones, the annexation of California. But it was not to be; in the final analysis, all that counted for naught. Shields sacrifices would go unrewarded as far as the Administration was concerned. The President, mindful of his political turf, was bothered that Shields had praised General

Scott publicly at a gathering in South Carolina. The newspapers had reported "General Shields speaking of General Scott, at Augusta, remarked "that though he entered the army prejudiced against General Scott, he considered him after his experiences under his command, having no living superior in the qualities of a great commander."[3] Polk, aware of Scott's Presidential aspirations, did not welcome such support for an opponent from anyone. At the same time, the Administration knew it could not totally ignore Shields either, since he was a wounded war hero. In a tepid acknowledgement of his gallant achievements, Shields was invited to a State reception at the White House, along with forty other military officers. There, he was not singled out for individual recognition even though he got a chance to chat with the President at the dinner, but that was the extent of the President's largesse.[4] Neither the President nor anyone else in the Administration was interested in hearing anything Shields had to say about how the war had been waged and won. Nor did they want to discuss any political appointments for Shields and, he found his cool reception in Washington hard to fathom after the white-hot heat of war.

The President had good reason to be nervous about returning war heroes. Successfully waged wars often rebound to the benefit of the Party in power, but not always and, it was so in this case. The President, who had started and implemented the war, had seen his stock sink lower than a sitting seagull on a sea wall. He was angered by the criticism heaped upon him, and his declining popularity was a major reason he did not seek reelection in 1848. On the other hand, the stock of General Zachary Taylor had soared to alpine heights. Despite his homespun manners, "Old Rough and Ready" Taylor was lionized and, his unpolished ways were converted into political assets. His long military record appealed to Northerners; his ownership of 100 slaves lured Southern votes, and he had not committed himself on any troublesome issues to arouse the ire of edgy naysayers. The Whigs duly nominated Taylor to run against the Democratic candidate, Lewis Cass, who favored letting the residents of territories decide for themselves, whether they wanted slavery. They were able to capitalize on Taylor's military victories to defeat the Party that had made his glory possible.

Shields could expect little from either the Administration, or the Whigs when they got into power, and was forced to face the unpalatable fact, that for him, the Washington cupboard was bare. At the very least, he had expected to be rewarded with a military promotion to the permanent rank of Major-General, which did not transpire. All he actually received were orders back to Tampico, Mexico, in other words, a one way ticket to political oblivion. While in Washington, he had stayed at the home of Secretary of State James Buchanan which may have aroused suspicions with Polk.[5]

Though bitterly disappointed, Shields had few options but to accept the cold shoulder as best he could. His friends could offer him nothing and his foes did not want him either. Some even saw him as a loose cannon with an inflated ego and, his star that had soared so high in Mexico was washed out by the cold gray Washington dawn. Forced to lick his wounds, he accepted his lot and left for the Land of the Aztecs again. En route, the General traveled via the mid-west and on April 17, 1848, stopped in St. Louis, where he was accorded a public reception that must have warmed the cockles of his heart. It was very different from his experience in Washington. In the Gateway City, Shields was loudly acclaimed with the pageantry of banners and bunting waving in the wind, and was met by marching bands and a dense and wildly cheering crowd. The history of Missouri notes "a special committee met the steamboat on which Gen. Shields arrived, and escorted by a parade he went to the Courthouse where he was met by the Mayor.[6] Gen. Shields responded to the Mayor's welcome with a speech, paying high compliment to both the regular army and "our citizen soldiers for their gallant conduct in Mexico." Neither the regulars nor the volunteers would have been so signally successful without each other he said and surmised that while the officers of both performed their duty well, it was the national impetuosity and indomitable bravery of the rank and file which made victory perch upon our banners.

"Men who had never seen a Squadron in the field vied with the veteran in the most trying scenes of carnage" he said to a wildly cheering audience.

"Freedom at home, and the prestige of an honored flag makes the American an invincible soldier" he concluded.[7]

Some, who saw the returned Shields, were shocked at how he had aged and commented that clearly he looked the worse for wear. One remarked "He is stouter than when we saw him, some two years at General Taylor's camp...Then, he looked like an elegant gentleman. He had not a wrinkle on his brow, and his countenance even wore a smile. His beard was closely shaven and his eyes were lighted up with the brilliant fire of hope. And yet how a short term of service alters a man? Yesterday he looked like the hero of many wars. His brow was seamed with the lines of fatigue and suffering, and his upper lip was garnished with a thick moustache. His complexion was bronzed, his arm, from a late wound, hung in a sling; but his eyes were still brilliant with martial fire. There were hundreds who flocked around him and sought to grasp his hand."[8]

Ornate ceremonial swords presented to Brigadier-General Shields by the states of South Carolina and Illinois following the Mexican-American War. The swords, purchased for $15,000 by the US Government following the General's death, were given to the Smithsonian Institution for safekeeping. They are now stored at the Armed Forces History Division of the National Museum of American History and may be viewed by special appointment.

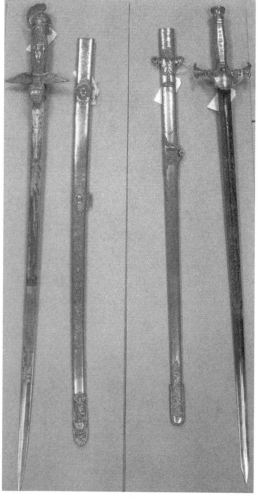

Following his threadbare treatment in Washington, this tumultuous reception in the "Show Me" state took his breath away, and had the salutary effect of raising his sights towards elective office again, only this time on the national scene. If others could parlay military achievements into success in the political arena where real power lay, could not he? As he reviewed his situation, he could see he was bright, had a ready wit, was as articulate as any politician on the stump and crowds resonated to him, all endowments that could propel him into political office. But alas, he sighed, that would have to be in the future, since he was still in the army and on orders out of the country. He had decided to remain on active duty, at least for the time being, and continued down the Mississippi to the brassy city of New Orleans. While he sat in the Crescent City, awaiting a steamer to take him across the Gulf of Mexico to Tampico fate, in the form of fresh orders from Washington, intervened. The newly cut directives commanded him to return to Frederick, Maryland for the court-martial of his former comrade-in-arms General Gideon J. Pillow who was accused of disloyalty to "Old Fuss and Feathers" Scott. While Pillow's "crime" included insubordination and supporting the secret Trist mission to bribe Santa Anna during the war, his real offense was to write critical letters about Scott to newspapers.[9] Shields was glad to return to Frederick to testify on behalf of his battlefield comrade and, when the trial was held, Shields came to the defense of his fellow officer. Shields testimony helped exonerate Pillow, who was acquitted and, even though Scott and the Administration were not satisfied, the charges were subsequently dropped.

At that point, General Shields decided to forego returning to the Mexican tropics. In characteristic style he abruptly mustered out of the army on July 20, 1848. Already he had formed plans for his future; he would return to Illinois, restoke the political fires beneath his boiler and run for elective office. On the asset side of the political ledger, his health had largely recovered and as a war hero he was highly popular; on the debit side, anti-immigrant sentiment was rampant and, it was nearly a decade since Shields held elected office. Perhaps he already had been forgotten? Nevertheless, General Shields raised his banner to test the political winds, with his eye on the Senatorial seat of Judge Sidney Breese which would become available the following year. At first Breese and his supporters were unconcerned. They complacently dismissed Shields' chances. Deriding the Irishman, they sniggered that he had been shot through the bowels - now if it only had been through his head, no one would have expected any serious result.[10] As an incumbent, Breese was in a strong position and, it appeared he had little to fear. He was a loyal Party man, had the support of a majority of the Democrats, especially the White House, and there were no controversial issues against him to bring him down. Shields, though liked by many, clearly faced an uphill fight. He had credentials with the electorate; now he was "General" Shields, a well known war hero, who had proved his courage in combat. As the Centennial History of Illinois later summed up, "Breese was an experienced legislator but not a statesman of eminence; Shields laid claim to neither qualification but had powerful personal friends, popularity as an Irish champion of liberty and the reputation of a military hero in the Mexican War."[11]

Still Shields had a hard row to hoe. William B. Plato, Senator from Kane County, commented in a letter to Breese on June 30, 1848 "Gen. Shields is here doing his best but your friends have as yet no fear of the result - and you can rest assured that he will achieve but little with all of his military achievements."[12] Still, Shields, a dogged and astute campaigner, traveled the length and breath of the state delivering patriotic speeches, receiving honors and quietly asking Party leaders for their support. He attended church meetings and gatherings and resumed his participation in freemasonry, which had dropped off during the war. His efforts began to pay off and soon sentiment began shifting in Shields' direction. Increasingly, his war record came into play. People came to hear him speak and stayed to shake the hand of the man that had been shot expanding the country. The Senate race tightened and, soon citizens changed the lampoon about Shields being shot in the bowel to the observation that "the piece of grapeshot that struck Shield's has killed Breese's chances of reelection."

Shields had a major hurdle to vault: his immigrant origins and, in a bold move, the General even turned that liability into an asset. He pointed out shrewdly, that because he had been born in Ireland, he could never be President of the United States, since that was barred by the Constitution. Therefore, he was no threat to the Presidential aspirations of Douglas or any other Democrat. Both Party leaders and the people of Illinois responded enthusiastically to that and Shields' increasingly public overtures.

By August 1848, Shields stock had risen so high that Breese's bubble of complacency had burst about his ears and, he began to devise a means of spiking Shields' guns. He floated an idea - suppose Shields were offered a prestigious political appointment that he could scarcely refuse, one that would remove him from the Senatorial race? That would solve Breese's re-election problem. Breese was on favorable terms with President Polk, who valued his support and many believe that Judge Breese approached the President for help in his tight race with Shields. Following that discussion, the President made Shields an offer that an ambitious politician on the eve of an uncertain election could scarcely refuse: Governorship of the Oregon Territory.

The Governorship was available now that the boundary dispute with Britain had been resolved and, Abraham Lincoln then a congressman was interested in it. He would have been glad to accept the Oregon appointment had it been offered to him, but he was a Whig and considered too small a political fish to be offered such a big political prize.[13] James Shields, on the other hand, was just the right fit and, the bait was cast into his waters on Aug 21, 1848. Then, the President and Breese sat back to see if Shields would bite. If the Irishman accepted, his decision would remove him from the Illinois Senatorial race. No one knows what went through Shields' mind when the tasty hook floated by. There is no doubt it had appeal and no doubt, Shields would have accepted the Oregon appointment gladly, had it been offered when he first came home from the war. But now things were different; he was running neck and neck for the Senate seat from Illinois. Sensing the Governorship was merely a sop to stop his gallop, Shields turned it down. According to the History of Oregon "The President's first choice for Governor was General J. Shields of Illinois but he declined the position."[14] Shields had set his sights on the Senate and wanted nothing less; his bandwagon was gathering steam. When people learned that he had turned down the Oregon appointment, Shields stock soared even higher and, he began receiving attestations of support. One came from his old friend and divisional commander, General Quitman, which included his analysis of the situation:

"…in spite of the hostilities of some high functionaries at Washington, you will be returned to the Senate from Illinois. I give you my hand upon your prompt rejection of the honor of exile, which our cool and calculating friend the President has proposed to confer on you… I hope to see you in the Senate."[15] Quitman had been appointed the civil and military Governor of the City of Mexico, and no doubt, would have welcomed a friend in the Senate in far away Washington.

What Quitman predicted was far from certain. Shields continued his campaign against Breese and also John A. McClernand, a downstate Democrat, who had entered the contest hoping that Shields and Breese would deadlock. Breese was the favorite of the conservatives and Shields represented the liberals and if they offset each other, McClernand could become the compromise candidate. That did not occur; Shields was not about to slip up allowing McClernand to slip in. The caucus was held on January 12, 1849 and, on the first ballot Shields received 32 votes, Breese, 27 and McClernand, 8.

Thirty four votes were needed for victory. On the second round of voting, three Breese supporters moved over to Shields and the final tally was Shields 35, Breese 24, McClernand 8. Shields was in. The full election was held the following day and Shields' victory was overwhelming. On the first and only count, he received 70 votes, more than double all the other candidates combined. Whig William Thornton received 26 and William Ogden 1. Shields triumph was well received except, of course, by Breese, who blamed his defeat on the fact that he was busy representing the state in Washington, while Shields, hampered by no such obligations, could campaign throughout the state as he wished. But Breese had contributed to his own downfall; he had been in trouble in some quarters because he had fallen short with federal patronage, was feuding with Douglas over land grants for the Illinois Central Railroad and had not brought benefits to the state as expected. Despite that, his defenders stoutly maintained that Breese's "defeat may entirely be attributed to the personal popularity of General Shields who was on the ground and became well acquainted with every member of the Legislature."

Nevertheless, Shields win was remarkable and truly against the odds. Behind the scenes, powerful forces had lined up against the Irish-American, both in Illinois and Washington, including officials at all levels up to the President. Ebenezer Z. Ryan of Springfield in a letter to James M. McLean two days after the election, wrote "I suppose you have seen through the medium of the newspapers, on Saturday last Genl Jas Shields was elected to the senate of the United States in opposition to the known instructions of the Administration at Washington and in opposition to the efforts of every office holder in the State of any magnitude, altho nominated by a Democratic Caucus. Yes they knew they had to do it or be defeated by the proviso Democrats with the aid of the Whigs. Consequently, they had no other alternative to save themselves from open and notorious defeat only by agreeing amongst themselves to elect Genl Shields."[16] Not all was sour grapes, however. The Democratic newspaper, the *Illinois State Register*, exulted publicly "The fame of General Shields throughout the United States precludes the necessity of any remarks of ours in relation to his fitness to the station to which he is about to be chosen..." The Whig press also seemed pleased but, as befitting an opposition publication, was less lavish in its praise of the Irishman.

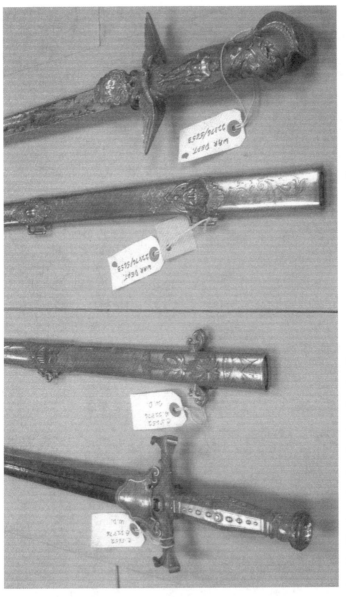

Close up of the intricate designs and encrusted jewels on the swords presented to General Shields by the states of Illinois and South Carolina. Note the emerald in the vase shaped pommel on the palmetto sword. For a complete description of the swords, see appendix T.

Shields relished his hard won victory and, with his mercurial quirk of character that sometimes converted his Nike victory wings into Achilles heels, was not above flaunting it. Shortly after the congratulations in Illinois had abated, he made his way to Washington as the new Senator-elect from Illinois. In the nation's Capital, he paid his compliments to lame duck President Polk on

February 24th[17] and, no doubt, relished doing so. Shields became reacquainted with his old comrade-in-arms, President-elect Zachary Taylor and they dined together. This time no anti-Irish slogans were bandied about the drawing room and the air was laced with *bon homie*. There were as many compliments as toasts at an Irish wedding and, Shields was described as "a brilliant jewel from the Emerald Isle." Shields reciprocated by hoping that Taylor's "Administration rebounds as much to the glory and good of his country, as his victories have to her honor and renown."[18]

All would have been well for Shields if he had left things at that and departed, but he did not. Through conceited recklessness, he took a foolhardy and fateful step, one that would cost him dearly, and nearly dealt a death blow to all his political aspirations. Though Shields did not have to take his Senate seat until the regular session commenced nine months later in December 1849, he decided to participate in the Executive session of the Senate called to ratify President Taylor's Cabinet appointments in March. This gave Breese and his cadre just the opening they needed to challenge the legitimacy of Shields' election. Not that they had not already started doing so. Immediately after his defeat by Shields, Judge Breese had started contesting Shields' election on citizenship grounds.

The US Constitution has three eligibility requirements for the Senate: that individuals live in the state they represent, that they be 30 or more years old and they must be US citizens for at least nine years. Shields satisfied the first two requirements but there was a question about the third. He had become an American citizen on October 21, 1840, which in March 1849 left him seven months shy of the required time span. He had cavalierly brushed off the Breese attacks on this issue in the past but, as it transpired, was unwise to do so now. Nevertheless, Shields pressed ahead and presented himself for the Executive Session of Congress on Monday March 5th, 1849. Douglas managed to have Shields sworn in for the special session, but Shields' participation proved his undoing. One week after attending the session, he was unceremoniously turfed out of the Senate by its select committee after his election was voted "void." According to the Congressional Quarterly's Guide to Congress "When he (Shields) appeared, March 5, 1849, to take his seat, at a special session of the Senate, the question of whether he had been a citizen the required number of years was raised... Although Shields was seated on March 6, the Senate on March 15 adopted a resolution declaring his election void on the grounds of insufficient years of citizenship."[19] Shields, now recognizing his awful mistake, tried to undo the damage, but it was too late. He fought back tooth and nail, but got nowhere. Frustrated, he decided an attack on Breese was his best defense and began a dubious disinformation campaign to discredit Breese. It did him no good and compromised whatever support Shields had.

In his counterattack, the Irishman alleged that Breese was in error about his naturalization and brazenly claimed that he had arrived in America as a child with his father and had become a citizen through the naturalization of his parent. According to US law, when a parent becomes a citizen, a minor child automatically derives citizenship at the same time. Shields claim, of course, was false; his father had died many years before Shields ever set foot in the new world and Shields had traveled alone. There was another, more egregious and quasi-comical aspect to Shields' false claim: the judge who had naturalized Shields in Effingham Court House in Oct 1840 knew all the circumstances of Shields naturalization, including exactly when it occurred, because that judge was none other than his political rival, the Honorable Sidney Breese.

Undeterred, Shields continued his broadsides at Breese, insisting he was wrong and Breese persisted in pointing out that Shields' claim was fallacious. Earlier, Shields had written Breese a hectoring letter warning him to stop his campaign against him and threatened rashly "if, however, you continue your course of injustice toward me, and refuse this request, I here give you fair warning - let the consequences fall on your head - I shall hold myself accountable both before God and man for the course I shall feel bound to pursue toward you."[20]

Breese, an experienced politician, recognized a gift horse when he saw one and rang alarm bells that Shields had threatened to assassinate him. This gained some sympathy for Breese and resonated with the people of Springfield who were growing tired of the unending struggle for the Senate. They remembered Shields' highly publicized shindig with Abraham Lincoln some seven years previously and that lent credence to Breese's claim, that the bloodthirsty Shields, though brave in battle, was unsuited for the Senate. Support for Shields evaporated faster than dew off dogwood in June. Even Shields' old friend, Stephen Douglas was aghast at Shields' ill advised actions. Distancing himself from Shields, Douglas even went so far as to recommend to

Illinois Governor Augustus C. French that someone else be appointed to the Senate in Shields' stead. French, finding himself pressed between the forces of two powerful rivals, demurred. Taking refuge in the Illinois Constitution, he maintained that, because Shields was a compromised candidate from the outset, no election had actually taken place.

Statue of James Shields erected by State of Illinois in Statuary Hall, U.S. Capitol Washington D.C in 1893. Before going to Washington, the bronze figure was displayed that year in the Illinois building during the World's Columbian Exposition in Chicago. The exposition, which celebrated the discovery of America, had an attendance of more than 27 million. The statue now is located in the Capital's Hall of Columns.

"Therefore I have no power to appoint anyone to the Senate"[21] declared the Governor in an adroit piece of political fence sitting. This would prove more of a boon to Shields than to Breese, because it gave Shields a much needed breather, and time to pull himself together. Governor French, in his wisdom, bided his time and waited until October before convening a special session of the Legislature to elect a new Senator. By then, Shields was eligible for the Senate seat, since he had been a citizen the requisite 9 years. If the Governor had done it as a show of support for Shields, it appeared to be an empty gesture, since Shields by his rash actions had alienated just about everyone. It seemed as though he had committed political suicide. The consensus among Democrats and Whigs was that Shields' stock had sunk so low that he was out of contention altogether and he passed a bleak summer. But once the election was announced in the fall, the previously despondent Shields gained new life and threw his hat in the ring once again. But this time he was involved in an uphill struggle, even steeper than his first. Unlike his previous campaign, where public sentiment had been in his favor, the currents of public opinion were definitely running him onto rocks. The Whigs had attempted to exploit the situation and accused the Democrats of being against foreigners. "No Whig had a hand in the business"[22] they declared self righteously while, at the same time, underscoring Shields foreign nativity. This time, there were no public receptions in Shields' honor, since he was no longer a heroic figure cast in bronze but the would-be assassin with feet of clay, a severe handicap, even for the politically nimble Shields.

For all that, Shields had had one thing going for him; a week is a long time in politics and six months a lifetime and, by the fall it was politics as usual again. Democrats had become hopelessly entangled in an internecine struggle about internal improvements and could not agree on a single Senatorial candidate. With such divisiveness, there was no clear cut favorite in the run up to the election and, once again, Breese was Shields' principal opponent, with McClernand waiting in the wings. The election was held on October 22 1849 and, voting was stubborn and contentious with 21 ballots in all. First one had the edge, then the other. Finally, it was over. Shields got the requisite majority by drawing on some of McClernand's supporters. The final poll was Shields 37, Breese 20, McClernand 12. For Shields it was bitter-sweet; he had won the seat nearly a year earlier, had lost it through his own recklessness, and finally triumphed through his own dogged efforts. It had been quite a roller coaster and he was well pleased with the outcome. At last, he was on his way to Washington, this time for the duration of the 31st Congress of the United States, but this time without any gloating

Condon noted "On Monday December 3, 1849, Mr. Mangum presented the credentials of the Hon. James Shields of Illinois elected as senator by the Legislature of Illinois, for the term of six years, commencing on the 4th day of March, 1849, which were read, and the oath prescribed by law was administered to Mr. Shields, and he took his seat in the Senate."[23] The session had run from March, but Shields was recognized as serving from Oct 27, 1849. In the 31st Congress of the United States, there were 112 Democrats, 105 Whigs and 13 Free-Soilers, who held the balance of power. Given such distribution, it is not surprising that there was bitter factionalism and almost everything was contentious. For example, it took three weeks and 63 ballots before a Speaker of the House, Howard Cobb of Georgia, was elected.

Questions of grave importance came before the Senate while General Shields sat there, none, perhaps more so than whether or not California should be admitted to the Union as a free-soil state. Compromise measures to preserve the Union had to be resolved before that could take place. In addition, the rail roads, public land grants and homestead law all commanded attention, as did Southern threats of disunion, which widened the breach between North and South. Shields attempted to play peacemaker and bridge builder, roles for which he was admirably suited, since he remained on good terms with politicians of all political persuasions. When John Calhoun, the South Carolina Senator, died a few days after his final speech in the Senate while participating in "The Great Debate" on the "Compromise of 1850," it was Shields who delivered his eulogy before the Senate.

Once Shields was in the Senate, he and Douglas mended fences and as junior Senator from Illinois, Shields tended to side with Douglas on most issues. But the moderately conservative Shields was his own man, sometimes to the chagrin of his supporters. On Dec 22, 1852, for example, the Irish-American's amendment to the transcontinental rail road bill, that none of the money appropriated in the legislation should be expended within any one state was "a bombshell cast into the camp of his friends."[24] This caused consternation, especially in California where it appeared the railroad would go no further than the towering Sierras.

Shields was industrious and served on various Senate committees including the Committee on Military Affairs.[25] He was Chairman of the Committee on the District of Columbia, a member of the public land committee, and was instrumental in getting recognition for military veterans. A supporter of railroad expansion, he was in favor of a transcontinental railroad along a central route, with Chicago as its eastern terminus. This placed him in conflict with the leadership of his Party, especially President Franklin Pierce and also Jefferson Davis both of whom wanted a southern railroad. Shields strongly supported higher education, particularly for state colleges, and voted in favor of giving more land to agricultural colleges in larger states such as California.[26]

Shields was disappointed when Franklin Pierce instead of Stephen Douglas, got the Democratic Presidential nomination in 1852. In the Presidential race, Shields as a loyal Party man did not withhold his support from Franklin Pierce over his old friend and former commander General "Old Fuss and Feathers" Winfield Scott, the Whig standard bearer. Charges were made during the campaign that Pierce was late getting into the war and had displayed cowardice in combat. War hero Shields, who had been Pierce's commander, charged to his rescue to refute those allegations. Shields was elated when his man carried the Presidency and anticipated that he would be rewarded with a higher position in Government. It was not to be, since President Pierce and the Democrats were suspicious of Shields' high regard for Scott, and were not about to facilitate any measure that might potentially assist their rival. So Shields, as happened before, was sent to political purgatory by the White House. Once again, there were no political plums for him to pick.

There was no more contentious issue in American politics in the mid 19th century than slavery and, the North and South had grown increasingly polarized. Just about everyone, whether they felt strongly about the issue or not, was forced to take sides. The North, for the most part, were free soilers, opposed to the spread of slavery, if not its total abolition. The South, on the other hand, wanted new territories to enter the Union allowing slave property on equal terms with the free states. Southerners, losing their hold on national politics, felt pushed to the wall, and defiantly insisted on the rights of their position. Should this be denied them, they declared, they were prepared to withdraw from the Union and to secure their rights with force of arms, if necessary.

Shields recognized that many from the South wanted to withdraw from the Union come what may, no matter what concessions were wrung from the North. In 1849 he wrote "My deliberate opinion now is that the leaders are secretly but anxiously desirous of a secession. They have reasoned themselves into the belief that the withdrawal of 4 or 5 states from the Union would force the rest of the Southern states to withdraw and that a Southern Confederacy would materially improve their condition."[27]

Like many of the people of Illinois, whom he represented in the Senate, Shields was not an abolitionist, but rather a pragmatist in favor of the status quo to preserve the Union. He saw slavery as evil and opposed it as a "violation of natural rights" but also opposed federal intervention in "domestic institutions," a political euphemism for slavery, in any state that already had it.[28] He did not want any free state turned into slave, nor the creation any additional slave states. On that he was solid.

His was not a popular position in downstate Illinois, where the census of 1840 reported there were still 331 slaves, down from 747 a decade earlier. Many downstate citizens had migrated from Kentucky and had been raised to see nothing wrong with

slavery. In fact, the Illinois constitution permitted slavery and when the Rev Elijah P.
Lovejoy, a clergyman, started publishing
abolitionist tracts in Alton in 1837, he
was set upon by an aroused mob and both
he and his printing press were tossed into
the Mississippi river.[29] A short time later,
Lovejoy was actually murdered when
another anti-abolitionist mob caught him
and set fire to his house.[30]

In his maiden speech in the
Senate on April 5, 1850, Shields
participated in "The Great Debate" and
supported the admission of California to
the Union as a free state. This was
critical, since the Union, at that time,
consisted of 15 free and 15 slave states
and, the admission of California as
entirely one or the other would upset the
delicate balance. Speaking from the floor,
Shields stated, "I am in favor of the
admission of California into the Union as
a state. I am also in favor of keeping the
question of admission unconnected with
any other exciting questions now before
the Senate. The people of California are
working out a great social problem, to
make labor, hard labor dignified and

General Shields adopting a Napoleonic stance. The black marks are due to scrapes on the glass negative.

respectable. Slavery can never be established there. Slavery, being in violation of natural
right, can only exist by positive enactment; and the Constitution of this country only
tolerates slavery where it exists, but neither extends nor establishes it anywhere. You

might as well undertake to plant orange groves in Siberia as establish slavery in California..." California duly entered the Union as a free state and the "Great Compromise of 1850," crafted by Henry Clay of Kentucky had the effect of saving the Union from dismemberment at that time. But it was not a permanent cure for the ills of America, and was merely a postponement of what in retrospect appears to have been inevitable - the forceful attempt at sundering of the South from the North.

Towards the end of Shields' term, Senator Stephen Douglas in 1854 introduced a measure that was to pull the rug from under Shields' bid for reelection the following year. By extension, the proposal also put paid to Douglas' own chance of ever becoming President of the United States. The contentious measure, which was supported by President Pierce, was the Kansas-Nebraska Act which threw out the Missouri compromise of 1820. For 34 years that compromise had held the Union together, because it stated that each new free state admitted to the United States should be balanced by the addition of another that was slave. The Kansas-Nebraska Act proposed to change that, by allowing the citizens of those territories to determine their own status, slave or free. Shields, at the behest of Douglas, voted for the act and by his action dug his own political grave, as he would learn when he ran for reelection the following year.

Chapter 8
Senator from the North Star State:
Dust and Bust

She sings her wild dirges, and smiles 'mid the strain;
Then turns to remember her sorrow
Men gaze on that smile till their tears fall like rain,
And she from their weeping doth borrow.
She forgets her own story: and none, she complains,
Of the cause for her grief will remind her:
She fancies but one of her kindred remains —
She is certain he never can find her.
Song by Aubrey De Vere (1814 - 1902.)

The seat of General James Shields in the United States Senate was the grand prize in the election of 1855 and, the Anti-Nebraska majority in the Illinois Legislature had their sights set squarely on winning it. It was within their grasp, since they held most of the high cards, and even pulled a series of anti-Irish jokers from the political pack to ensure the General's defeat. But Shields, the old war horse, did not succumb easily. Against the incumbent Senator were: Abraham Lincoln, "a champion of antislavery" and Shields' old nemesis Lyman Trumbull. Shields, for his part, scarcely stood alone; he could count on Douglas, the other Illinois Senator, who believed Shields was being attacked, not because of his politics but, because of his place of birth. "I am confirmed in the opinion that our friends in the Legislature should nominate Shields by acclimation, and nail his flag to the mast, and never haul it down under any circumstances nor for any body. The election of any other man would be deemed not only a defeat, but an ungrateful desertion of him, when all the others who voted for him have been sustained... At all events our friends should stand by Shields and throw the responsibility on the Whigs of beating him because he was born in Ireland. The Nebraska fight is over, and Know Nothingism has taken its place as the chief issue of the future. If therefore Shields shall be beaten it will be apparent to the people & to the whole country that a gallant Soldier & a faithful public servant has been stricken down because of the place of his birth."[2] declared Douglas unequivocally during the bare knuckles campaign.

Shields, on the other hand, was less sure that his place of birth was the principal issue. The General thought some Democrats were against him, not so much because he was Irish but, because he was so closely allied with Douglas, the upstate upstart. Shields correctly perceived that an attack on him was a strike at Douglas, and surmised that the rebel Democrats had cut an unsavory deal with Lincoln to gut his friend. Shortly before the election, Shields said as much to Charles H. Lanphier, a longtime Douglas supporter and publisher of the *State Register* newspaper, "They don't care two pence about Nebraska, But Douglass they have sworn to destroy. My election will help him so they have already made an arrangement with —.[Abraham Lincoln][3]

Led by Judge Sidney Breese, the dissenting Democrats had various positions but agreed on one thing, to unite against Shields, even though they did not rally around a single alternate candidate. That was good enough for Judge Breese, who was still smarting from his defeat by Shields six years previously, and for him, it was pay back time. Breese self righteously declared, that he "repelled with scorn the attempt to foist this bastard plank (Kansas-Nebraska) into the Democratic Creed"[4] and, it is possible that he felt similarly disposed toward Shields. The *Chicago Tribune* and other newspapers made war upon the senator, and his ally the "Little Giant" Douglas, whom it called the "Little Whelp" and, since Chicago's influence in Illinois politics was growing, its opinion counted.[5] The railroads had reached Chicago in 1852 and the road to Springfield now ran through that city. New immigrants were arriving on every train and no longer was the state dominated by pro-states' rights supporters down-state, which boded badly for James Shields.

In contrast with the low opinion of Shields held by many in Illinois, the General had earned accolades for honesty and hard work from his colleagues in the Senate. John M. Clayton, Senator from Delaware, attested to his industry. Clayton, a Yale educated lawyer and former Secretary of State was the antithesis of Shields and what he stood for. Nevertheless, he was in a position to observe and judge the Irish-born Senator from Illinois on his merits. While commenting on the appointment of non-natives to high political office, Clayton said that no general rule could be laid down excluding them. "I can give you an example, sir, to illustrate my meaning" he said. "There is James Shields of Illinois, now a candidate for reelection in that State to the Senate of the United States. I have been a Whig always, and he is a Democrat. I am a native and he is an Irishman by birth. I do not know what his religion may be, but I suppose he is a Catholic, and I am a Protestant. If I had a hundred votes for a Senator from Illinois, I would cast them all for James Shields. He is a statesman, a patriot, and, in my opinion one of the best men in the Senate. Such a man is an honor to any station he may hold, and I should grieve to learn that he is not to return to the body of which he has been so useful and valuable a member."[6]

But the Honorable Mr. Clayton's vote of confidence cut no ice with the electorate of Illinois on a wintry, Feb 8, 1855. There was an expectant hush as Dr. Charles Ray of the *Chicago Tribune* intoned the totals following the first round of balloting. All breathed again when no outright winner was declared. Abraham Lincoln, who had resigned his recently won seat in the State Legislature to make himself eligible for the US Senate, was ahead with 44 votes. Shields was a close second with 41 and everyone else was far down the field. Trumbull trailed with 5 votes and 8 votes were scattered. Shields' lips must have tightened when he noted that five dissident Democrats, including his former law partner Gustave Koerner had bolted the Party and not voted for him. This was the first time in the history of Illinois that such a thing had happened. Shields knew if all Democrats had supported the official ticket he would have been in front, and in a strong position to carry the day. Now, his situation was precarious, but he was not prepared to succumb without a struggle. Like a tired boxer clinging to the ropes, he fought tooth and nail for his political life, button-holing one delegate after another, seeking their hearts, their heads and their help. Despite his best efforts, the next few ballots produced little change. The deadlock stood and no one could garner the requisite 52 votes.

Political arm twisting continued in all corners and the wrangling was intense. Afterwards, the Democratic defectors complained that "Tremendous pressure was brought to bear upon them to vote for Shields or (Gov. Joel A.) Matteson. One of the participants (George T. Allen) later charged that bribery as well as persuasion was attempted upon him. Just when the bolters were on the point of abandoning Trumbull and joining their brethren to elect Shields, Lincoln, convinced that it was impossible to secure his own election, instructed his Whig supporters to unite at once on Trumbull as a candidate who could be elected."[7] Lincoln, seeing that his own strength was not sufficient to carry the day, threw his total to Trumbull, even though Trumbull was a rival Democrat. Thus, Abraham Lincoln sacrificed his chances of the Senate to shut out Shields. Trumbull was duly elected on the tenth count and went on to represent Illinois in the Senate for the next twenty years.[8]

The reasons for Shields' loss were debated afterward. Some wondered if Lincoln had thrown his votes to Trumbull because of personal pique against Shields for the incident on the banks of the Mississippi river thirteen years before, but there is no evidence of that. Douglas pointed to Shields' foreign birth and the xenophobic Know-Nothing movement for his undoing,[9] but there is no firm evidence for that either. Douglas could not accept that the loss was due to Douglas's own hapless brainchild, the Kansas-Nebraska act.

To most, it appeared that what transpired was simply political expediency making strange bedfellows. Lincoln surmised he could not win and, did not want Shields, albeit Douglas in Shields' clothing, to carry the day either. That is why he supported Trumbull. Afterwards, Lincoln wrote to Elihu Washburn, the Harvard-trained Whig congressman from Galena, "I regret my defeat moderately... On the whole, it is perhaps as well for the General cause that Trumbull is elected..."[10] One is left to speculate of what the General cause might be - Lincoln's personal ambitions, the abolition of slavery, or something else. Another reason for Shields' defeat was suggested by Douglas during the Senate campaign of 1858. Douglas intimated that Lincoln had struck a bargain with Trumbull at the expense of Shields in the political wrangling during the voting. In exchange for Lincoln's support against Shields, Trumbull was expected to cross Party lines and support Lincoln against Douglas in the Senate election three years later. Lincoln denied the charge in August 1858 during his debate with Douglas at Ottawa, saying that there was "no substance to it" and "no man – not even Judge Douglas can prove it." Thus, that allegation against Lincoln and Trumbull was never substantiated.

Koerner probably provided the most accurate assessment of Shields' fall from favor when he wrote in his memoirs "Shields felt very much mortified, particularly as I, being then Lieutenant Governor, could not actively support him because I had from the start been violently opposed to the Kansas-Nebraska Bill... But his ill success was his own fault. Both I and Governor Bissell who was then a member of Congress, tried our best to prevent him from voting for the ill-omened bill, and I prophesied that it would defeat his election; I also told him from the start that I could not support him unless he severed his political connections with Douglas."[11] Shields, either out of loyalty to Douglas or due to his own tenacious beliefs, did not take his former law partner's advice, and paid the full political price.

James Shields, U.S. Senator from Minnesota, in a photograph by Matthew B. Brady. Brady, reportedly born in Co. Cork Ireland in 1823, had opened a photographic studio in Washington three years earlier "to preserve the faces of (the country's) historic men..," which included Shields. Shields, wiry and thin most of his life, was at his plumpest around this time and the photograph may have been taken after he had returned from six months relaxation by the sea.

Shields himself did not accept that his defeat was due solely to his Irish nativity even though he recognized that where he was born did not help. The Know-Nothings were able to fan the flames of anti-Irish and anti-Catholic sentiment because feckless immigrants not infrequently set themselves up for it. Shields saw himself as a positive force, one capable of offsetting the negative image engendered by the actions of some of his fellow countrymen. At the same time, he recognized reality, in calling a spade a spade. "The Irish have excited a strong prejudice against themselves here. When I first came here that was not so much so; this, of course, reflects on me. I share in this feeling to some extent and yet the wonder is how I succeed. I never got any support from my own countrymen here. They are proud of me but, if I depended on them, they would drop me immediately" Shields noted a few years later.[12]

The Centennial History of Illinois, quoting from various newspapers of the time, summed up the ambivalence many in Illinois felt towards the waves of immigrant Irish in the 1850s. "To the people of Illinois there seemed to be two strains, sometimes combined in the same individuals in the Irish population of the state. There were on one hand the brilliant idealists who supported the cause of civil liberty and liberal institutions in all its forms and expressions, whether in the Irish struggle for independence or in European contests for self-Government.., men like Senator Shields, held themselves in readiness to join in the redemption of their native land when the hour to strike should come.

But to the people of Illinois, the Irishman more often appeared in another guise. To them he was pictured as the noisy, quarrelsome seeker after excitement, who found it in the company of John Barleycorn, in bloody street brawls, and even in the lower depths of crime…. Why do our police reports always average two representatives from 'Erin, the soft, green isle of the ocean,' to one from almost any other inhabitable land of the earth?… Why are the instigators and ringleaders of our riots and tumults, in nine cases out of ten, Irishmen?" chided the *Chicago Tribune* in 1853.[13]

There followed in the *Tribune* a report of a riot at La Salle, south of Chicago, and of the murder of a contractor by a gang of Irishmen. The newspaper, aroused to the point of approving action under lynch law, outrageously declared "Had the whole thirty-two prisoners that were taken been marched out and shot on the spot, as the citizens did the Driskells in Ogle County, some years ago, the public judgment would have sanctioned it at once."

The *History of Illinois* went on to provide a balance that was generally lacking in the inflammatory anti-Irish tirades of the *Chicago Tribune*. "A more careful analysis, however, revealed a situation that scarcely warranted such a superficial judgment. The railroad contractors were often shrewd schemers and hard men who sought to impose upon the ignorant Irish laborers and to direct matters to their own advantage. Palpably unfair treatment was almost certain to arouse the temper of the hot-headed Irishman. As it was, however, thousands quietly submitted to conditions upon the public works that brought death or ill health, 'from exposure to miasmi, bad accommodation in camps and shanties, and from improper diet;' when sickness fell upon them they were discharged and turned loose upon the world."[14]

An example of bias against the Irish had surfaced ten years earlier when Shields took over as Commissioner of the General Land-office in 1845. The New York *Morning Post* had sneered at him as "a bog of a boy."[15] In addition, there was no shortage of anti-Irish propaganda in the publications of the day and *Barney O'Toole,* a satiric piece of doggerel about a disreputable Irish politician, is one such example:

> *"Then he lit up his pipe and he put on his coat,*
> *And he ran for an office; they counted the vote.*
> *And they figured it out by the Tammany rule,*
> *And who was elected, but Barney O'Toole.*
> *Then he bought a new coat and a diamond so fine,*
> *And a lad for five cents give his boots a nice shine.*
> *Then he talked about court, legislation and school,*
> *For now he was a statesman, bold Barney O'Toole.*

Twenty years later, Shields opinion of many of his fellow countrymen had scarcely altered; he remained critical of their failure to take advantage of the myriad advantages America had to offer, especially in the area of education, which had been lacking in Ireland. "What the Irish need is education. Protestants send their children where they can be best taught, some to nuns and some to monks. The Irish (are) going to no school very often. Education is the first necessity everywhere. Without this they are as much slaves in this country as at home" and "The Irish here do little for their numbers. They are generally ignorant without any taste for reading or improvement, hence they spend their leisure time in whiskey shops."[16]

The lamentable fact was that not infrequently the children and grandchildren of Irish immigrants remained at the bottom of the social heap because, neither their parents nor they appreciated the value of education.[17] Of course, some Irish became bettered or battered over the years depending on one's perspective, as depicted in an 1871 parody of *Kincora,* a poem by the 11th century Irish poet Mac Liag:

> *"Where are now the Roughs I cherished?*
> *Where the voters I once called mine?*

> *Some too much rum have perished;*
> *Some the prison walls confine*
> *Voting early, voting often,*
> *Voting morning, noon and night.*
> *And ready, ready, always ready,*
> *For a riot or a fight."*

James Shields' defeat in Illinois was a supreme loss of face for him, not just because of betrayal by former friends like Koerner, whom he had counted on, but because he had lost to his archenemy Trumbull. Abandoned and alone, he faced an uncertain future. He could return to practicing law, but had little stomach for that. He could not run for the Senate the next time, since it would have pitted him against Stephen Douglas, his friend. Who knows how things would be six years in the future, when he could again take on the crafty Trumbull? But by then the country could be vastly changed, and in fact it was, with a bloody conflagration raging. There

Sign to General Shields Lake, Rice County, Minnesota, one of many entities named after the nomadic Irish-American.

was talk of Shields running for Governor but he did not pursue it and instead, made a hasty and private decision. Without consulting anyone, he decided not to run for political office in Illinois at all, but to run from the state altogether.

Within six weeks of his heart-rending defeat, he packed up his jeweled swords, his few belongings and departed for the Minnesota Territory. In those days, the route, to what would become known as the "Gopher State," ran across Illinois to Galena on the Mississippi, and then up river by steamer to St. Paul, at the head of navigation. By April the ice on the upper reaches of the river was breaking up and steamers, after hibernating for winter, were firing their boilers and starting to move. Shields found himself traveling alongside hardy pioneers with their boxes and bundles, corn and corn shells, wooden barrels and bales and a variety of farm animals and equipment. Like the time of year, he was in a mood for a fresh start, unencumbered by his battered baggage from Illinois.

General Shields had been thinking of the opportunities available in Minnesota while he was still in the Senate. The speculative land boom that began in 1854 was still going strong and, Shields knew there was money to be made. Why not try his hand at that? On his way to Minnesota, the General was thinking of the future but as he looked back on his life, he saw a scene as speckled as the Sperrin Mountains back in County Tyrone. Like an eagle, he had soared to dizzying heights but then, buffeted by stormy turbulence, had spiraled precipitously to earth. He knew it would be hard to reach to such heady heights again, because the country was changing. In his early years in the new world, Shields, an immigrant, had found acceptance because of a relative shortage of talented natives on the frontier; he had embraced the country's mainstream which had carried him along. Now, as his image reflected in the gray river, he was seeing the country in a different light and his rejection at the polls, as time would show, had marked him. He began to question tenets he had taken for granted, such as his smooth assimilation into American society and his ready acceptance by the electorate. In his heart, Shields knew that even though he had lost in Illinois on political grounds, his defeat had been due, at least in part, to being an Irish Catholic immigrant.

In his plan for the future, General Shields decided to make some changes and started with the spiritual. Though he had not been outwardly religious in Illinois, he mended fences with the Roman Catholic Church in Minnesota and became a devout churchgoer. This, as it turned out, was not some fleeting fix, a transient search for solace during a bleak hour of his life, but rather, demonstrated a major reorientation. His active participation in church affairs would continue from then until his death, some twenty five years later. Previously, Shields, had often been mistaken for a Scotch-Irish Protestant in Illinois and, in fact, had complained that Southern Irish discriminated against him. He pointed out that the Irish north-south divide worked to the detriment of the sons of Eireann, both at home and abroad. "In the Legislature that elected me there were four Irishmen; three of them opposed me. They were Southern men and opposed me, I believe, because I was from the North."[18] he commented in a letter to Patrick in January 1858.

In his personal habits, Shields continued to remain as abstemious as ever, and was not a man given to ostentation. All his life he adopted an austere, frugal life style for himself, though he was generous with others. Carl Schurz., a German revolutionary and friend of Lincoln who visited Shields in Washington in 1854, wrote that Shields was "a jovial Irishman who… lived in a modest boarding house near the Capitol, and the only ornament in his room, in which he received me, consisted of a brace of pistols attached crosswise to the bare whitewashed wall. He welcomed me with effusive cordiality as a sort of fellow revolutionary from Europe…[19]

At the same time, Shields was no recluse. He enjoyed a rich and varied social life and the company of both men and women. While living in Washington he was invited to a Christmas party in Baltimore in 1845, because "the fair Miss Ellen" was going to sing for him,[20] and he was not above composing verse to impress the fair sex. Koerner quoted a sample written in 1851 for Henrietta Mitchell, a Washington damsel, which shows a credible poetic hand. Shields had asked his friend to comment on the work, because Shields and the young lady had "differed in opinion about the style and spirit of it."

> *Yes, Dear Henrietta, I think of thee still*
> *And see thee in spent fountain and rill*
> *I hear thee in whispers, in prairie and grove*
> *That speak to my ear like a spirit of love.*
>
> *I dream while awake of thy sweet sunny smile*
> *A beam from the soil of my own native isle*
> *I dream while I sleep, of isle o'er the sea*
> *Where love would be transport and rapture with thee.*
>
> *The eye and the smile and the heart touching tone*
> *Though far from me now are in spirit my own*
> *Thus fancy brings visions of love and delight*
> *To cheer me and bless me by day and by night.*[21]

General James Shields' attitude toward his native land across the Atlantic was not one-dimensional. Though he followed events there, he did not try to influence them directly and merely offered verbal support. He was not indifferent to Ireland's political and social travails and commented on them, but never played an active part in Irish affairs. He said he adopted his "hands-off" policy, because he did not want to compromise his position in the American Congress, where he was vulnerable to attack had he done so. He believed that political enemies would have branded him disloyal and accused him of engaging in foreign intrigues, which was probably true. Shields contended that he did not become involved in the Fenian revolutionary movement after being warned not to by Lord Napier, the British Ambassador, who threatened to report him for violating the Logan Act if he did.[22] The General was justifiably proud of his equal status with Lord Napier and chortled in a letter, "Here I am on equal footing with Lord Napier, the British Ambassador - dine with him on equal terms, and so with all others. There (in Ireland) it would be different."[23]

For all that, Shields supported Ireland whenever he could. He sympathized with the Young Irelander revolutionaries who had tried to overthrow English rule in 1848 and sought a resolution in Congress denouncing Britain's subsequent treatment of the Irish rebels. He decried their transportation to the dreaded Australian penal colonies and he understood the subtly, that the on-going subjugation of Ireland was not so much by England, as by Protestant Anglo-Irish land owners, who were descendents of English and Scots who had been planted in the country 200 years previously.

In a speech entitled "Resolutions Expressive of Sympathy for the Exiled Irish Patriots," Shields declared "There is something so unnatural in what the English law denounces as treason the Irish heart recognizes as Patriotism. Poor Ireland! Her history is a sad one. It is written in the tears and blood of her children. Ireland has never been governed by the English people. It has been governed by an Anglo-Irish oligarchy. They may exterminate the Irish race but they will fail to make it Anglican. Ireland is at this moment as feeble, helpless and hopeless as the most anti-Irish heart can desire. Her nationality is gone; her hopes are crushed; her ancient generous race is becoming extinct. She has no future to speak of, if it is it is a dark one."[24] To a crowd in Galena, in Western Illinois the following year, Shields acknowledged Ireland's contribution to America by saying "The immigration to a country is generally in proportion to its prosperity and often one of the chief causes of that prosperity.[25]

Shields was a strong supporter of Thomas Francis Meagher, one of the exiled Irish rebels, who escaped from the antipodes and made his way to America. Shields squired him around the Capitol and introduced him to his colleagues in the Senate in March 1853.[26] At the same time, Shields was a realist who was not uncritical of his fellow Irish and the harsh realities of life both in Ireland and America. He probably agreed with Patrick Ford, the publisher of the *Irish World* when Ford stated "I felt that next to England, whiskey was the enemy of my race."[27] In a letter to his brother Patrick, the General stated "Our unfortunate country men always suffer most. They are thoughtless, thriftless and improvident, and when a change comes they are thrown out of employment and sink into destitution. They congregate about the cities instead of seeking homes in the country and as they are dependent upon others for employment in hard times their condition is deplorable. Every day some of them call on me hoping to be relieved. This is painful to me."[28]

Shortly before Shields arrived in Minnesota, the US Government concluded treaties with the Minnesota branch of the Sioux Indians. This opened millions of acres for settlement and in turn, led to a speculative land boom that had not been seen previously in Minnesota. Shields was aware of the rich potential of the "North Star State" from his time in the land office. The territory was fertile and well watered and even today the State bears the sobriquet "land of 10,000 lakes." Migrants also heard about its Eden-like qualities and were flocking in by the thousands. The population of the territory jumped five fold from 32,000 in 1854 to over 150,000 three years later and, land sales for 1855-57 were more than 1,500,000 acres per annum.

Scenic General Shields' Lake. The several square mile expanse is administered by the State of Minnesota and is used largely for recreation and boating.

In the "North Star State", Shields came into contact with Alexander Faribault, who had been born in Prairie du Chein, Wisconsin and had migrated to Minnesota in 1826 to become a fur trader and entrepeneur. Faribault had established a permanent trading post on the Cannon River to do business with the Wahpekute Indians in 1834, and later formed the Faribault Townsite Company to develop the area. Faribault, impressed with Shields, "offered him such liberal inducements to act for the townsite company, that he at once came here (to Faribault.)[29] Shields became a partner in the townsite company on September 11, 1855 and immediately began "looking over" the area, especially the "Big Woods" west of Faribault. The undulating land, a change from the flatness of Illinois, consisted of almost continuous forest - Norwegian pines, oaks, maples, ash and walnut interspersed with lakes sporting an abundance of fish and pink and white lady slippers, butter 'n eggs and other wildflowers along their banks. According to the *New York Tribune*, Shields, on one outing, "came to a lake with such picturesque surroundings that he was tempted to explore it. Fastening his horse to a tree, he strolled through the country, and, on trying to retrace his steps, found that he had lost his way. Night was falling when he descried a Sioux village of fifty tepees or wigwams. Entering the largest tepee he saw some forty Indian warriors. They took no notice of his entrance, and he approached a young and intelligent-looking Indian and took hold of a string of beads, which he wore around his neck and (Shields) pulled a trifle too hard, for the next moment the beads strewed around the floor. The young man rose, seized his rifle and (Shields thought it was his end. Instead, the Indian,) pointing to the beads, ordered a squaw to pick them up. He then pointed to (Shields) to precede him, and they marched out of the village at a point opposite where he had entered and, either by accident or design on the part of the Indian, made a beeline for his lost horse, which they found still securely fastened to the tree. After making his guide happy by giving him a five dollar gold piece, the traveler made his way without difficulty (back to town.) Delighted with the fertile spot he had discovered, he purchased the tract, including the lake and village and returned after a few months with a party of ten and formed a settlement."[30]

After accepting Faribault's offer to join him, Shields went to work resolving a dispute over ownership of the land. In this, Shields' legal knowledge and contacts in Washington proved invaluable, and he became the company's land agent, lawyer and lobbyist. On May 29, 1859, Judge Andrew G. Chatfield of the third judicial district of Minnesota gave a deed of warranty to Shields "who thus became nominally the owner in fee of the whole town site. This, however, was only for convenience in making sales and confirming titles by deeds of warranty to lands before conveyed by quit claim, the real ownership being determined by the agreement previously made and recorded."[31]

Shields also bought land for himself, both within the town and without. "Shields drove out of town about 10 miles to a small settlement on the Dodd Road between Forts Snelling and Ridgely. There, on May 29, 1855, he bought 282.42 acres from a bois brule by the name of Moses Latourelle.[32] The land consisted of mixed terrain which at once provided "a picturesque and challenging picture" since it "presented a view of undulating surface, with here and there a tendency to hilly, timber, marsh and meadow land. The wild forest, with groves of oak and all sturdy varieties of timber... and the tranquil and glassy lakes embedded in the mist of the hills, combined to make (the area) a pleasant and picturesque spot."[33] Shields, whose ideas were generally larger than his purse, used his Mexican war bounty and repayment of a loan he had made to Douglas to obtain the property.

With shrewd vision, Shields knew that if his land was to prosper, it needed people, lots of them. For that, Shields thought the area could be a God-send for the Irish, who were still immigrating to America at a rate of nearly 100,000 a year and being shoehorned into eastern coastal cities. He traveled to New York to recruit settlers, but ran into an unexpected obstacle in Archbishop John Hughes, the flinty first Archbishop of New York. Hughes, who had been born in Ireland only a stone's throw from Shields, ruled his diocese with an inflexible cross and rigid crosier. He adamantly opposed the General's plan, because he feared that his flock might founder in the western wilds of Minnesota. Shields did his best to reassure Hughes that he should not fret, and that the migrants would be well looked after. "Once people are there, a priest will come" he is reported to have said. Hughes was not swayed by Shields' eloquence, arguments nor pleadings.[34]

"It's too bad about your eye trouble" said Shields finally in disgust.

"I was not aware that my sight was failing" His Grace responded tartly.

"It's quite evident you can't see beyond the length of your nose" snapped

Shields, as he picked up his hat and stalked out.

The General expressed his frustration to his brother Patrick saying that the Irish "congregate in the cities instead of seeking homes in the country and as they are dependent on others for employment in hard times their condition is deplorable."[35]

Following his failure in New York, General Shields turned to Illinois, this time with more success. He recruited 600 Irish in the "Prairie State", who followed him, like the pied piper, to what was initially known as "General Shields' Colony" in Minnesota. There, Shields had divided the land into lots next to his own farm for sale to the settlers. Before long, there were more buildings than tents and tepees to be seen on the plains around Faribault. The Irish who arrived found themselves in a strange new land. One newcomer noted "Looking across the valley, the most conspicuous objects that met my sight were numerous scaffoldings elevating by rude pole structures ten or twelve feet above the ground the bodies of dead Indians, according to the custom of the Sioux to help their departed warriors on their way to the happy hunting grounds. All along up and down the river were the tepees of the Wapakootas, far more numerous than the habitations of the white man, and the intermingling of tepees, log cabins, frame houses just begun, with four or five steam saw mills plying a busy trade in their midst, with the rude monuments of an Indian cemetery in the background, pictured a blending of civilization and (Indian culture) never again to be seen on this continent."[36]

More than 250 permanent housing units had sprouted by the fall of 1856 and the population had jumped to 1,500.[37] Improvements that year amounted to $100,000 and Shields' house was "an imposing residence," valued at $2000. Business was booming and Shields "advertisements in eastern papers…attracted the attention of his fellow countrymen and they thronged in."[38] Clearly, Shields had bounced back from his crisis in Illinois and was putting it behind him. He began to show his hallmark signs of optimism and, pleased with his progress, he got over his indignation at his old friend Gustave Koerner and started corresponding with him. In October 1855, Shields wrote "Here I am doing well, collecting property around me. I have a hundred head of horned cattle and sheep and horses. I have taken an interest in the town from which I write, one of the prettiest spots in the territory, and I might say in the United States."

As part of the land deal with the Indians, the Federal Government set aside some of the territory for people of mixed Indian and European heritage. People who were at least 50% Indian were awarded notes, called "Half Breed Scrip" for up to five lots of 160 acres each. The Indians could hold onto the land or sell it as they wished. Shields lobbied his friend Douglas in Washington for authority to open a Government land office to sell the scrip. He was rewarded when the Government commissioned him to do so. Things were progressing well and "Shields Colony," about ten miles northwest of Faribault, soon had a Catholic church, sawmill, creamery and several stone buildings.[39] Faribault had its first hotel, the Nutting House, built using boards from Shields' saw mill and, the hotel ledger shows that Shields was paid seventy five cents for the lumber. The Shields settlement was incorporated into a town on May 11, 1858 and "the residents voted that he town should be named Shieldsville in honor of General James Shields.[40] Suddenly, the Minnesota land boom went bust.

There were a number of reasons for the plummeting price of land. One had to do with the unsettled situation between settlers and the Indians, and Indian tribes with each other. An uprising by the Sioux occurred in March 1857 at Big Bend in the blue earth country, where they massacred 40 settlers and, for a while, the Indians threatened Faribault itself. Also, rival Indian tribes skirmished with one another, especially the Sioux and Chippewa. In one battle, Sioux scalped and then beheaded four of their rivals. Shields knew, if his development scheme was to prosper, that could not continue. Raising an armed posse, he scared the Sioux away, by a process of intimidation rather than bloodshed. According to Mrs. Anna Whitney, a resident of Faribault at the time of the threatened attack, the General "organized all male residents of the city able to bear arms into a military company and drilled them daily. He armed the company with such guns as he could procure and sent to St. Paul for an extra supply of ammunition. He put pickets on the outskirts of the city and prepared in every possible way to give the Indians a warm reception should they appear here... To lead the Indians to believe he had a large force of men under his command, (Shields) put on his General's uniform, mounted on a fine horse and galloped up and down the principal streets, waving his sword and issuing orders in a stentorian voice as though he had thousands of men."[41] Shields ruse worked and the Indians retreated, and did not attack the town.

Rotunda of State Capitol of Minnesota showing the commanding presence of General Shields on the second floor atrium. This is the spot where legislators congregate and discuss issues during breaks.

That encounter was not the first between Shields and the Sioux. A year earlier, according to Judge Martin M. Shields of Minnesota,[42] Shields had acquired some fresh cattle, shipped up the Mississippi by steamer. One morning, the General's hired hands discovered that the animals were missing from the farm when they went to attend to them. The men trailed the cattle along the Dodd Road toward Millersberg, until they came across Chief

Inkpaduta, a renegade Sioux, and about thirty Indians herding the stock into a wooded coulee.

"Try taking them back and you'll be scalped" snarled the Chief as the men approached. The unarmed hands, not waiting to see if the chief was serious, turned tail. As soon as General Shields heard what had happened, he was livid.

"If I had a score of men from my Mexican brigade, I'd whip all the Sioux in the state" he yelled, grabbing and loading two double barreled pistols. "I'm getting my cattle back from that thieving band and no one's stopping me."

About ten men followed the General, as he rode out after the Indians. When he reached them, the General rode straight up to Chief Inkpaduta, who at first was not prepared to relinquish his spoils.

"Try taking them and you'll lose your scalp" threatened the Chief ominously.

Shields wasted no words, but drew a pistol from its holster, cocked both hammers and placed the muzzles close to the Chief's head.

"By God Almighty, if you and your buck renegades don't drive those cattle back to Shieldsville this instant, I'll blow your brains out. You're a dead red man" he spat. Inkpaduta, seeing that Shields meant business, gestured to his braves to do as Shields bid. Soon the cattle were back grazing peacefully in Shields' corral.

Though the Indians were repulsed, it was not before great damage was done. Reports of the Indian uprising had reached Eastern newspapers with the speed of the telegraph. Gruesome accounts were published, which slowed the westward flow of settlers. Shields, tried to counter the negative press by sending letters of his own to newspapers. On April 15, 1857, he denied rumors of Indians "burning houses and killing settlers" and maintained "There is not the slightest foundation for these absurd reports. I hope the papers of the territory will hasten to correct any false impressions on this subject, as we know if they get into circulation in the East, they will have the effect to deter emigrants from bringing their families to this territory. You may declare with truth that there is neither hostility or sign of hostility among the Indian tribes in this territory."[43]

Another reason, besides irate Indians, accounted for the land bust: politics. The Federal Government distributed notices that it planned to auction additional public lands at favorable prices. No one was willing to buy land pivately with that prospect in store and sales slumped. Shields campaigned against the proposed Government scheme and his efforts partly paid off. President Pierce postponed the sale of public land but even that move failed to re-ignite enthusiasm. Land prices continued to remain low and Faribault did not prosper as Shields had hoped, even though he kept up a good front. "We have plenty of property which will become very valuable but at present our money is all out and in that respect we are poor" he wrote bluntly to his brother in Ireland.[44]

Shortly after forming his partnership with Faribault the latter became seriously ill and the burden of work fell on Shields' shoulders. The Irish-American displayed prodigious energy but, the tasking was more than he could handle alone. Facing the prospect of losing his large investment, Shields tried another track. He had a vision of connecting Chicago to St. Paul by rail, by extending the railroad that had reached Chicago in 1852. Realizing that a railroad venture could not be achieved without a great deal of political support, Shields, became involved in Minnesota politics. With Alexander Faribault ailing, the General desperately needed another partner and approached Henry Sibley, an able congressman, to interest him in buying out Faribault. Sibley declined, but was attracted by Shields' railroad ideas.

Author standing next to statue of General Shields in the rotunda of the State Capitol of Minnesota, St. Paul. Notice the shiny toe of the General's right boot which people rub as a talisman for good luck

Together, Sibley and Shields worked on a railroad plan that would connect St. Paul, not with Chicago as Shields had first envisioned, but with Dubuque, Iowa, on the Mississippi, which they called the Minneapolis Cedar Valley Railroad.

Shields efforts paid off and the seventh Territorial Legislature granted a charter to the duo for the railroad on March 1, 1856. The proposed route from the Iowa state line would follow the Straight River Valley and push through the "big woods" to Minneapolis, a distance of 100 miles. Shields predicted that the road could be completed within three years, and would start generating revenue even before that. The company's initial meeting was convened at the law office of Shields & McCutcheon in Faribault on Jan 28th, 1856, where Shields became President. Shields immediately traveled to New York where he successfully secured stock subscriptions of $200,000 in Eastern financial markets. In addition, the Minnesota Legislature passed a $5 million loan bill in 1857 and it appeared that at last Shields had backed a winner. But once again, like so many opportunities in his life, it was not to be. There were ongoing fiscal problems. The bonds did not sell well and work on the railroad ground to a halt. The failure of the railroad and the land bust left Shields near destitute, and he had little to show after his longest sustained attempt at business.[45] But all was not lost, since he still had the world of politics.

There were two long time rivals for control of the Democratic Party in Minnesota, Henry Hastings Sibley who owned considerable property, including the Minnesota *Pioneer* newspaper, and Henry M. Rice, a former territorial representative, who had been a partner in the American Fur Company. Rice was now allied with the anti-fur Democrats, while Sibley was Shields' business partner. Though Shields and Sibley were close, that did not stop Shields, in his customary fashion, from being on good terms with the rival Rice faction and, he was constantly healing rifts between the two groups. Shields attended the state Democratic convention on Dec 2, 1857, but was not seeking elected office. His main interests were support for his land and railroad ventures.

In anticipation of Minnesota entering the Union the following year, the convention had to nominate two Senators to take their seats, once that came to pass. Another order of business was to nominate a candidate for Governor. The latter went as anticipated to Sibley, who was supported by his rival Rice. Most believed that Rice threw himself behind Sibley so that he, Rice, would get the Senatorial nod, which happened. Rice was elected easily as the first Senator from Minnesota. That still left the second Senatorial seat; who would get it? Since that had not been prearranged, the outcome was more uncertain.

Three long time Democrats, former territorial Governor Willis Gorman, Franklin

Steele, a regent of the University of Minnesota and John W. North placed themselves in contention. Then Shields, at the suggestion of Sibley, tossed his hat into the ring. Sibley supported the Irish-American because of their business connection and, Shields obvious attraction was his Washington contacts. But that scarcely seemed sufficient to gain his election, since he was such a newcomer to the state. No one gave Shields much chance and his candidature got scarcely a second glance. According to Mrs. Daniel Robertson, the wife of a prominent politician, Shields was "attractive and captivating in spite of his irascible temper" and another noted that he was "a graceful and engaging speaker, possessed of an unusually rich and sonorous voice which he used with art. His attractive and charming personality made it easy for him to win friends."[46] But that was the extent of it.

The voting commenced and it was obvious that dark horse Shields, was almost no body's favorite. But, as it turned out, he was nearly everyone's second pick in the event of deadlock. On December 15, three separate ballots were held without a clear winner and on the fourth, the long shot pulled through. Shields, now supported by Rice as well as Sibley, nosed ahead. According to William W. Folwell. "The magnetism of his presence contributed to his success as a candidate."[47] Shields election was ratified by the full Legislature on Dec 19, and according to accounts "The expectation was that his personal influence would procure many good things for the state."[48]

On the evening of his election Senator-elect Shields was tendered a banquet in his honor at the American House, St. Paul, which was attended by some 300 citizens, including members of the Legislature. The toast to General Shields ran: "The soldier, statesman and citizen. His antecedents give full promise that his future will be devoted to the interests of the state of Minnesota... His re-election to the United States Senate will afford infinite satisfaction to the country..."[49] But not everyone was satisfied at Shields' political success. His victory was a bitter pill for his opponents and the St. Paul *Minnesotian*, decried Shields' election saying that the "North Star State" did not want "the cast off trousers of Illinois... rejected by the people of that state."[50] Steele, a man of affluence who would later donate much of the Minneapolis real estate on which the University of Minnesota now stands, was furious and "never forgave Rice for failing, as he claimed, to throw the election to him."[51]

For outsider James Shields the victory was as sweet as it was unexpected, and it meant he was going back to Washington again as Senator-elect, this time not from Illinois but from Minnesota. He could scarcely have asked for more. He could forget about personal business problems for the time being, and put his mind to work on the political ills of the country. There remained an outstanding item of business. Shields and Rice had to decide which of the two would get the shorter term ending in 1859 and whom would sit for a full six years. The pair drew straws and Shields picked the shorter one.[52]

Shields and the Minnesota delegation rolled into Washington on a bleak January day in 1858, hoping to take their seats in Congress right away. But that did not happen. Their reception inside the Capitol was as cool as the Washington wintry weather outside. In a scene reminiscent of his frosty reception nearly a decade earlier, when he first tried to take his seat from Illinois, Shields and the other Minnesotans were refused admission. Congress declared that Minnesota was still a territory and should not be admitted until statehood was ratified later that year. Shields, though he was a junior member of the delegation, took a leading role and almost succeeded in getting the representatives recognized, by using a novel argument. In *A History of Minnesota*, William Watts Folwell states "General Shields, doubtless acting for all, had made a statement of their case in a letter which was read to the Senate on February 25. The position taken in this letter was that the Territory of Minnesota, having conformed to the enabling act in framing and adopting a constitution, had thereby been instantly transformed from a territory into a state. He expressed the hope, therefore, that the Minnesota representatives would be promptly admitted. This novel proposition excited enough interest to be referred, after an interesting debate, to the judiciary committee. Crittenden of Kentucky, who presented the letter, presented also General Shields' credentials as a senator from Minnesota, supported the claim, and declared that he could 'see no reason why the gentleman in question had not a just, constitutional, and lawful privilege to take his seat here.' Pugh of Ohio gave hearty approval, citing an example from his own state. Seward announced his intention to vote for the seating of General Shields and his associate on the ground that swearing in the senators and representatives from Minnesota would work her admission to the Union."[53] While there were constitutional and legal reasons for the cool reception afforded Shields and his fellow Minnesotans, they were also buffeted by political gales swirling around Washington. Democrat James Buchanan was now in the White House and, though Shields and the Minnesota delegation were also Democrats, they were too proDouglas for Buchanan's palate. And because they were Democrats, the newly forged Republican Party did not want anything to do with them either. The delegation was denied recognition and forced to cool its heels until spring, after Minnesota officially entered the Union on May 6, 1858. When that happened, Shields and Rice took their Senate seats the following day.

Almost from the outset, Shields and Rice began to disagree. Like two disparate highways, their views diverged on almost everything and, Rice made no bones about his disaffection with Shields. He wanted all the federal patronage he could get and cosied up shamelessly to the Administration. Shields, on the other hand, quickly found himself at loggerheads with President Buchanan and the majority of Democrats. The General had a more lofty vision than pure political pork and, his first disagreement with the Democrats was over the proposed Lecompton Constitution for Kansas. Kansas was in turmoil over it with armed posses everywhere. Lecompton would have given Kansas citizens the right to hold and own slaves, making it a slave state. Shields was

Potawatamie Indians around 1860. While Shields had run ins with various Indian tribes, it was generally for cause. The Irish-American treated the native North Americans better than many settlers and even signed a treaty with them.

utterly opposed to that. Even though President Buchanan had declared "The great objective of my administration will be to arrest, if possible, the agitation over slavery," his policies had an opposite effect. Before "Old Buck" left office, the infamous Dred Scott decision, saying that Negro slaves were not citizens, had been handed down by the Supreme Court, the Confederacy had been established, the Covode committee had found the executive department guilty of improper patronage and bribery, and the nation, following the actions of abolitionist John Brown, was on the brink of war. Brown had raided the U.S. arsenal at Harper's Ferry, Virginia to get arms for a slave rebellion and was captured and hung. Because Brown's raid was financed by Northern funds, and had enjoyed widespread Northern approval, it greatly angered the South. Resentments that had smoldered for more than a decade reached flashpoint after that and culminated in war.

All that was of concern to Shields, who saw presciently that a rupture between the States was coming. Because of his stand, Shields found himself, along with Stephen Douglas, ostracized by the Administration and proLecompton legislators. It was not a happy time for Shields nor the nation as a whole and clearly, he was perturbed. A letter to his brother Patrick written in Washington lacked his usual upbeat tone. In it, James said he was "Chairman of a very Laborious Committee in the Senate" doing "laborious investigation" without specifying the nature of his laborious work.[54] He summed up his pessimistic thoughts to William B. McGrorty, an Irish supporter in Minnesota "As soon as the poor fellows heard I was not for Lecompton they fled from me like rats deserting a falling house... Let me know the feelings at home. Of course, they are afraid to oppose the Administration... Rice has sold out body and breeches... They are buying up voters here like sheep in the market. Not with money as our friends in St. Paul but with the public trusts... Can I depend upon [Sibley] and the Pioneer...(newspaper for support?)"[55]

It was a good question, because without federal patronage, Shields had little to offer back home. He had no long-term reservoir of goodwill to draw from and, his principled stance had weakened him both in Washington and Minnesota. Gov. Sibley, for his part, stuck by Shields and continued to offer him support, but he was one of the few willing to risk his political skin to do so. Sibley had a pragmatic reason; he still hoped something would come of their abortive railroad venture.

Then suddenly Shields disappeared. He vanished from the Washington scene in May 1858 like springtime snow in the Nation's capital. No one heard from him for months, nor could say where he had gone; it was a strange mystery. It seems the General, reeling from political and financial pressures, thought that his ship, instead of coming in, was going under. He was depressed and, it appears, had begun to contemplate his demise. In a pessimistic letter to his brother Patrick he wrote "I began to think my health declining and felt I had not long to remain here... If I quit public life I may go to Europe for a while. I know I ought to retire and seek repose but once in this life it is hard to get out of it.... I once thought of going back (to Ireland) but my habits would not do for you now."[56] Obviously, his mind was muddled and he needed time to put it back together. Not that there were not good reasons for General Shields' disaffection, since his situation was not good on any front. His business ventures in Minnesota were falling apart; the Buchanan Administration was not willing to support the Minneapolis and Cedar Valley Railroad; he was on the outs with his fellow Senator from Minnesota, and what little political base he had, had melted away. There was no where he could turn. In May, he had written to Gov. Sibley that Washington politics that spring were as "dull and cold" as the weather."[57] A letter from Senator Rice to Governor Sibley underscored the extent of the rift between Shields and the Washington Democrats. Clearly, Rice did not want Shields reelected to the Senate under any circumstances. "I saw the President today" wrote Rice to Sibley, "...under no circumstances could Shields' reelection give anything but pain to the National Democracy."[58]

In the Thirty-fifth Congress, Shields was Chairman of the Committee on Revolutionary Claims and he found himself opposing the Administration day in and out on many matters - not only domestic policy but foreign issues as well. The British had taken over Honduras in Central America and the Administration, invoking the Monroe Doctrine, wanted them out. Shields opposed such a move and was warned by the Chairman of the Foreign Relations Committee that he would be bucking the Party if he continued to dig in his heels. Shortly after that, he disappeared. He was not seen nor heard from all through the Lincoln - Douglas debates, which took place in Illinois from Aug 21 to Oct 15, 1858. Lincoln had challenged Douglas, his opponent in the Illinois Senatorial race, to a series of joint debates that have since become legendary. In all, there were seven debates and they covered the ground of the slavery controversy and its impact on politics, law, and Government. Lincoln emerged from these debates as a national figure, which in turn provided the impetus to propel him into the White House two years later.

Just as suddenly as he had vanished, Shields magically reappeared. He returned to Washington in November and said he had been undergoing rest and recuperation at the Atlantic seashore. He was delighted by Douglas's success in the Senate race against Lincoln. Though Lincoln had won the Illinois popular vote by a narrow margin, Douglas had carried the day in the Legislature 54-41, where it counted. By this time, the national Democrats abhorred Douglas and saw him as a millstone around their necks. He was nearly as unpopular with them as the Republicans and, the Democratic caucus tried to deprive him of the chairmanship of the Committee on Territories. Nevertheless, Shields continued to support his friend unreservedly. "Douglas' stock" he chortled "is now above par in the political market... My opinion is that they [the Democrats] will now defer to Douglas."

Lord (Sir Francis) Napier, British Ambassador to the United States in 1859. Shields was delighted to dine with him on equal terms in Washington. Napier, who left Washington before the Civil War, was later Minister to the Netherlands and Governor of Madras.

Shields health continued to be indifferent through the remainder of his term of office, which ended in March 1859. His illnesses appeared to have been respiratory in nature - frequent colds and difficult breathing, possibly aggravated by his internal wounds from the Mexican War. The grapeshot induced fibrosis of his lung had reduced his pulmonary capacity. This left him winded and short of breath following mild exercise, but he was still able to make effective political speeches.

Once Shields term of office as Senator from Minnesota was over, he left Washington for Springfield Illinois, where he became a house guest of former Governor William Bissell, a comrade in the Mexican War. Again, he was facing an uncertain future, one that looked as bleak as the Northern winters he was tiring of, and where his political star had set. He had burned most of his political bridges in the "Gopher State" and could scarcely return to Illinois. He was tired of political and financial setbacks and began to consider seriously the "Golden West," the newly minted State of California. "I must set my sights for the far West" he wrote to his New York friends, Judge and Maria Daly. But with uncharacteristic self-scrutiny, he fretted about becoming simply a rootless drifter and what that implied. "Change seems to be my destiny. Too much change is as bad as monotony" he wrote, with some insight, to Maria Daly on April 8, 1859.

Nonetheless, Shields was not sure he would actually go west and decided to try one last roll of the dice to recoup his financial fortune in Minnesota. When Shields returned to the "Gopher State", he was dismayed to find the Democrats in deep disarray, which boded badly for him. Republican platforms were resonating with Minnesota voters and the Democrats were operating on thin ice. The Grand Old Party had found a winning formula; "Vote yourself a farm." The Democrats tried to counter the Republicans with a land packet of their own, but it was too little, too late and not popular with Party rank and file. Certainly, it did not sit well with Shields, the land entrepreneur who mustered all his oratorical prowess to shoot it down.

"If you give land to the landless, why not n*****s to the n*****less" he thundered angrily in the raw political vernacular of the day.[59] Shields spent the summer of 1859 in Faribault "taking a lively interest in the progress of the young city"[60] and in June of that year, "he presided at a meeting of citizens to select a committee who were to choose a site for the state deaf and dumb school and we ascertain that he continued friendly interest in the welfare of his Irish colonists in and around Shieldsville."[61] As he ran for reelection, Shields activated his ethnocentric plan to turn the Irish settlers in the plains of Minnesota into a potent political base. It did not work. The Irish had no compunction about supporting him, but their support made Shields less attractive to mainstream America and, he found himself under attack. Not only was he skewered by Republicans but by Democrats as well. Former territorial Governor Samuel Medary, a one-time Ohio Journalist, denigrated Shields as an "Irish Catholic Politician" and William Wallace Kingsbury, a businessman and US Representative, in a letter to Governor Sibley denounced "the influence of an immigrant rabble."[62] In the election, the Republicans routed the Democrats and that was the beginning of a long period of Republican rule in Minnesota. In fact, there would not be a non-Republican Governor there until the turn of the twentieth century, when the state elected, not a Democrat, but an independent.

Even though he was not reelected, Shields had one bright spot; he prevailed on the Minnesota Democrats to support Douglas for President. Though pleased by that small success, he recognized the damage his failure to get reelected had inflicted upon his political career. "Douglas from present appearances will triumph over all their efforts. But do not think of any place in the cabinet for me. There is no more chance of that now than for me to be President. This last election has settled that point. Had I been returned to the Senate I could have commanded anything... So far as Douglas is concerned — I am for him against the world…"[63]

Shields did not attend the Democratic National Convention in Charleston in April 1860. The reason: he was broke. "I need not conceal from you that I find it impossible to get money from my debtors for any purpose. People owe me in Belleville, Marcy and several other places as well. You know that I would not want to go to Charleston without funds. But I tell you I never was in such a way before. I can't raise enough to pay my taxes."[64]

Archbishop John Hughes first Archbishop of New York. Born in Annaloghan, Co. Tyrone, he was responsible for the construction of St. Patrick's Cathedral. Hughes opposed Shields' plan to assist Irish immigrants to move to the interior of the country.

It was probably a good thing that Shields did not go to the convention, because he would have been dismayed to see the Democratic Party fracture so badly over the issue of slavery. The convention could not agree on a Presidential nominee and delegates from eight Southern states felt so strongly that they walked out in a huff, planning to hold a separate convention to nominate their own candidate. Meanwhile, the regular Democrats packed their bags and reconvened in

Baltimore in June. Shields was not there either. If he had, he would have been delighted to see his friend Stephen Douglas get the Presidential nod.

By now, the curtain was coming down on Shields' mixed career in Minnesota. Though he had become a Senator, a land agent and president of an embryonic railroad, he had not become a Minnesotian of destiny and wealth. His visionary ideas remained unfulfilled. He was unable to pay for his own lands or deliver proper deeds to the settlers he had brought to the Faribault-Shieldsville region, which troubled him deeply. In order to support himself, he started lecturing about the Mexican War and his life as a Senator. He applied for a war pension and was granted $30 a month. His well had run dry and there was little left for him in Minnesota. In May 1859, he pulled up stakes, boarded a steamer and headed down the mighty Mississippi for St. Louis and the far West. Before he departed, he handed his mortgaged holdings to his nephew Patrick who had come out from Ireland to join him.[65] Clearly, he was hoping for better fortune in the Golden State of California.

Chapter 9
Success in the Shenandoah:
California, Marriage and Civil War

I wish I were on yonder hill,
'Tis there I'd sit and cry my fill
Till every tear would turn a mill,
Is go tee tu mavourneen slan!
Shule, Shule, Shule aroon
Shule go suckir, augus shule go cuin
Shule go deen durris augus eiligh lume
Is go dee tu mavourneen slaun!
Old Irish ballad popular with troops during US Civil War.[1]

When General Shields ventured across the country along the California Emigrant Trail in June 1860, the trip was fraught with danger. Regular transcontinental passage, begun less than two years previously, consisted of an arduous trek along deeply rutted tracks through sagebrush desert, steamy swamps, and towering snow-scarfed mountains. There was merciless heat sucking the strength from one's very soul, and the ever present danger of Indian attack, marauding bandits, and other hazards, both natural and man made. The mountains, where frothing horses toiled against the traces, brought relief from the stifling heat of the plains, but the heights exacted their own toll: cold and air hunger exhausting one's body in the rarefied atmosphere. Nor was there any comfort in the jolting overland stagecoach where passengers chewed and swallowed dust, instead of trying to spit it out, to preserve precious saliva. After a while miserable travelers gave up swatting the incessant swarms of flies, pouncing on any exposed skin, to save their strength. By the time the stagecoach breasted the Sierras and descended to the blue Pacific rim, they felt they had gone through hell in the alternate fiery and freezing three week trip from St. Louis.

As soon as General Shields reached the sun-drenched west coast, he took up residence at the prestigious Bella Union Hotel in Los Angeles,[2] the social and political hub of the area, and was greeted as a visiting dignitary.[3] His warm reception was appropriate, since he was a former US Senator not merely from one state, but from two, and had advocated strongly for the Golden State's inclusion in the Union a decade earlier. This made Shields a celebrity, and the local newspaper recorded his arrival. Shields said he had made the long trip, not because he was broke and seeking fresh opportunities, but ventured that "a wound received during the Mexican War prompted my coming."[4]

Senator David Broderick, the stone cutter son of Irish immigrants, who had sat with Shields in the US Senate, was the magnet that drew Shields to California. Broderick painted a glowing picture of the state, and encouraged Shields to see it for himself. Unfortunately, by the time Shields followed in the footsteps of the forty niners, Broderick was deceased, killed the previous year in a duel with California Supreme Court, Justice David S. Terry.[5]

Shields was not as much taken with the City of the Angels as it was with him and found it stifling hot after the winters in Washington and Minnesota and too undeveloped for his taste. After scouting the area for close to a month, he made his way to Northern California, by means of stagecoach instead of steamer. On Aug 1st, Shields arrived in the bustling port of San Francisco and took up residence at the fashionable Metropolitan Hotel. Once again, he said he had come "for the purpose of recuperating his health" and added "to see the wonders of the Pacific Coast."[6] By the same token, people of Northern California were pleased to see him, the *Alta* Newspaper noting that "his name will be mentioned with respect." As a former Senator, who had sat in Government in far away Washington, he was living proof of California's connection to the rest of the country.

Though Shields said he had come to California to recuperate, he did not spend much time resting. For one thing he was short of funds and could not afford to sit around, and another, he was not the type of person to let grass grow under his feet. The General made himself at home in the City by the Bay and, after renting an apartment at the North-east corner of Mission & Brady, followed his customary pattern by opening a law office in partnership with Lewis Shearer at the North-east corner of Montgomery & California Streets.[7] This provided Shields with means of support while making political and social contacts and, he met the influential Irish community, which had started holding annual St. Patrick's Day parades seven years earlier in 1853. He put out political feelers to local Democrats including Lt-Governor John G. Downey who had left Co. Roscommon as a four year old boy less than thirty years previously. (Downey was the only foreign-born Governor of California until 2003 when Austrian-born Arnold Schwarzenegger was elected.) Because of his sterling reputation Shields was invited to make political speeches which he did enthusiastically. His actions showed that he aimed to make his mark in the Golden State, as he had previously in Illinois and Minnesota.

Shields strolled the hilly streets and could see that commerce was king. The population was exploding and ships' manifests in 1860 told the story of the boom: 30,700 passengers disembarked from vessels in the Port of San Francisco that year, while only 14,100 departed. It was estimated that an additional 50,000 individuals arrived overland. According to *The Annals of San Francisco,* at that time, "The wharves are constantly lined with clipper and other ships, the discharge of whose cargoes gives employment to an army of sailors and boatmen, stevedores and 'longshoremen. The streets are crowded with wagons and vehicles of every description, bearing goods to and from the huge stores and warehouses. The merchant and his clerk are busily buying and selling, bartering and delivering; and fleets of steamers in the bay and rivers are conveying the greater part of the goods disposed of to the interior towns and mining districts."[8]

When General Shields arrived in California, the Presidential campaign of 1860 was in swing and, he stumped vigorously for his old friend, Stephen A. Douglas. Douglas was up against not one Presidential candidate but three, Abraham Lincoln who had been nominated by the Republicans, John Breckinridge of Kentucky, the champion of the Dixie Democrats, and John Bell of Tennessee, a standard bearer of the die-hard Whigs and remnants of the Know-Nothing Party. Douglas' electoral effort was doomed from the outset, since the division among the Democrats was too great and Douglas was getting no help from the White House. An investigation by a committee under the chairmanship of Rep. John Covode (R. Pa.) demonstrated that the Administration had sought the ruin of Douglas with bribery. The editor of the Philadelphia Press was offered government printing contracts worth $80,000 to support Presidential policy against Douglas. In addition, Lincoln's lead was too much to overcome.

The teeming port of San Francisco, its wharves filled to capacity with ships, in the 1850s. Shields arrived here in August 1860 following a two-month overland trip.

Lincoln, as it turned out, failed to garner a single Southern vote, but his strong following in the North, gave him a clear majority. Shields, for his part, was doubly disappointed at the outcome: despite his best efforts for Douglas, Lincoln carried California, though the count was close. If it was any consolation to Shields, the Township back in Illinois bearing the Shields name went for Douglas 71 - 55, even though Illinois overall had Lincoln on top by 12,000.

Following the election, a dejected Shields knew that he could abandon any thoughts he might have harbored about obtaining a federal position either in California or Washington. With Douglas in the White House, it would have been easy; instead, Republicans ruled the roost and there were no pickings for him. As Shields mulled his future, the future of the country turned dark. Immediately after Lincoln's election, the South Carolina Legislature called for a state convention to reject his Presidency. Meeting at Columbia on Dec 20, they passed, without a dissenting vote, an ordinance declaring that "the Union now subsisting between South Carolina and the other states under the name of the 'United States of America' is hereby dissolved." It was not long before the Palmetto State was joined by ten others that abandoned the Union altogether to form the Confederate States of America .[9]

Shields, a strong believer in the Union, grieved to see it dismembered and decided to do what he could to save it. As news of what had happened in South Carolina reached California, Shields let everyone know where his loyalties lay and began speaking out against Southern secession. On Saturday May 11, he gave a speech at the Pavilion in San Francisco, which according to Charles E. De Long, a California politician, "came out very well."[10] Less than three weeks later, on June 5, after another anti-Confederate speech, Shields "was repeatedly applauded and when he concluded three cheers were given for him. He arose again and made a patriotic response."[11]

Shields' plain but eloquent speaking style and, his ability to orate at length without notes or prompting, made him a popular figure. He wooed crowds with a self-effacing style of delivery which elevated audiences to his level. Since people did not feel talked down to, they responded warmly. As the *Sacramento Union* recounted of one presentation, "General Shields said at the outset he was no orator, aimed at no display, and his only expectation was to throw off some suggestions which his audience could take up and improve upon." The report also noted that "General Shields spoke some two hours without notes, and was frequently interrupted by hearty applause. His remarks were eminently suggestive, and listened to with close attention by an excellent audience."[12] By such methods, Shields resonated in harmony with his audience, which in turn, went a long way toward explaining his success at the ballot box. He was able to articulate what was on people's minds, but as yet unexpressed, so that their thoughts crystallized with his words and they could then say them aloud. He did this so smoothly that Koerner observed "He did not seek popularity, but yet had a sort of winning way about him that made him friends quite readily."[13] Extracts from a presentation delivered at the Sixth Street Congregational Church, Sacramento in January 1861, shortly after the secession and, an analysis of audience response demonstrates how he wooed and won audiences with carefully chosen words and phrases. Entitled "The Character, Life and Times of Andrew Jackson," the Sacramento speech was to "a large audience of Ladies and Gentlemen," that had been profoundly shaken by recent events in the East. The *Union* stated that

Shields "was introduced as 'the distinguished lecturer, General James Shields' but the General said he begged leave in the outset to correct that complementary statement. He was not a lecturer, but for the first time in his life had commenced here in California to deliver, not lectures, but little talks. I believe he said that we all commence trying to do things here in California that we could not or dare not attempt to do anywhere else. (*Applause and laughter.*)"

"Having by this felicitous turn placed himself *en rapport* with his audience, the lecturer announced his subject, and entered upon its consideration. He said he did not feel competent to do justice to the character of General Jackson - a character which few men could even appreciate, much less delineate, but his apology for the attempt was that the subject had long been in his heart, from that had got into his head and he could not help talking about it. (*Applause.*)"

Shields went on to describe the leading incidents of President Jackson's highly dramatic life. "*At the age of 13 years, Jackson was captured by a British band, cut down and wounded by the officer in command and thrown into prison, from which he was only liberated by the heroic exertions of his mother. This incident told more than five hundred Fourth of July orations of the nature of that struggle by which our liberties were secured; and long, he trusted in God, we might continue to enjoy the fruits of that struggle.* (Applause.) ...

We have had as yet but three great Presidential eras - those of Washington, Jefferson and Jackson" continued Shields.

"*The Washingtonian was the Constitutional era; the Jeffersonian, the Democratic era, and the Jacksonian was the Popular era. What the next era will be denominated, God alone, from the events that are now shaping, can foretell; Heaven send that it is not to be recorded as the disastrous era.* (Applause.) *There existed, at the beginning of Jackson's Administration a gigantic political, financial internal improvement system which Jackson believed to be wrong and against which, therefore, he waged war although the warfare convulsed every interest in the country. The consequence was that everybody seemed to oppose his Administration. Capital, talent, the press and even the pulpit, appeared to conspire against him. His friends deserted him. Even his cabinet fled ingloriously. In the midst of the conflict, South Carolina, a generous and high spirited but*

impulsive State rose up against the same system, but not confining herself to that, she
unwisely rebelled against the laws. General Jackson had sworn to uphold the laws and
therefore, South Carolina became an obstruction in his path.

Then it was that he uttered these words, historic and yet to be trusted prophetic
'The Federal Union, it must be preserved.' The words as they passed through those lips
rang through the land like a blast from a trumpet and from that moment nullification was
doomed. South Carolina saw the blow coming and even Calhoun trembled before the
strong arm of Jackson. Then a mighty coalition was formed against Jackson. Its forces
were led by the colossal Webster in the North, by the eloquent Clay in the West and by
the brilliant Calhoun in the South. Behind these - giant intellects stood the moneyed
influence and nearly every interest in the country. The press denounced him and the
pulpit which never does its duty when it goes into politics (Applause.) *joined in the*
crusade. Another man would have fallen but Jackson stood firm and defiant. He knew he
did not stand alone. Such a man never does. If we had such a man now, the American
heart would rise beside him again. (Applause.) *Down went internal improvements and*
tariff. The bank was this Sebastapol where they made their final stand. At length the blow
fell and down came Bank and Biddle and all. (Laughter.)

.... In 1845, the cold grave closed over his large strong heart and the tears of a
nation flowed in sorrow... Oh! If we could only recall him now from that cold tomb. If
God could only lend him to us for eight years, or even eight months to be replaced in the
Presidential chair and again to rouse the cry "The Federal Union; it must be preserved!
(Applause.)

I do not mean to give offence; I trust the time has not yet come when a man who
speaks of his whole country shall give offence but nothing so astounds and pains me as
the indifference, the torpor that seems to have seized upon our people as to the great
danger of the times. Don't you think this is an hour of peril? Ten years ago how would
the heart of America have beaten to witness what is now happening in the East? Yet
everyone seems to take it as a matter of course. If anything could indicate that the disease
is mortal, it is this apathy... to the present peril. I cannot comprehend it. They are
fighting about their places on the floor when the house is on fire. They are scrambling
about the pantry instead of taking holds of buckets and fire engines to save the building.

(Applause.)

They are like the Legislature of Louisiana, which was wrangling about a doorkeeper, while the British columns were marching against New Orleans. For me, I dare not say like General Jackson, The Federal Union must be preserved; would to God I could and were able to carry it out, (Applause) *but I say the Federal Union ought to be preserved, and I say the Federal Union can be preserved. I cannot tell you how, for you would call me a partisan. How can a man speak in these days without touching some of our contemptible small parties.* (Laughter) *I only say this; I am not for a Southern Republic, for a Northern Republic, nor for a Pacific Republic. I am for an American Republic, one and indivisible.* (Great Applause.)

... I do not want a mutilated Republic. I want the whole. Some men say 'Let South Carolina go, she is only an annoyance, anyhow' I give you my word that, if I am ever called upon to select an army, I will leave all such men out of the ranks. I am a military man in a small way, and I tell you if one regiment can rise up in mutiny and be permitted to march out of the camp with colors flying and drums beating, I would not give a pinch of snuff for the army it leaves behind. (Applause.)

I do not know how Andrew Jackson would act in this crisis; I dare not say - but I believe in that at any hazard, he would execute the laws and let the consequences be what they may. (Applause.)

...I do not despair of this Government even if ten States should withdraw, for the race which originally constructed it is capable of its reconstruction. But here in this new State, you should hold an even balance between the sections. Men of all sections fought for this soil, paid their money for it, and it has been open for the settlement of all. For God's sake then, let not this great and new State take up a position untrue to the whole Union. (Applause.)

I think God will not suffer this Government to go down. A dissolution of the Union would be Mexico over again but ten times worse. Civil war in this country would be too fearful to contemplate. We have great work to do, in the hands of God's Providence, both on this continent and in the old world on the other side of the Pacific. Put not your trust in politicians or in presses or in anything else but go back to the heart of the people. The people and they only, can save the Union. (Applause.)" The reporter noted that General

Shields spoke for nearly two hours and at the close the audience sang in a 'spirited and effective manner' *The Flag of Our Union.*[14]

As can be seen, even though General Shields was billed to speak about a dead President he quickly resurrected him and made him part of the living present. In so doing, he adroitly shaped a lattice work of old issues into contemporary concerns for his listeners. He never wandered too far away from what had been billed as his subject, nor traveled anywhere without bringing his audience along with him. Because of that, they never felt lost, cheated, nor manipulated, even though he continuously directed their thoughts and conclusions.

Senator David Broderick, whose parents came from Ireland, encouraged Shields to migrate to California. A former stone mason, Broderick had died in a duel by the time Shields arrived in the Golden State 1860.

Shields made his case not only with eloquence and humor, but with inspirational appeal to all the senses, achieving this through the use of strong metaphor and imagery, both auditory and visual. As he spoke of the house being on fire, one almost felt the heat and heard the flames crackling and might have had to stifle an impulse to grab a fire bucket to save the building. The "blast from a trumpet" did more than wake everyone up; it was a clarion call to arms to save the Union and, there were few in his hearing who could not relate to the worthlessness of a "pinch of snuff." Even the most unfeeling must have felt shivers as Shields, stroke by stroke, painted a picture of Jackson's noble heart being stilled and entombed in a cold gray crypt. Shields so masterfully coupled Jackson's heroic struggles against the moneyed class thirty years earlier with the current crisis that the audience learned lessons for the present. His use of inspirational language was not over done. Even though he was speaking in a church hall, he was not afraid to rebuke churches for daring to dabble in politics. Appeal to the deity on high was *de rigeur* in that era, and he sprinkled it appropriately on the dish he was serving. Finally, Shields' culmination, his *coup-de-grace,* was ingenious as he ended with an ultimate and audacious role reversal. He exhorted the audience not to put their trust in politicians, of which of course he was one, and by so doing, he garnered even more of their trust. His twist ensured that they would repay him tenfold with unmitigated loyalty and support, and would be only to happy to get in line for whatever he proposed.

There were other speeches of a similar nature, and in them, General Shields presented a graphic picture of how Civil War would sunder the nation and he predicted the enormous loss of life and limb that would ensue. For a military man, he was remarkably candid about horrors of combat and it being neither glorious nor grand. Overall, General Shields could generate a *tsunami* of patriotic fervor and few left his meetings without a feeling that whatever he said made sense and it was for the good of the country.

The Civil War commenced on April 12, 1861, when Southern shore batteries, under the command of Gen. Pierre Beauregard, opened fire on Fort Sumter, a Northern controlled fortress, in Charleston Harbor. On hearing of the hostilities, Shields was ready to re-enlist, and applied for a regular military commission, hoping that at last he would achieve his cherished goal of becoming a command Major General and would direct events. Instead, he heard nothing back from Washington, and concluded that his offer of services had been declined. Deciding to move on, his life then took a dramatic turn, when he forsook persistent bachelorhood and got married, apparently at short notice.

Over the years, General Shields had been pursued by and dated various women, but had never shown any propensity to settle down. One might conjecture that he never really did, but he finally took a bride, Mary Ann Carr, an Irish-born woman who had grown up in America. The wedding took place on August 15, 1861 in St. Ignatius Jesuit Church, San Francisco,[15] and when he tied the nuptial knot, he, like his father, chose for his wife, a woman 30 years his junior. There are two versions of how the two met and subsequently wed. The first states that James and his bride-to-be got to know one another back in Minnesota in the home of Judge Corkery, a friend of Shields, where Mary had been employed as a housemaid. She had been born in Loughgall, County Armagh on Aug

15, 1835 and had come to the US with her parents in 1845 at the age of 10. Within two years of her arrival she was orphaned and working to support herself. After the General went west, he sent for Mary and she came to him.[16] A slightly modified version places Mary higher up the social scale.[17] It states that she was the daughter of Tarence (?Jerome) and Sarah Carr who came to America in 1847. Her father, a prosperous linen merchant, had lost his fortune by endorsing a friend's note. Seeking to regain his wealth, he had settled in the City of Baltimore, where he resided until his death in 1850.

His wife succumbed a year later leaving Mary to live in a convent with nuns. This account states that Mary and the General were introduced while she was visiting relatives in California and he "pressed his suit and won."[18] Condon also contended that the Carr and Shields families had been friends back in Ireland. While that is certainly possible, since counties Tyrone and Armagh abut each other, there is no record of a Carr - Shields family friendship.

President Andrew Jackson in 1845, the year of his death. Much like Shields in character, the charismatic yet feisty Jackson championed the "common man" and served Shields as his alter ego. Jackson, from Tennessee, once killed an opponent in a duel and he did not hesitate to aggressively confront international powers whenever American interests were threatened. He several times risked foreign wars - against Britain over West Indies trade and Sicily and France over debts owed to the United States. At home, he was an ardent expansionist who fought tooth and nail against the tight-fisted policies of the Bank of the United States and its President, Nicholas Biddle.

Not everyone was glad that wedding bells had finally chimed for the reluctant

General and his youthful bride, especially not Maria Daly, the gossipy wife of Judge Charles P. Daly of New York.[19] The Dalys were close friends of Shields and, whenever Shields was in New York, their home was his. Early in Shields' political career, Mrs. Daly, a society mover and matchmaker, looked upon Shields almost as her protégé. She advocated for him and did whatever she could to promote his political career. She also did everything in her power to inveigle him into marrying her good friend, socialite Harriet Whetten.[20] Mrs. Daly could not contain her dismay when she learned of the General's nuptials and could scarcely believe it. Even though she had never met the bride, she wrote cattily about Shields' "girlwife" and said "she has followed the General now to my knowledge for four years with relentless perseverance, declaring that she was engaged to him long before the old gentleman ever thought of such a thing, as I know from his own letters. I hope that he will not repent, but such a bold *lover* (when a maid) rarely makes a very attractive wife."[21] It is possible that Mrs. Daly was confused about the bride; there may well have been a maid named Mary Cahill in Minnesota whom Shields dawdled with, and told Mrs. Daly about, possibly to fend off advances from Maria and Harriet, but that Miss Cahill was not the woman he finally chose.

Once Shields married, he thought once again about trying his hand at commerce, since he had a wife, and might soon have a family to support. He purchased an interest in a silver mine down the coast from California in Mazatlan, Mexico and, the day after his wedding he and Mary boarded a steamer and sailed along Baja to it. He had given up on being recalled to the military but, as it happened, three days after his departure, his commission came through from Washington, even though it took some time for the news to reach Shields in Sonora, Mexico.

Once again, to Shields' disappointment, his appointment specified the rank of Brigadier, not Major General, as he had hoped. Since he craved a second star, he immediately set about trying to get it, by writing letters, putting his political connections to work and pushing General Scott, the Dalys and various others to intercede for a him.[22] Shields was not able to call on help from his old friend and ally Stephen Douglas, because the Illinois Senator had died three months earlier, aged 48, a victim of typhoid. Douglas's death would have been a blow to Shields, since he could have counted on him. The "Little Giant" had been stricken as he toured the country urging support for President

Lincoln and his policies. Shields' efforts were to no avail and no second stars fell on his shoulders.

Kernstown Battlefield as it looks today. Stonewall Jackson's Virginians, including the 1st Virginian (Irish) Battalion, advanced from left along Cedar Creek (at woods in background) against Gen. Shields' infantry division under Cols. Kimball, Tyler and Jeremiah C. Sullivan on the right. Union forces included regiments from Ohio (5th, 7th, 13th & 62nd) Indiana (7th) Pennsylvania (110th), West Virginia (1st) and Illinois (39th.) The Confederate front and flanking movements faltered when they came under withering artillery fire from Prichard's Hill (located to right rear of photographer.) Following several hours of intense fighting the rebels were forced to flee. This battle, on March 23, 1862, marked the opening conflict of Jackson's famous Springtime Shenandoah Valley Campaign and was the only battle ever lost by him.

Shields understood quite well the military situation confronting the rival forces and wrote insightfully "The North will crush the South - but what of that. We are only weakening ourselves. We may kill them and overrun their country but will that make them loyal... The North has to act and act nobly but the result no human being can foresee. Are we to keep a permanent army in the South to keep them down? Then we must change our system and have a military republic... The future is dark to me... My heart shudders at the prospect beyond. Do you know that the feeling for war is as strong here as it is with you but what is curious - the preachers are the most belligerent. Our civilization is a show... God save our country and God Save the Union."[23]

Nevertheless, Shields, "the old war-horse" was not going to miss the action for the sake of a second star, and sailed north to California, where he was cheered and feted. But all was not puffery; he had to weather a political storm that had been brewed by Senator John McDougal of California during his absence. McDougal, the second Governor of California, leveled charges against Shields in Jacksonville Illinois, accusing him of being a secret secessionist. There was no truth to McDougal's allegations and his motivations for making them are unclear. Some speculated that Shields might have been contemplating a run for the US Senate from California at the time, which could have been a factor.

Shields did not take the widely reported allegations lying down, and immediately fired off a pugnacious letter to the *Alta* newspaper. In it, Shields declared "Since my return to the State a few days ago my attention has been drawn to the following paragraphs that seem to have gone the rounds of the papers in my absence. The Jacksonville *Journal* in a sketch of his (McDougal's) remarks referred to an interview between himself and General Shields in San Francisco in the fall of 1861 which shows that Shields was enlisted in the secession movement at that time. He visited California to further its interests and tried to induce the speaker to join his fortunes with it. This paragraph, short as it is, contains three separate and distinct falsehoods: "That Shields was enlisted in the Secession movement at that time" (or any other time) is falsehood number 1. "That he visited California to further its interests" is falsehood number 2.

"That he tried to induce the speaker (Senator McD.) to join his fortunes with it," falsehood No.3

If Senator McDougall is correctly reported in the above paragraph, it is only left for me to pronounce him the author of a base lie and a despicable calumniator.

Your obedient servant, Jas. Shields. Dec 6, 1861.[24]

The former Governor choose not to respond to Shields' angry denunciations according to the mores of the time, even though McDougal was no stranger to dueling. Ten years earlier, he had wounded A.C. Russell, editor of the San Francisco *Picayune* in just such an encounter. McDougal remained "mum" and the *Alta* wholeheartedly endorsed Shields rebuttal, noting, on the day Shields departed for the war, that "although he (Shields) has been resident of the state but a short time, he has become identified with our interests and has endeared himself to a host of friends. Like many others, his loyalty in this crisis has been assailed by the tongues of slander, but 'actions speak louder than words.' While we with others regret that our young state is being deprived of a sound and able person in his departure we are consoled with the knowledge that he leaves us to devote his talent and energies in behalf of the cause we have so much at heart: the perpetuity of our Union"[25]

On December 11, 1861, Shields was escorted to the port with all the pomp and pageantry the Shields Guards, a company in the California Militia named after him, could muster. The troop consisted of naturalized Irish-Americans, who drilled out of the Montgomery Guard armory at the corner of California and Kearney Streets, and their flags and banners fluttered briskly in the breeze as they marched along the bayshore. Upon reaching the wharf, the Shields Guards saluted *Slainte,* as the General stepped aboard the SS Golden Gate, the steamer that would take him down the coast on his first step to the cataclysm in the East.

Edwin Stanton, Lincoln's Secretary of War, a capable man who was no friend of Shields.

When he sailed, Gen. Shields left behind his pregnant wife, Mary, since she was carrying their first child, who would also be named Mary, after her.

General Shields journey east via the isthmus of Panama took three weeks. He arrived in a snowy New York on Jan 4, 1862, where, as usual, he stayed with the Dalys. Judge Daly was glad to see him, but his wife Maria had reservations. She was put out, not only by Shields marriage but even more so, by his refusal to discuss it. Despite her discreet and sometimes unsubtle probes, he kept his own council. Maria wrote acidly in her diary "I think he seems desperate and will probably scarcely come out of this war. I

186

am glad my brothers are not with him." General Shields had an ulterior motive in visiting the Dalys this time round, shortage of funds. Military officers were expected to equip and uniform themselves and his assets were tied up in the Mexican mine. What little ready cash he possessed, had been deposited with his pregnant wife on the other side of the country. Because of that, he was forced to borrow $500 from the judge to accouter himself. After he left, Maria confided in her dairy "The General left this morning... I wish he would confess about his marriage. I hope the report that he has married his servant woman is not correct." While staying with the Dalys, Maria noted that Shields was visited by "some Army officers from Oregon who came on with him, came to see him in the evening and they took out the map and planned out the campaign. One Lieutenant seemed military man and General."[26]

General Shields during the Civil War. His Brigadier star is visible on his epaulet.

Though cool to Shields, he warmly toward her. rebuff by Gen. the Union confided in her, "It find that hardly of here but there is change here done. These people anything without anything. The new Lee inspires a great [in the South.] chaos... Men are

to me a very able devoted to the Maria Daly was continued to feel Later, following a George McClellan, Commander, he is soul sickening to anything is thought offices... Unless nothing will be will undertake qualification for [General Robert E.] deal of confidence Everything is in appointed for

commands that are fit for nothing."

Shields decried the bungling by the high command and noted that "General McClellan has lost the confidence of the public here. I fear he will soon fall... I know we can take Richmond. I will risk my reputation to do it but not in the present way. They are frittering away the strength of the nation in childish expeditions. Sherman's party might as well be in Africa for all the good it is doing... Is all this folly, imbecility or ignorance? The raw material is here to do anything. But this is like a political campaign. It is not like a military one...

Chomping at the bit throughout February, Shields was frustrated at not being summoned immediately to action. He had traveled a long way to take part and did not want merely to sit on the sidelines. The war was not going well for the North and, Shields clearly thought he could correct that, if given the chance. At this low ebb, Judge Daly suggested to Shields that he establish a "Hibernian Brigade," and set himself at the head of it. Daly had a point. The Irish-born, having arrived in America in large numbers during the previous two decades, were enlisting in droves as both sides sought their services. Altogether, about 200,000 Irish-born served in the war, three quarters in blue uniforms and the remainder in gray. The Irish were the largest single ethnic group serving the South, though they did not enlist under a single banner or Irish Brigade as they did for the Federals. (Irish born Confederate heroes included Patrick Cleburne from Cork and Lt. Dick [Richard W.] Dowling from Tuam, Co. Galway.)[28] In Shields Township, Illinois alone, 83 of 104 eligible, mostly Irish, males enlisted in the Federal Army, the majority even before the draft was initiated.

Declining to follow Judge Daly's advice, the General preferred a regular command. He was painfully aware from the Mexican-War that ethnic or reserve units were not highly valued by army regulars, and were considered expendable. An Irish Brigade was organized later that year, under the command of Thomas F. Meagher the former Young Irelander who had also been commissioned a Brigadier General. The Brigade was virtually wiped out, in what many consider were "expendable" orders, on Marye's Heights at the Battle of Fredericksburg in December 1862. More than sixty percent of the Brigade were casualties in that battle. Shields had sound ideas about how to conduct the war and bring it to a speedy conclusion. But without two star rank, he knew that his views would scarcely be countenanced by higher command. Nevertheless, Shields sent a copy of his strategy to truncate the war to Gen. George McClellan and, as it turned out, this was the plan, with minor modification, that would finally bring the war to a close three years later. Shields could see that the natural objectives for the Union army were Richmond and Memphis. With their rail links severed, they would quickly fall and once that happened the Union could crush the South.

As H.A. Castle summed up "On January 10, 1862, in a letter to General McClellan, commander in Chief of the Army, General Shields, outlined the military operation which he deemed necessary for the suppression of the Rebellion. Secretary Seward in an official communication a few days later, submitted this letter to the Secretary of War, urgently inviting his attentions thereto.

The letter is published in the Rebellion records, Serial Volume 5, Page 701 to 703. It is one of the more important papers relating to the conduct of the war and stamps its author as not only brave, but capable as a strategist of great ability."[29] McClellan, the professional soldier who thought little of all non-career military officers, was unimpressed with Shields plan and ignored it. A short time later, Shields wrote to Maria Daly that "Little Mac" was cold to him as he was "to all old officers who come to the service with reputations. There is no encouragement to men who are ready to risk their lives in all this."[30]

Stonewall Jackson, legendary Southern commander, whose only defeat came at the hands of Gen. James Shields. Jackson evened the score some three months later and that defeat effectively ended Shields' military career.

Early in March, much to Shields delight, he finally got an assignment he prized. Ordered to the Shenandoah Valley to command a division of 10,000 men, he would be under another politician-General, former Speaker of the House of Representatives, Nathaniel P. Banks. Shields was dispatched to replace General Frederick

W. Lander, who had died from pneumonia on March 2nd, and took command of his division at Paw Paw Tunnel, Virginia shortly after Lander's death. As much as Shields was happy, his officers were not. Feeling left out of the main action, they took little satisfaction in their defensive role, protecting the flank of the Nation's Capital. The real war, they figured, was McClellan's Peninsular campaign ascending on Richmond. Little did they know that their situation was about to change and they would soon see all the action they craved, and then some. The men were pleased to see Shields and George A. Huron, a trooper in the 7th Indiana, stated "Upon General Shields' arrival the army instantly felt the magic of his touch, and though only a few men of his new command had previously been in battle, we at once recognized the fact that our commander had brought with him his master hand... he came to us wearing his fighting uniform."[31]

Upon Shields' arrival, Banks received fresh orders to protect the Baltimore and Ohio Railroad west of Harper's Ferry, and for that, his troops had to cross the Potomac river and occupy the town on the opposite side. The long lines with their cassions and wagons snaked slowly across a hastily constructed pontoon bridge without incident, as the Confederates under General Thomas J. "Stonewall" Jackson fell back toward the town of Winchester, Virginia.[32] Jackson's army, the 1st Virginia Brigade had survived a hard winter, but his numbers had dwindled to 4,200. His forces had occupied the area since November 1861, but were not in a position to hold on to it. Jackson knew it would be folly to face the foe in his withered state, and conceded ground.

As Banks, aided by Shields, pushed deeper into enemy territory, Jackson continued his tactical retreat, pulling out of Winchester on March 11, 1862. It was none too soon since the Union Army moved in and occupied Winchester the following day. The area around Winchester was important, because of its geographic location at the head of the Shenandoah Valley and as a valuable Southern breadbasket. Bounded by the Allegheny and Shenandoah mountains on the west and the Blue Ridge mountains on the east, capturing the valley denied valuable food and other supplies to the South. The area was also strategically important because it was a route the Southerners could use to outflank the Union Army and threaten Washington and, these were the reasons it changed hands 72 times in the course of the war.

The Shenandoah river, running north to meet the Potomac River at Harpers Ferry, bisected the picturesque valley bounded by fertile fields plowed for wheat, buckwheat, rye and clover. Its waters seemed of little consequence when Shields first scouted the region. It would complicate matters markedly for him later that year, though he did not know it then. Banks consolidated his position in Winchester and issued orders to Shields on March 17th, St. Patrick's Day, to pursue Jackson to Strasburg 18 miles further south. The trenchant Shields wasted no time and ordered his troops on a fast march through enemy territory. Unopposed, they made rapid progress and Shields was in his element. The weather had turned warm, the magnolia was in bloom and the red wing blackbirds and mocking birds had returned and chirruped at every step. Shields was pleased that, even though he had been in command but a short time, his troops were responding well. Shields occupied Strasburg without much ado and pressed on another five miles to Woodstock. Still, the foxy Jackson eluded him. Shields had no way of knowing that the Southern commander had moved his entire command an additional 37 miles south of Woodstock to Mount Jackson.

Statue of Thomas Meagher in front of State Capitol, Helena, Montana. In 1867, then Acting-Governor Meagher, who was born in Waterford, Ireland, fell off a docked steamer into the fast flowing Missouri River near Fort Benton, Montana. His body was never recovered and he was presumed drowned. Shields had introduced Meagher, who was sentenced to death for his part in the Irish rebellion of 1848, to the US Senate after he escaped from Australia and made his way the US in 1853. Meagher, like Shields, was a Brigadier General in the US Civil War. This equestrian statue, erected in 1905, was funded by contributions from Irish miners in Butte and from Co. Cavan-born Copper King Marcus Daly, a founder of the Anaconda Copper Mining Company.

Shields continued sending out scouts to locate Jackson's forces, but had scant success. Some of Shields' cavalry actually reached the Mount Jackson region, where they skirmished briefly with Jackson's cavalry, under the command of Col. Turner Ashby but Ashby performed so ably that, they were rebuffed, and learned nothing of his superior's whereabouts. Shields, unable to locate Jackson, then brought his entire division back to Winchester where he set up camp on March 19. He then reported to Banks that only a small contingent of Confederate cavalry remained in the Shenandoah Valley which, of course, was wrong.

Shields' erroneous communication was only the first of several inaccurate intelligence assessments on both sides that were to culminate in the Battle of Kernstown less than a week later. After hearing what Shields had to say, Banks, satisfied that the rebels had been routed, decided to implement a bold tactical plan of his own. Leaving Shields at Winchester, Banks deployed the remainder of his troops toward the east. Banks planned to cross the Blue Ridge Mountains, link up with McClellan, and their combined forces would advance on Richmond to crush the Confederate capital.

Unknown to Shields, as he was returning to Winchester from Strasburg, Ashby's cavalry had shadowed him all the way. When Ashby observed the bulk of Banks' forces pulling out on March 21st, he sent word to Jackson that large numbers of enemy soldiers were leaving for the east. Jackson was furious. His orders were to defend the valley and tie down as many Union troops as possible, so they could not be used against Richmond. When Jackson got word that the Federals were moving out, it seemed that he had failed. But he was a brilliant tactician and decided to rectify the situation. Ordering his troops to decamp immediately, he let Ashby know that he was coming and, Jackson's Virginians made a forced march on Saturday March 22nd, covering 25 miles, but did not arrive at Winchester until next day. Meanwhile, the impetuous Ashby decided to harass Shields and, at four on Saturday afternoon, ordered his men to start shelling Shields' forces in front of Winchester.

At first Ashby was successful, catching the Union forces off guard, and driving them back into the town. But Shields soon regained his footing and brought up reinforcements, leading them into battle himself. The exchange of fire was withering and Ashby's forces faltered, since they had only light guns. When the shooting died down around sunset, Union soldiers had had much the better of things, and were about halfway between Winchester and Kernstown, a small village about 4 miles south. But all was not well for the Federals; great damage had been done to Shields. While positioning his artillery, he had been wounded and suffered a broken arm. Shields reported "While directing one of our batteries to its position I was struck by the fragment of a shell which fractured my arm above the elbow, bruised my shoulder, and injured my side."[33] That hit had not happened by happenstance; Shields had been singled out for injury and possibly worse. Some fifty years later, J. M. Meade speaking at the unveiling of a statue of Shields in Carrollton in 1914, gave an eye witness account of what transpired that Saturday afternoon.[34] Meade had been a Southern sympathizer and, the action had actually taken place on his father's farm, where he had had a clear view of the incident. He recounted "My first knowledge of General Shields was in the Spring of 1862, when General Stonewall Jackson engaged him in battle. It was on Saturday afternoon, March 22, 1862, that General Ashby of the Confederate cavalry, picked out General Shields and his staff with his field glasses. Ashby had in Caskie's battery a crack shot, named Phillips.[35] He asked him to fire on General Shields party. Phillips planted a little three inch smooth bore gun brought from Belgium by General Wade Hampton. He fired. A confusion followed in General Shields party and he was seen to fall from his horse, struck in the shoulder. This shot crippled him for life."[36] Though Shields was down, he was not out. He ordered Col. Nathan Kimball another veteran of the Mexican war, to take charge in the field and, at the same time, directed the ongoing battle from his sick cot, using his aide Col. J. T. Mason of the Fourth Ohio as his liaison. During the night, Shields issued orders to Kimball to press Ashby and clear his forces from the field. Shields stated in his report to Maj-Gen Banks "The injuries I had received prostrated me but were not such as to prevent me from making the required dispositions for the ensuing day. Under cover of the night I pushed forward Kimball's Brigade nearly three miles on the Strasburg road."[37] In addition, in a brilliant tactical move that was to pay rich dividends later, Shields dispatched a brigade of Union troops to the rear to confuse the enemy, but kept the men within marching distance so they could be recalled swiftly, as needed. Shields' ruse achieved its intended purpose and he stated "Ashby's cavalry, observing this movement from a distance, came to the conclusion that Winchester was being evacuated and signalized Jackson to that effect. We saw their signal-fires and divined their import."[38] Ashby then figured that Shields had only 3,000 men in four regiments, a small horse force, and one battery of artillery.

Next morning, Kimball continued to implement Shields' plan and pushed Ashby further back. Despite Ashby being reinforced with four companies of newly arriving infantry from the South, the Confederates had to give ground, and retreated all the way past Kernstown. In so doing, they conceded a strategic piece of terrain, Pritchard's Hill, the only high ground in the area. Kimball advanced no further and adopted a strong defensive position on the knoll, placing two artillery batteries there.

Jackson finally arrived at Kernstown in the mid-afternoon, and was reluctant to do battle, since it was the Sabbath; as a devout Christian, he would have preferred to spend his time praying instead of peppering the enemy with shot. Besides, his men were dog tired after marching more than thirty miles in two days. Surely they should rest on the Lord's Day? As Jackson surveyed the scene, Ashby gave him misleading intelligence information about Yankee strength. Whether from fatigue, or some other factor, Jackson did not check the details for himself, and accepted Ashby's figure at face value. It was the last time he would do such a thing, and afterward, always surveyed battlefields for himself. Ironically, that would be the reason he would meet his fate the following year.[39]

Believing he had superior strength, Jackson ordered his troops into a battle he hoped to settle by sunset. Under covering fire, his men were to advance along a dense wood on the left, ford a shallow stream and out flank the enemy on the knoll. The terrain would protect them from the Yankees, who would find it difficult to bring their guns to bear, thought Jackson. After the rebels opened up, the return fire from the Federals was stronger than anticipated, and the Southern advance stalled. The scrap continued without much change on either side until sunset, at which point Shields ordered the brigade he had held in the rear into the fray. When they appeared, a subordinate reported to Jackson that there were 9000 Yankees pouring down the valley and, that is when Jackson realized a trap had been sprung.

"Say no more of it. We are in for it" Jackson is said to have cried.

Indeed they were. The rebel lines broke as they ran for their lives. According to John Selby, a Jackson biographer, Stonewall was "greatly angered when he saw his old brigade falter and fall back."[40]

Jackson attempted to stop the rout, but there was nothing he could do. His troops departed in such disarray that they left behind many fallen comrades. Afterward, Shields reported that he had suffered 150 killed and 300 wounded and his estimate of enemy losses was 500 killed and 1000 wounded.[41] Southern dispatches were at variance with Northern numbers and said that their losses amounted only to 80 dead, 375 wounded and 263 captured or missing. In addition to the prisoners they took, the Federals captured two artillery pieces, four caissons and about a thousand stand of small arms.

Afterwards the *Richmond Whig* described the battle as, "the most desperate contest of the war" and that compared to it, "Manassas was childsplay."[42] The Honorable George A. Huron held a similar view, stating a half century later, "This battle has been dismissed by the historians of the war with the barest references and still, those of you who remember know, that in proportion to the numbers engaged, it was one of the bloodiest of the Civil War."[43] Bruce Catton, a popular Civil War historian, was of the same mind and wrote, "Jackson was roundly whipped and he had to retreat up the valley after a savage little battle which Shields' boys recalled later with vast pride theirs was the only outfit in the Union army which could say it had licked Stonewall Jackson in open fight."[44]

The victory could not have come at a better time for the Union, since, apart from some gains out West from U.S. "Unconditional Surrender" Grant before that, the South had been getting much the better of things. According to the *Freeman's Journal* "The Confederates continued to win victory after victory all through the summer, the fall and the winter of 1861. The Union forces were not only nearly everywhere beaten on land, but in the early spring of 1862 the Confederates won a tremendous victory on the water. On March 8, the Confederate ram *Merrimac* steamed out from Norfolk to Hampton Roads and sunk the United States warships *Cumberland* and *Congress* with (loss of) nearly all on board. That blow struck consternation into the friends of the Union. The engagement between the *Monitor* and the *Merrimac* that followed resulted in a drawn battle, but, though it afforded a sigh of relief, failed to dispel the gloom that hung like a pall over the Nation."[45]

Stonewall Jackson's first account of the battle tried to put a good face on his failure which was difficult to do. Nonetheless, in a report to Joseph E. Johnson commanding the Department of Northern Virginia for the Confederacy, he stated: "As the enemy had been sending off troops from the district and from what I could learn was still doing so, and knowing your great desire to prevent it, and having a prospect of success, I engaged him yesterday about 3. P.M. near Winchester and fought until dusk, but his forces were so superior to mine that he repulsed me with the loss of valuable officers and men killed and wounded; but from the obstinacy with which our troops fought and from their advantageous position I am of the opinion that his loss was greater than mine in troops, but I lost one piece of artillery and three cassions."[46]

The morale of Jackson's troops plummeted following the unexpected Shields' success, and Jackson, taking punitive action to reestablish his command, lashed out at his own men. Immediately after the Battle of Kernstown he cashiered Gen Robert S. Garnett, his best field commander, because Garnett had not advanced in the face of withering fire from Shields' forces.[47] In addition, a month later, he relieved Col. Turner Ashby his able cavalry commander, of his command, saying that Ashby failed to exercise sufficient control over his troops during the Kernstown battle. Clearly, it galled him to be beaten in that encounter, the only battle of his career that he would ever lose.

On the other hand, Shields was ecstatic with the outcome. Two days afterward, he wrote triumphantly to Maria Daly "In the first conflict which occurred in the evening previously I was struck by a fragment of a shell which broke my left arm and severely injured my shoulder and it was from my bed, I issued orders and directed the movement the next day. As yet, I am still prostrate but hope to be well soon and at the head of my command."[48] Shields wound at Kernstown put him out of commission for five weeks and, he did not resume command until April 30, 1862.

Shields received accolades on his success; General McClellan congratulated him on his "energy, activity and bravery" and expressed concern for Shields' well being. McClellan stated that he was "pained to learn that the wound you have received in the skirmish on the day before is more serious than at first supposed."[49] A joyous Maj-Gen. Banks, Shields' immediate superior, penned "The Commanding General of the Fifth

Army Corps congratulates the officers and soldiers of General Shield's division, and especially its gallant commander on its auspicious and decisive victory gained over the rebels on the 23d inst. The division has already achieved a renown against superior forces and a subtle and barbarous enemy."[50]

But not everyone was so laudatory. Owlish-looking Edwin Stanton, the Secretary of War, while acknowledging Shields' victory as "a brilliant achievement," was more tepid than thrilled. Compared with the other congratulatory chain-of-command letters, Stanton's communication was surprisingly circumspect and foreshadowed problems for Shields, should the Irishman stumble at any time in the future. The square-bearded Stanton wrote "While rejoicing at the success of your gallant troops, deep commiseration and sympathy are left for those who have been victims in the gallant and victorious contest with treason and rebellion. Your efforts as well as your success prove that Lander's brave division is still bravely led, and that wherever its standard is displayed rebels will be routed and pursued." The subtext of Stanton's communication suggests, that in Staunton's mind, the Kernstown victory belonged more to the dead General Landers than the living General Shields and indicates that Shields would be wise to watch his back. The Secretary of War's antipathy toward Shields was to prove a factor in the latter's fall from favor some three months later.

Paradoxically, though Jackson lost the battle, he became victorious in defeat. President Lincoln and Stanton, afraid that Washington could be taken through the Shenandoah back door, ordered Banks back across the Blue Ridge to make sure it stayed shut. Rightly or wrongly, they did not subscribe to the military maxim that cutting off a serpent's head disables its tail. Lincoln, at least, believed the real strength of the South lay, not its metropolis of Richmond, but in its military. "I think Lee's army, and not Richmond, is your true objective point" Lincoln wrote to General Joseph Hooker and also said "The strength of the rebellion, is its military—its army. That army dominates all the country, and all the people, within its range."[53] Banks' forces never linked up with McClellan and the Peninsular Campaign had to go on without them. Three months later McClellan actually came within 6 miles of Richmond, but the attack was snuffed out. With Bank's extra might from the Shenandoah Valley and the doughty Shields by his side, who knows what might have happened?

Chapter 10
Triumph and Tragedy:
La Belle Rebelle

The stars stand up in the air,
The sun and the moon are gone,
The strand of its waters is bare,
And her sway is swept from the swan

The cuckoo was calling all day,
Hid in the branches above,
How my stoirin is fled far away
' Tis my grief that I gave her my love
Two Songs from the Irish by Thomas MacDonagh (1878 - 1916.)

Sharp pains emanating from the war wounds of General James Shields scarcely tempered the pleasure surging through him, as he basked in the warm afterglow of the Battle of Winchester. Here was vindication, if any were needed, that he was an able commander worthy of the highest respect and a similar command. His victory reinforced his belief that the Union forces were fettered by a bungling bureaucracy and, that if he were in charge, the Federals would have already rolled into Richmond. Now at last, his long hoped for promotion to Major-General was in the cards and, his outstretched hands were eager for it. Even though Congress had capped the number of Major-Generals at 30, Shields expected to be one of them. But, as was his wont, Shields, at his very moment of triumph, overplayed his hand. To move things along, he wrote an injudicious letter to the *New York Herald* accusing General Banks of being overly cautious.

That piece, penned about a week after the Battle of Winchester raised eyebrows in high places. A subordinate does not usually comment publicly about a superior's perceived shortcomings when bullets are flying. Not surprisingly, Banks was furious and an acrimonious rift developed between Shields and the former Speaker of the House, costing Shields whatever good will he might have expected from his commander. It need not have come to that and, there is no good explanation for it. Possibly Shields euphoria, or the medication he was receiving, impaired his judgment; or maybe, it was simply his make up and, like heroes of Greek tragedy, Shields was doomed to be undone by his own hubris. Whatever the reason, support for Shields slipped, and as Maria Daly noted "I am sorry that the letter of General Shields has been published in which he speaks so confidently of himself and abuses General Banks... Vanity, vanity both for men and for women is the parent stem of many other vices. The General is by no means free of this moral weakness." The bottom line was that Shields, despite his fine showing, did not get the cherished recognition he so desperately craved.

As Shields recuperated in Strasburg, there was no fear of further attack, since the Southerners were too degraded for that. The dogwood broke into resplendent bloom and the orchards blossomed, filling the air with fragrance and, Shields became more concerned about attacks from civilians than armed Confederates. The valley, predominantly Confederate territory, contained many Southern sympathizers and some of these had taken to harassing anyone who collaborated with the North. In response, Shields proposed that Southern civilians be taken and held as hostage.

In a letter to Col Lewis, Provost Marshall at Winchester on April 7, 1862 Shields wrote: "It becomes our imperative duty to afford protection to loyal citizens from the persecution of secessionists in their respective neighborhoods. This duty we cannot perform by armed guards in every neighborhood. The secession leaders have organized a system of terror by which they intimidate their neighbors - expelling them from their homes - and preventing them from returning, under apprehension of arrest and sometimes even threatening their lives... I would recommend in every neighborhood where Union men are kept from their homes by fear of violence, two or more leading secessionists be arrested and retained as hostages until you learn how the loyal citizens are treated."[2] The Provost Marshal, recognizing that to incarcerate civilians would cause more ill will than the harassment engendered in the first place, had the good sense not to implement Shields' request. Harassment was something the Federals and the population at large would just have to put up with.

By the end of April, the Administration's fears of a direct attack on Washington had subsided to the point where they began to think of mounting another offense against Richmond. Shields was to play a larger role in this and, his brigade was detached from Banks and ordered to Fredericksburg under General Irvin McDowell. Deploying Shields' forces was part of a plan to build up McClellan's army for another assault on the

Southern Capital and, this time, with Shields in the field, the Union Command hoped for better success.

Belle Boyd, the "Rebel Spy." Her unconventional behavior titillated the North and scandalized the South. She became an actress after the Civil War and died in 1900.

Once Shields received his orders, he set about implementing them; if other commanders were slow to act, he was just the opposite and did not hesitate to push his troops. Shields' Brigade arrived at Fredericksburg ragged and footsore after marching 80 miles in four days and found President Lincoln waiting to greet them. Buoyed by Shields late March victory, Lincoln had come from the Capital to shake Shields' hand and review his troops.

"I want to see the boys that whipped Jackson" he declared enthusiastically.

The President's enthusiasm did not last, once he saw the shoddy appearance of Shields' troops. A crestfallen Lincoln later commented that "Shields' division has got terribly out of shape, out at the elbows and out at the toes"[3] Despite Shields irrepressible optimism, Lincoln was concerned for the morale of his men. Shields discounted their discomfort and said he wanted to be present when the *coup de grace* was administered to the Confederacy at Richmond. Shields was still hoping his success would lead to a second star. The President was partial to Shields promotion and actually recommended it, but members of his cabinet maintained that such advancement of a reserve General would be "unpopular with the officers of the regular army and likely to create trouble for the Administration."[4] In addition, some thought that Shields was a "lose cannon," and insane, and that the Republican dominated Congress would refuse to ratify his promotion.[5] "I would like to have had a few more such crazy generals," Lincoln is said to have responded to those allegations.[6]

About this time, Gen. Robert E. Lee, the capable Southern commander, got wind of the Federal build up against Richmond and decided to reemploy the earlier tactics used by Jackson in the Shenandoah Valley. He ordered Stonewall to go against the weakened Banks whose central command was still at Strasburg. With his forces depleted, Banks was justifiably concerned about what might befall him and thought that the Confederates, spotting his degraded state, would strike. His nightmare soon became more than a bad dream; the Confederates attacked in force at Front Royal in mid-May and Banks was forced to abandon Strasburg and retreat to Winchester in an overwhelming Yankee defeat. Banks casualties were enormous and he lost 1500 killed and wounded and 3000 of his best troops taken prisoner. The Confederates also captured vast quantities of stores, arms and ammunition and achieved their strategic goal of creating chaos in Washington. The panic-stricken Administration responded to the Jackson thrust by pulling Shields back from advancing along the Peninsula.

Shields, for his part, had predicted that the Confederates would attack Banks as a diversion, but that they could not possibly reach Washington. His letter to Peter Watson, the Assistant Secretary of War on May 9th on the matter had been ignored. Following Bank's loss, Lincoln ordered Shields back across the Blue Ridge to reinforce Banks, and the Confederate Capital of Richmond was forgotten. Shields, dismayed, as were his dispirited troops, turned back reluctantly and began the long return trudge. To lighten their load, the troops traveled without tents and were exposed to the heavy Spring rains. Feeling miserable, they bivouacked at Rectortown on May 28th and next day arrived at Front Royal. Despite being drained from their long forced march, Shields' men had sufficient in reserve to chase the Rebels out of Front Royal, and were able to recapture portion of the booty and prisoners seized earlier by Jackson. Shields did not press his exhausted brigade any further and awaited the arrival of Generals McDowell and Ord before resuming hostilities. They arrived on June 1st and, following a three day rest, Shields advanced against the Confederates along one bank of the Shenandoah, while General Fremont edged cautiously along the other.

The wily Jackson watched their coming and conceived a daring strategy. Jackson figured he could concentrate his forces on one side of the Shenandoah river and then destroy the bridges across it. This would make it virtually impossible for the Union forces to link up to reinforce each other if attacked. Jackson would fall on one of the Union forces and when he finished it off, he could turn on the other. This required precise timing and more than a modicum of skill and luck. The latter, as it happened, would come from an unexpected quarter, Miss Isabelle Boyd, the infamous Rebel Spy.

Today, Belle Boyd is better remembered than General Shields, at least in that part of Virginia.[7] She was the well endowed daughter of a Southern officer, who was articulate, resourceful and an accomplished horsewoman. Some accounts say she was a student at Mount Washington College,[8] while others suggest she was more schooled in villainy than any known virtue. After the war, Miss Belle became a successful actress in England, where she became known as "La Belle Rebelle," and wrote her popular memoirs. These became the basis for a melodrama, *Belle Lamar*, written by Irish playwright Dion Boucicault.[9]

General Shields first made Miss Belle's acquaintance in Winchester when Union forces occupied the town in March 1862.[10] She was then 18 years old and obviously engaging, so much so, that the beguiled General, like many of his officers, turned a blind eye to the perils she presented. Employing her vivacious personality, Belle wheedled information from Yankee officers and became an invaluable Southern agent.[11] General Shields, if he ever read her book, might have been flattered by her description of him as "an Irishman endowed with all those graces of manner for which the better class of his countrymen are justly famous; nor was he devoid of the humor for which they are no less notorious."[12] On the other hand, he would have been less amused with her account of how she spied on him for the South.

Port Republic as it looks today. Nestled among oaks, willows, ashes and elders, the village sits on a narrow neck of land between the North and South branches of the Shenandoah River. This is the view from Madison Hall, Stonewall Jackson's headquarters just before the Battle of Port Republic, June 9th, 1862. The area has changed little in the last century and a half and remains rolling farmland owned mostly by descendants of German Baptists. In Shields day they were called "Dunkards," because of their rite of adult baptism. The Blue Ridge mountains can be seen dimly in the haze in the background beyond the trees and village.

Before long, Belle had accumulated a dossier of information about Northern troop movements, strengths and supplies, which she passed on regularly to the Confederacy. In her not quite tell-all memoirs, she related how a certain Irish Captain, Daniel J. Keily smitten by her, gave her not only his heart but the best of intelligence as well. Keily, (later Brig. Gen.) an aide to General Shields, was seriously wounded at the Battle of Port Republic on June 9, 1862, when he was shot in the head and jaw, but survived. Belle wrote "General Shields, introduced me to the officers of his staff, two of whom were young Irishmen. And to one of these, Captain K(eily), I am indebted for some very remarkable effusions, some withered flowers, and at last, not least, for a great deal of very important information, which was carefully transmitted to my countrymen. I must now avow the flowers and the poetry were comparatively valueless in my eyes; but let Captain K(eily) be consoled: these were days of war, not love, and there are still other ladies in the world besides the "rebel spy."[13]

Not everyone who saw Belle was taken by the comely red head. Nathaniel Paige, war correspondent for the New York *Daily Tribune,* wrote: "In personal appearance, without being beautiful, she is very attractive. Is quite tall, has a superb figure, an intellectual face and dresses with much taste... She would go at will through our camps, flirt with our officers, and display their notes and cards to her visitors. She is a native of Virginia, but professes to be an ardent South Carolinian, at heart - wears a gold palmetto tree beneath her beautiful chin, a Rebel soldier's belt around her waist, and a velvet band across her forehead, with the seven stars of the Confederacy shedding their pale light therefrom. It seemed to me, while listening to her narrative, that the only additional ornament she required to render herself perfectly beautiful, was a Yankee halter encircling her neck."[14]

Miss Belle's espionage activities eventually brought her to the attention of the Federal marshals, who placed her under house arrest. But that scarcely cramped her style. She still gadded about, using her charm and passes issued by none other than General Shields himself. As the net closed in, the future actress decided it was time to take her final bow. She and her maid sat in the rail road depot waiting for the train to leave the valley, when she was recognized by a Federal officer and arrested. She was released by the bemused Federals a short time later and continued to spy fortuitously for the South. (For her colorful account, see her own story in Appendix S.[15])

The Federal Administration, at the end of May, determined to eliminate Jackson, who had being causing them so much angst, and decided to throw the full weight of the Union army against him. President Lincoln kept firing off telegraph messages to Shields to entrap Jackson and, on Sunday June 8, Shields marched south from Luray against "the Stonewall" expecting a repeat of Kernstown. But this time Jackson, armed with more accurate intelligence and more men than Shields, was determined on a different outcome. While the exact numbers on either side are debated, it is known that Jackson had more than 13,000 against less than 10,000 for Shields, even though the Union army had more total troops in the area. There were additional Union forces under General Fremont nearby at Cross Keys on the other side of the Shenandoah.

Jackson was fortunate to have in his command a man named Jeb Hotchkiss, who had been a topographical engineer for railroads before the war. Hotchkiss skillfully mapped out the arena and directed Jackson to the highest terrain, the village of Port Republic where Jackson strategically positioned his troops. From this vantage, Jackson had a commanding view of the Luray Valley and watched as Shields forces struggled and became bogged down in muddy roads. Shields, unsure of Jackson's whereabouts, wanted to cross Massanutten mountain where he expected to encounter the Southern General in New Market, further to the west. Jackson, already knowing Shields intentions, determined to surprise Shields and sent word to General Richard S. Ewell, a cunning and skillful commander, known as "Old Bald Head," to join him for an attack on Shields the following dawn. Stonewall proposed that after disposing of Shields, the combined forces of Jackson and Ewell could wheel about against Fremont. Ewell, who had tangled with General Fremont at Cross Keys earlier on Sunday June 8th, knew that the danger was, if Fremont mounted an attack while both he and Jackson were engaged with Shields, the Confederates would be beaten flat like hot metal on an anvil. The Confederates considered their plan a reasonable risk, since the only bridge still standing across the Shenandoah was at Port Republic and the river, after ten days of rain, was running too high for fording. Jackson, anticipating losses, was still mourning the death of "the black knight" Turner Ashby who had fallen in a skirmish with the Pennsylvania Bucktails two days earlier.[16] He wondered if he would be next, since he had dispatched Ashby to "Cut off the Federal view at every roadway, every lane, every ford; engage the pickets, drive off the cavalry, do all possible to confuse Shields and Fremont and delay their junction."[17] Jackson was more worried about Shields' Brigade than any other Union force because Shields' troops were mostly Westerners and unlike the Easterners were familiar with weapons from boyhood. "As Shields' division is composed principally of Western troops who are familiar with the use of arms, we must calculate on hard fighting to oust Banks" Jackson wrote.

In 1862, a covered bridge stretched from this point about 200 feet across the North Branch of the Shenandoah River at the entrance to the village of Port Republic. On June 8, 1862, an advance guard of Shields' Division under Col. Samuel Carroll scattered Southern pickets and surprised Stonewall Jackson, who was headquartered in a farmhouse just outside the village. Jackson, forced to flee, galloped across the bridge as Union fire and shot crashed into its timbers. Jackson, surviving a close personal call, made it safely across but, two of his party did not. Next day, a counterattack by the Confederates drove Union forces from the bridge and the village. After Jackson had moved all his forces across the river and had no further use for the bridge, he torched it to prevent Union forces under Gen. Fremont from linking up with Shields.

Holding the more strategic terrain, Jackson deployed his artillery skillfully along Luray Road on Shields' flank. As Shields approached, he felt enemy resistance stiffening and surmised that the real battle would commence on the morrow. He knew it would be bloody. Both Shields and his men were in fine fettle and Shields was recovering well from his wounds. One of Shields officers wrote from Luray on June 8th that "The General's arm is entirely well now and he is able to use it, though he tells me it is still weak. It would do your heart good to hear the hurrahs the men give when they see the General riding past with his black stallion and body guard. He is beloved by the men and they would follow him anywhere for they have confidence in his ability and courage."[18]

206

At first light on June 9th 1863, Shields troops advanced with banners flying, their swords gleaming in the sun, across a farm owned by the Lewis family, toward Port Republic. They were a formidable sight. The clouds of the previous day had vanished and the air from the left over rain was hot and sticky. The Blue Ridge Mountains, living up to their name, were painted their deepest hue. It was a tough trudge across rising terrain and sweat ran down the faces of the men. Soon their woolen uniforms were soaked through. As the Federals labored, contending with increasingly steep foothills and gullies, they came under withering fire from the entrenched Confederates. Nor surprisingly, they faltered. Shields urged them on, and the Federals continued to press. The fire was as fierce as any the war had seen and this time the Confederates flinched. "General Shields made a very stubborn fight and by nine o'clock things began to look very serious for us. Mules kicked, plunged and squealed and Winder's brigade had given way" recalled General John Imboden, a Southern officer later.[19] Jackson, to his chagrin, could see his men falling back and had visions of another Kernstown. So had Shields.

Jackson could not stomach a repeat of their previous encounter and rushed headlong into the fray. "The Stonewall brigade never retreats, follow me" he yelled to rally his troops. The fighting was intense, hand to hand combat, as blue and gray lines surged back and forth for five hours. Despite their fewer numbers, the Federals were slowly getting the better of things. Jackson's forces suffered cruelly and still there was no sign of General Ewell. Jackson called urgently for reinforcements. At the same time, Shields wondered about Fremont's forces - "Couldn't he hear the sound of guns booming across the valley and take action?" pondered Shields. This time fortune favored the South; Jackson's call was answered soon after, to the detriment of Shields.

The key to the battle was the Coaling, an elevated plateau with a large hearth for making charcoal from timber on the surrounding hills. Shields had positioned three batteries of 12 pounder parrotts and mountain howitzers there to inflict mayhem on the Confederates. General Richard Taylor, son of the former President who had been Shields' commander in the Mexican war, and his Louisiana Tigers were dispatched against the artillery. Coincidentally, there were many native born Irish in Taylor's ranks, yet they did not hesitate to attack fellow-countryman Shields and, in fact, were rearing for it. Shields rushed to rally his forces to the new threat and Taylor too was thrown back, not once, but twice. Clearly, Shields men had superior morale and mettle, were giving more than they were getting and Taylor later acknowledged that he was sure he would fall in the savage fight. "It was not war on that spot. It was a pandemonium of cheers, shouts, shrieks and groans, lighted by flames from cannon and musket - blotched by fragments of men thrown high into trees by the shells in the words of a post-war newspaper account of the assault. Vicious hand to hand fighting marked the collision, as the Federal gunners resisted savagely and bravely, with men on both sides employing bayonets, knives, clubs and bare hands. 'Men ceased to be men. They cheered and screamed like lunatics - they fought like demons - they died like fanatics' reported one newspaper account. 'To lose the guns was to lose the battle. To capture them was to win it.' The fighting in and around the battery was hand to hand, and many fell from bayonet wounds. Even the artillerymen used their rammers in a way not laid down in the Manual and died at their guns" wrote James Gannon in *Irish Rebels Confederate Tigers.*[20] Jackson had thrown all that he had into the field and it was still not enough; he was being forced back. It looked like history was about to repeat and he would suffer the torment of another loss at the hands of the resolute Shields. Then, as suddenly as a storm cloud shutting out the sun, day became night for Shields and his men. "It was then that Ewell emerged bringing with him the 34th and 58th Virginia regiments. In this instance, with coordination as precise as if it had been planned, three assaults fell on the Federals. The fierce, skillful fight of the men of Shields went for naught. Within ten minutes Jackson's (impending) defeat became an overwhelming victory. Despite heavy casualties, Jackson was delighted…, in front of him was Shields, the most formidable of his Valley opponents, going into retreat."[21] Shields tried desperately to rally his troops, but to no avail. Bleeding and broken, they streamed to the rear, overwhelmed by Ewell's fresh forces and superior numbers. Ewell had tipped the scales at the vital moment.

General Fremont had not made an assertive move against Ewell all day and, his passivity enabled Ewell to slip away from Cross Keys and join Jackson, the critical factor in the fray. Ewell had left only a small force behind under Gen I. R. Trimble and if Fremont had mounted a drive as soon as he heard the guns across the valley, the outcome would have been different, since he had both the men and means to make it so. By the end of the day, Shields reported he had 67 killed, 300 wounded and 558 captured, but the magnitude of the defeat was much larger than that.

In a strange paradox, the large number of Irish fighting for the South contributed greatly to Shields' loss. Beforehand, they had been apprehensive knowing they were facing their formidable fellow countryman, after coming against a series of Teutonic regiments. "Them Germans is poor creatures, but Shields's boys will be after fighting" one Irish Confederate had predicted, wrote General Taylor in his memoirs, *Destruction and Reconstruction.*[22] Taylor, a Southern blue blood, went on to say of the victory over Shields "I thought the men would go mad with cheering, especially the Irishmen. A huge fellow, with one eye closed and half his whiskers burned by powder, was riding cock-horse on a gun, and, catching my attention, yelled out, "We told you to bet on your boys." Their success against brother Patlanders seemed doubly welcome. Strange people these Irish! Fighting everyone's battles, and cheerfully taking the hot end of the poker, they are only to be found wanting when engaged in what they believe to be their national cause."[23]

For the next two days, Shields regrouped his forces and awaited Jackson's further attack which did not transpire. Jackson slipped away and Shields was blamed for letting that happen. As it turned out, Port Republic was the climactic battle of Jackson's Shenandoah Valley campaign.

Shields still thought he had a chance to turn the tables on Jackson and made provision to combine with Gen. Fremont to pursue Jackson towards Gordonsville and defeat him with their combined forces. After that they could push on towards Richmond. But they were unable to effect their plan and, President Lincoln ordered Shields to return to Front Royal. Shields considered bucking the order, but in the end deferred to the Commander in Chief. That order to retreat by Lincoln effectively ended Shields military career and a short time later, he was recalled to Washington and never again was he favored with a field command. General Fremont, perhaps assuaging guilt for his passivity at a critical juncture, opposed the recall of Shields and wrote Lincoln to that effect. In addition, he sent a conciliatory letter to Shields saying "Most deeply I regret the order you received to abandon our movement for the march on Richmond...."[24] Shields took his defeat hard; he knew that victory had been within his grasp, but had slipped like quicksilver from between his outstretched fingers. Shields lashed out at members of Congress and blamed his defeat more on enemies in the Administration than those in uniforms of gray or feminine attire.[25]

The low hill known as the Coaling at the foot of the Blue Ridge Mountains with the author in the foreground. In 1862, the area was largely bare of trees, since they had been cut down to create charcoal. Six Federal artillery batteries, manned by the 1ˢᵗ Ohio Light Artillery, on top of the hill, (above the author's right shoulder,) rained death down on the Confederates. Gen. Richard Taylor's "Louisiana Tigers" made a flanking move through thick underbrush (to the author's left) and charged repeatedly. In desperate hand to hand fighting, the Confederates slit the throats of mules and men to prevent the guns being moved. Following three desperate assaults, the reinforced Confederates, finally captured the Coaling, forcing the Federals off the hillock in what was the key to the battle. Though Shields remained on active duty for another nine months he was never again entrusted with a field command after this defeat.

At this time Shields, riding an emotional roller coaster, was at Virginia Station and precipitously tendered his resignation from the army on June 24. He rescinded it just as abruptly three days later. In Washington, he pleaded for a fresh command, but got nowhere. Some attributed his cool reception in the Capital to dislike of Shields by Secretary of War Staunton, who blamed Shields for letting Jackson slip away, and jealousy on the part of others, stating "Many officers of high rank were jealous of any other officer whose success called public attention to himself. General Shields was early marked for a victim of this."[26] Shields called on Treasury Secretary Chase, and afterward Chase wrote in his diary "General Shields came to breakfast and to visit the Ohio men of his command at Cliftburne Hospital. He told me he desired greatly to have a command of 5,000 men, and be allowed to dash as he could, breaking the lines and communication of the enemy."[27] It was wishful thinking.

The recall and pass-over for promotion galled Shields, who made his disgust known to his confidant, Maria Daly. Maria, with her ear close to the ground, quoted a fellow officer saying that General Shields "was going to Washington and it would not be his fault if General Shields was not either in the Confederate Army or in Fort Lafayette.[28] The General is not a well-balanced character, but his military talent is unquestionable. Had he been let alone, the disaster at Richmond would not have occurred. Jackson was in his power, everything ready for battle, the position a superior one when a peremptory order came at Fort Royal from the President to retreat and join McDowell. Stanton and the President are responsible for all this."[29]

Shields calmed down and after a while began attending meetings at the War Department along with Lincoln, Chase and Stanton, where he chafed and made impassioned pleas to be allowed once more to "pursue the war vigorously." It was during this time, Shields later claimed, that Lincoln, through Seward, offered him the job of supreme commander and that he, Shields, turned it down.[30] No documentation has ever surfaced to support that assertion and it is of doubtful veracity. At the same time, Lincoln was considering a new supreme commander and it is possible he may have considered the mercurial Shields for the job, but, in the final analysis, did not select him. Two weeks later on July 11, Gen. McClellan was replaced by Maj-Gen Henry "Old Brains" Halleck as General-in-chief of the US Army. The bookish Halleck, a cautious commander, was an 1839 graduate of West Point.

On July 1, 1862, Shields was dispatched to New York to recruit fresh troops for the Union army and as usual, visited the Dalys. Maria Daly wrote in her diary: "General Shields came here yesterday and came directly to see me. He has come on business to raise, if possible, 300,000 men... He speaks despondently of the way in which the war is carried on. His plan was to divide his command into three columns to attack Charlottesville, Lynchburg, etc., the railroads which lead west from Richmond and cut off their supplies. He went to Washington to propose his plan, where he says he was looked upon as a crazy man."

Back in Washington, Shields pushed for the Union to concentrate on cutting the railroads since they were the arteries supplying the life blood of the war. But he had no success. There is no doubt Shields understood the role of railroads in a way few others did at that time. General George McClellan, a West Pointer who before the war had been a railroad manager for the Illinois Central, for all his experience, had failed to put his knowledge to good effect. Eventually, the War Department decided to follow "General Shields original plan to attack the railroads and cut off the communication with the South and their supplies." However, by this time, Shields political and military stocks were spent and there was no role left for him.

The Bonnie Blue flag still flies today from a front porch on Main Street, Port Republic, Virginia.

By now it was clear that, as far as Washington was concerned, Shields was a "has been" and the handwriting was on the wall that he was going no where. Even Shields, much as he disliked that unpalatable fact, had to own up to it. His command now consisted of a personal staff of four. He could remain on active duty in a supporting role but that did not satisfy his thirst for action and the spotlight. Shields decided it was time to place his sword back in its scabbard and put in for transfer to the Department of the Pacific, where he planned to retire. The Government would pay for his transportation to the West Coast, where he would be close to his wife and child. Before leaving, Shields visited the Dalys in New

York and discussed politics and the war. Maria, as usual, chronicled the visit: "The General thought that the party in power had acted with consummate art. They had, he said, gradually got everything into their hands and meant, he thought, to keep the Government, only going through the form of an election in 1863. He thought that they intended it from the beginning. The West he thought would not stand it …"[31]

Shields sailed for San Francisco on February 22, 1863 and upon arrival, tendered his resignation to become effective March 28, 1863. His career in the Civil War was over and it had been a mixed bag. While troops under his command had inflicted the only defeat Stonewall Jackson ever suffered, Jackson, had evened the score. Shields had had a clear vision of how to pursue the war to bring it to an early closure, but he was never given the command authority to implement his plan.

Shields, a one star reserve officer, was far from a failure in the Civil War and performed admirably, in fact, better than many professional military officers, including some of two-star rank, such as Major Generals Samuel Heintzelman and Don Carlos Buell. Both, like many of the generals on both sides, were West Point graduates. Heintzelman, an able administrator, proved so clumsy in combat that he had to be relieved and relegated to administrative command in 1862, while Buell failed to pursue a beaten foe and had to be replaced in October of the same year. Such a situation would scarcely have been permitted by Shields.

Despite being tagged as "vain" by some,[32] Shields, never claimed credit subsequently for his victory over Jackson, possibly because the reversal proved so devastating to Shields' military career and his self image. During a debate in the Missouri Legislature a decade later, Shields was asked "did you ever whip Stonewall Jackson. To that, Shields instantly responded "No Sir, and no other man ever did."[33] Frances O'Shaughnessy, whose father had been an intimate friend of Shields, told a similar tale. At a public gathering, Shields was introduced as "the only man who ever conquered Stonewall Jackson. In reply, General Shields modestly stated that although he had come nearer perhaps than any other soldier in whipping Stonewall Jackson, yet the truth of history impelled him to say that Stonewall Jackson was never conquered."[34] In Shields' mind the outcome at Port Republic loomed much larger than the victory at Kernstown. Of course, he was deeply troubled by his removal by Staunton and "through life he constantly bore the impress of the chastening he had received."[35] The mercurial Shields showed surprising modesty at other times too. Once, when the General, with seemingly more lives than a cat, was asked "When during the Mexican and Civil wars, or during life, in your opinion were you nearest death, he surprised his listeners by replying "In a bar-room at St. Louis before the war in Mexico." He had gone there as a lawyer to confer with a client, and was drawn into an argument between a man and "the worst desperado in Missouri." The enraged desperado came at Shields with a long bowie knife and, Shields slugged him across the head with a glass tumbler, showering blood all over the place. Shields then pulled a pistol and forced the man out of the room.[36]

Dion Boucicault, Irish playwright, actor and producer who was popular during Shields' lifetime, in a villainous pose. Boucicault created the "stage Irishman" as a conniving yet charming fellow much beloved by audiences on both sides of the Atlantic. Born in Dublin in 1820, Boucicault wrote *Belle Lamar*, a play about Shields in the Shenandoah Valley, based loosely on Belle Boyd's memoirs. The melodrama was first produced in 1874.

Upon his return to California, Shields, despite any private misgivings about his performance, was treated as a war hero. There was a public reception at the Occidental Hotel, where a military band and a large crowd turned out in his honor. Shields accepted the salutes and plaudits with good grace, but remained haunted by the memory of lost opportunities in the Valley of the Shenandoah. Picking up the pieces of his life as a mine operator, he went about his business, but with no more financial success than before.

At that juncture, Mexico was at war with France and, Shields was arrested by the French, charged with being a spy, and for a while, it appeared would face a firing squad. Fortunately, American authorities intervened and gained his release. Shields had trouble with the Mexicans as well; guerrillas stole his mules and he was unable to work the mine, which never realized a profit.[37] For all that, Shields had known what he was getting into when he started doing business in Mexico and had stated "Everything (in Mexico) is for sale - the Government is for sale - justice is for sale, and armies and parties are for sale. Parties fight one day and fuse the next - but whether in conflict or in concert, they never fail to plunder the people."[38]

Agnes Robertson, Dion Boucicault's second wife, appeared in many of the Irish impresario's productions. Her outstanding talent and stunning beauty made her an excellent choice for the role of the tempestuous Belle in *Belle Lamar*. This picture, by Matthew Brady, was taken in New York after Boucicault and Robertson had eloped to America in 1853 following a disagreement with Charles Kean, Robertson's guardian.

Finally, the disgruntled Shields had had enough and gave up on the Land of the Sombrero; he returned to California in 1865, but did not remain in the West for long. Unable to settle down, the Irish rover packed his bags once again and returned east, this time bringing with him his wife and child. The family arrived in New York in the fall of 1865 and, once again, Shields called on the Dalys. Now, Maria Daly was sharply critical of the General, who was accompanied by his wife. On Oct 20, 1865. Maria wrote "General Shields suddenly made his appearance. He looks very well, but I do not feel towards him as I did. He stayed all night, much to my astonishment. As he ignores his wife and child, we do so likewise. His manners have very much deteriorated. He chews and spits in a most disgusting manner. His conversation interesting as usual. He has new ambitious schemes, had been to see the President [Lincoln in 1863] and told us many anecdotes of his magnanimity."[39] While in the east, Shields contacted John F. Callan, an expert in military law in Washington to correct his date of resignation from the army. Shields maintained that his resignation should not have become effective until August 17th 1863 instead of March 28. By that reckoning, the General would have been entitled to an additional 5 months pay. The War Department refused to budge and his resignation date remained as of March. Shields then put out feelers for a federal job but here again he had no luck. Giving up on Washington, the restless Shields started considering other alternatives. Upon hearing that the altitude of the Rocky Mountains would be kind to his ailing lungs, he decided it would be beneficial for him and his family to make the trek to the Mile High City of Denver. Again, the footloose General without ever unpacking his bags in the east, would set out across the country. This time he was determined to settle down.

Chapter 11
Senator from the Show
Me State, And Carrollton

The long, long wished-for hour has come
Yet come astore,[1] in vain;
And left thee but the wailing hum
Of sorrow and of pain
My light of life, my only love!
Thy portion, sure, must be
Man's scorn below, God's wrath above —
A cuisle geal mo chroidhe.[2]
A Cuisle Geal Mo Chroidhe by Michael Doheny (1805 - 63.)

Early in 1866, the nomadic James Shields was on the move again, retracing his steps back across the country toward the snow capped Rocky Mountains. "Pike's Peak or bust" was the mantra of the day and, Shields thought that the high altitude would be beneficial for his breathless lungs and infuse him with new life. When he, his wife Mary and their 3 year old daughter, Mary, reached St. Louis, they paused at the Plantation House Hotel to catch their breath. Mary, pregnant with their second child, found the going hard, while the General, impatient as ever, quickly regained his vigor and was eager to push on. The war had ended and, with many other veterans heading west too, Shields did not want to be among the last to arrive and miss out on a fruitful claim.

Because Mary was not able to continue immediately, the couple faced a dilemma - to stay or press on. Eventually they reached a compromise; Mary would remain behind with their daughter, while Shields continued across country. As soon as he found a suitable place for them to live, he would send for her and would finally stop the pursuit of his impossible dreams. Bidding farewell to his wife, Shields boarded the old Missouri train to take him across the "Show Me" state to St Joseph and places west. As the train puffed across the countryside belching smoke and cinders, Shields found himself watching the trackside telegraph wires hypnotically rise and fall and gazed wistfully at the smooth rolling Missouri hills. They were green, fresh and fertile and moved his mind back to Ireland, a place that was but a distant memory after forty years. The affluent farms with smoke curling lazily upward, intermixed with small cabins with clothes drying on bushes, induced a sense of nostalgia. He had seen the world, but had little to show for it. Now, he was on his way to Colorado with its pine forests and sparse vegetation and for what? That was the question. At Chillicothe, halfway across Northern Missouri, the impulsive Irishman suddenly changed his plans. Upon hearing that Boonville was booming, he decided to go no farther and left the line.[3] Obtaining a horse, Shields struck out overland for Boonville about a hundred miles away in the center of the "Show Me" state. It was late in the evening when he reached Carrollton, the County Seat of Carroll County about 70 miles east of Kansas City. There, he got a room at the Kendrick Hotel. As he checked in, the General learned that Judge George Pattison, an old friend from his days in the Legislature in Illinois, was living in the town and, Shields decided to renew his acquaintance. According to Alice, the Judge's daughter, Shields, displaying his impish sense of humor, "thought he would give my father a surprise. A messenger was sent to tell my father a man at the hotel wanted to see him. My father, thinking it was someone wanting to see him on business, asked why did not the man come to his office? Then he was told who it was and he joyfully hurried to the hotel to meet his old friend."[4]

Both men were delighted to see each other again after so many years, and talked away the night. As they reminisced by the warm fire, Shields let the Judge know he was on his way to Colorado for a fresh start, but he wanted to check Boonville first. He said he was finally going "to retire from active life and thought it would be ideal to live on a farm."[5] At that, Judge Pattison picked up his ears. He suggested that the General look no farther than where he was in Carroll County. Why not make a home there? At first, the General demurred but, the Judge persisted. He was persuasive, noting that the area was rich and fertile, with relatively mild winters and hot summers, words that were music to Shields' ears. What the Judge was saying had appeal - why go beyond a place named after a prominent Anglo-Irish Catholic family that had immigrated to the U.S. in the late 17th century?[6] There was another advantage to the area; the journey from St. Louis would put a lot less strain on his wife Mary, who would not have to travel an additional five hundred miles to the high country of Colorado. Who could foretell what might happen if Mary was forced to make the trip in her condition? Shields, in typical fashion, quickly made up his mind to abandon his perennial end-of-the rainbow quest for a pot of gold and immediately dropped anchor. For the first time in his life, he would put down permanent roots.

A few days later, the impetuous Shields purchased from Henry Winfred a small farm in Eugene Township about six miles outside town. The General then "sent for Mrs. Shields and their little daughter Mary, a dear child."[7] The farm overlooked the Missouri River Valley, was well watered and appointed and became the Shields family home for the next 12 years. "Its quiet shade, it's spacious and comfortable house, its orchard burdened with fruits and its natural scenic beauty appealed to the General."[8] In fact, the family remained there until just a year before the General's death, when they moved into the town of Carrollton itself.

Shields found life on the farm anticlimactic following his tempestuous career. He did not care for farming and it showed. Apart from planting a small vegetable patch and keeping a cow or two, he avoided agriculture altogether. It was with good reason he could refer to himself as "the poorest farmer in Carroll County" and, his correspondence frequently recounted his impecunious situation. It was sometimes difficult to know if he was talking about himself or the country when he wrote about the poor state of the economy. In a letter to the Right Rev. John J. Hogan, Catholic bishop of St Joseph, requesting aid for the Carrollton Catholic church, he said "I can see no other way of getting out of debt. Crops are poor and money is scarce."[9] To his brother Patrick in Ireland a few years later he wrote "our finances are all in chaos just now, yet the country hardly feels it." Later there was more of the same, "This country has seen its happiest days. Debt and extravagance have exhausted our resources. Business is paralyzed, finances disarranged and enterprise dead. If we escape general bankruptcy it will be owing to the illimitable resources of the country. Farmers and working men can hardly live now."[10]

At other times the General was more sunny in outlook and commented that he did not believe in endowing children with material wealth; he thought they should be trained to paddle their own canoes. In 1873, while recovering from a broken leg, he sent his brother Patrick a letter stating "My family are all well. We are not only well but very happy and sufficiently prosperous to be independent. While my health lasts I have no fear for though not saving or economical I have wonderful energy and resources of mind. My present object is to educate my little family. Leaving fortunes to children is an injury - in this country - but a thorough education, not a mere school education, with the discipline of all the facilities, is more than fortune; it commands success."[11]

On the other hand, General Shields did what he liked to do; he opened a law office and used it as an entrée into local politics. He started a small real estate practice and became very much part of the community. It was obvious that Shields, the inveterate politician, simply could not stay away from public life, and soon was appointed overseer of roads by his new neighbors. In that capacity, he had to make sure roads were maintained and that farmers did not scour their ploughs on the highway or otherwise interrupt public passage. Shields also remained active in the Catholic Church, opened his home to all for Catholic religious services, and contacted Bishop Hogan to obtain a priest for the congregation. He also received visits from American and Irish relatives, since, finally, he had a home where he could accommodate them. His nephews Patrick, John, James and Litton Shields came from Ireland and the General's first cousin Mary Quinn Talley visited from New York.[12] When Mrs. Tally saw that the Catholic community in Carrollton had no church, she provided $1000 to build one. She had enjoyed a lot more financial success than her improvident first cousin, and now was prepared to use her means for charitable works.

As Shields settled down, he took time to write to his relatives in Ireland and waxed nostalgically for the "old Sod," and resumed his interrupted correspondence with Gustave Koerner. Initially he was dispirited, as much for the state of the country as for himself, but gradually regained his optimistic outlook. Shields' state of health remained as indifferent as the state of country, which was struggling with the aftermath of the Civil War and the assassination of Abraham Lincoln. It was a difficult time all around. The process of healing the nation's deep cleavage was slow, and split Republicans and Democrats alike. Lincoln's policy of "Malice toward none, charity for all" was strongly endorsed by Shields and he had no time for the radical Republicans and their punitive approach toward the South. He thought they were tearing the country further apart instead of helping it heal.

Shields stayed close to home to assist his pregnant wife and daughter during the electoral campaign of 1866, but following the birth of their son, Patrick, Shields picked up his political pace once more. He remained a conservative Democrat, but was in favor of Andrew Johnson's Republician platform. The General spoke at a large meeting in Chillicothe, Missouri in Oct 1866, where he denounced Secretary of State William H. Seward and the Reverend Henry Ward Beecher, brother of Harriet Beecher Stowe, author of Uncle Tom's Cabin, for their vindictive anti-Southern stance. "These tyrants of the gutter are so low now that even a decent Missouri dog would be ashamed to bark at them" he harangued.[13]

Shields saw similarities between England's treatment of Ireland and the occupation of the South by northern carpetbaggers. At the conclusion of a St. Patrick's Day speech in St. Joseph, Missouri in 1866 he stated "The English Government in Ireland is one of the greatest failures in history. It has failed to crush, and it has failed to conciliate…"[14]

Because of Shields' name recognition and obvious voter appeal, he was drafted by the Missouri Democrats to run for Congress in 1867 against an incumbent moderate Republican, Robert T. Van Horn owner and editor of the Kansas City *Journal*. Shields gladly accepted the nomination and stumped the district with real reconciliation as his theme. That was particularly important for Missouri, a former slave state that had many Southern sympathizers, but had not been formally part of the Confederacy. He successfully cast his opponent as a flaming radical, even though the mild mannered Van Horn fell far short of that on almost anyone's scale. He, like Shields, had been a "Douglas Democrat" and did not espouse the Southern cause nor the extreme sectional views of the North. He had enlisted in the Union Army, led a battalion of Kansas City volunteers and afterwards became a Republican. Despite Van Horns moderate position, the Shields strategy worked and the Irishman topped the poll by 109 votes. He seemed set to make his way back to Washington, this time as Representative from the seventh Congressional district of Missouri. But there were road blocks looming ahead.

While Shields supporters celebrated their against-the-odds victory, Van Horn registered a protest, claiming that many Shields voters had supported the South, and had not taken the new "iron-clad" loyalty oath.[15] This was a requirement to be eligible to vote. A red signal flashed and, Shields' Washington bandwagon was halted abruptly in its tracks. His election placed on hold. According to Condon, the State was now "ruled by carpetbaggers" and the Missouri Legislature refused to ratify Shields' victory.[16] Following an investigation, a canvassing board threw out the votes from two counties, thereby eliminating Shields. The General was not going to Washington after all and was denied the Congressional seat he had just won. Though Shields did not go to Congress, his effort did not go totally unrewarded. The Missouri State Legislature, in a tacit admission that its decision was tainted, awarded Shields $5,000, the equivalent of one year's salary for a Congressional Representative.

General Shields remained anti-radical and opposed U.S. Grant in the Presidential elections of 1868 and 1872. He disliked Grant's acrimonious treatment of the South and maintained that the Northern military occupation of the South was something that should end. Shields did not change his mind four years later, when he jumped ship and supported liberal Republican, New York publisher, Horace Greely for President. In justifying his decision to support Greely, Shields described Greely as "a born Democrat and genuine Republican, the natural foe of every kind of oppression; he abhors proscription and persecution; he makes war to the knife on every kind of rascality; he is for the weak against the strong, for the oppressed against the oppressor, and for the poor, the friendless and the wretched against the world."[17]

Shields traveled extensively to lambaste Grant and laud Greely, the man whom had urged young Americans to "Go West" some 20 years earlier. In a speech in Chicago, Shields was cheered and applauded when he stated "General Grant as President is a decided failure. His Administration is the greatest failure in our political history. *[Applause]* He saw the Southern people of his own blood and race, crushed in hearth and broken in spirit, with their eyes turned to him in Washington as next to God their only hope. But the man is by nature incapable of any great, generous or magnanimous action *[Applause]* He preferred to give up his time to fast men and fast horses and to other kindred fast attractions, and to disport himself and his gift carriages right royally at Long Branch and other places of dissipation; and he abandoned this generous people to the tender mercies of a ring of Radical politicians, who, for meanness, rapacity and vindictiveness, have no equals."[18]

Predictably, as Shields aged, he also mellowed and this was reflected his speeches which became less fiery than before. He showed an increased awareness of social issues that had not been present previously and became more proletarian in outlook. He decried the increase in the number of Republican millionaires, whom he excoriated for exploiting workers. "More of the profits of labor finds its way into the coffers of speculators than even into the treasury of the United States." he complained.[19] "The number of millionaires is increasing annually… It needs no great foresight to see the end of this state of things. The end will be inevitable, irretrievable ruin."[20] Shields also stumped for politicians in other states whom he thought deserving and crossed the river to Illinois to speak in Springfield on behalf of his old law partner Koerner who was running for Governor. Shields swallowed his perpetual distaste for Republicans and justified his support for Koerner, who was now a member of the GOP, on the grounds that he was a good man. "I would rather have you than any other man in the State" Shields declared unequivocally. The General's efforts brought forth an enthusiastic surge for Koerner, but it was not enough to get him over the top. Koerner, who also suffered from anti-immigrant bias, lost to Richard Oglesby, who garnered 55% of the vote. For his part, Shields was delighted to be back on his old stomping ground and even mended fences with his old foe Lyman Trumbull, who was still the incumbent Senator from Illinois.

Around this time, Shields supported himself mostly by speech making and addressed gatherings all over the country. He generally recounted anecdotes from his days in Government or his military memoirs and at times spiced up the truth. While this undoubtedly entertained his audiences, it created difficulties for Shields biographers later. Shields' embellished stories were sometimes reported as fact, when they were more likely fancy and afterward, it became a challenge to separate some of his genuinely extraordinary achievements from ornate oratorical embroidery. For instance, while speaking to an Irish American audience, Shields claimed a connection with the Young Irelander Revolutionaries of 1848, saying that he had dispatched two emissaries to the rebels to learn what they wanted. That may have been the case, since he knew several of the "forty eighters" personally, but Shields was not by inclination a violent revolutionary and preferred constitutional methods. That did not stop him from befriending violent revolutionaries when they came to America and, he was chairman of the Senate committee that welcomed Louis Kossuth, the Hungarian who led an armed revolt against

Austria; he also introduced Thomas Meagher, the Young Irelander to his Senate colleagues. Shields sympathized with the Irish rebels and offered them verbal support, but that was as far as he went. "I am not a Fenian.., I find myself unable to approve of the secret character of the organization"[21] he once declared, even though Michael Doheny, co-founder of the Fenians who had been a Young Irelander, dedicated his history of the forty eight rebellion to "General James Shields, whose Irish breast has been so bravely bared in defense of his adopted country."[22]

Following the failure of the Fenian movement in the late 1860s, Shields could see no future for Irish nationalism. He became resigned to Ireland continuing in England's shadow indefinitely, not an unreasonable position given the reality of English power and Irish poverty at the time. Shields stated pessimistically "I have arrived at the conclusion that the present policy of Ireland is to abandon all idea of political separation from England. Her old nationality is gone. She should cooperate on all occasions with the most liberal English party.... I see great changes and progress in Ireland, exercising a powerful influence in the British Empire and throughout the Empire and the world. The traditions of Ireland are all Christian and Catholic, and no country in the world is holding as fast to its traditions... these traditions will make them a leading people in this world."[23] At that time the idea of "Home Rule" was taking root in Ireland as a hot political issue and Shields, viewing the movement from an American context, wondered why England opposed it. He pointed out that the balance of power distributed between the central Government and the states in the United States worked to America's advantage overall. "Your Home Rule is a commonplace in this country. It is a principle admitted by all. The American would say "Let the Imperial Parliament provide in imperial affairs but let each division of the Empire have a local Legislature to manage local affairs."[24] he wrote to his nephew in Ireland in 1873.

As General Shields aged, he also showed increased periods of nostalgia for the land in which he had been born, but had not seen for fifty years. Like other exiles, he longed like Oisin to return, if only for a day, to see old faces and places. "I wish to God I could be in your corner a while to talk the old talk, and sing the old songs. I pray sometimes that we may all have a meeting before we die" he wrote wistfully to Patrick in 1873 and, he infused his children with an appreciation of Irish culture. "Our life here is as simple and happy as your own. We sing the old songs that you sing at your fireside. I teach the little ones and the big ones too." Two years later he wrote "I am bringing (my children) up as Irish children. They will be as Irish as if born at Altmore. Irish songs, Irish music, Irish traditions and Irish feeling are kept more alive in my family than in any family in Tyrone."[25]

Irish-born Mary Ann Carr Shields (1835 - 1928) aged about 70. She was a woman who stayed in the background. She and the General had five children, but no grandchildren.

There is little extant material dealing with the quality of General Shields' marriage and his relationship with his wife Mary. What little is known about her shows she was a retiring, possibly shy person, who kept very much in the background. Whether that was due to her own inclination or, as appears more likely given the Generals dominant personality, by his desire is unclear. Shields and Mary, to outward appearances, were reasonably happy, each in their own way. She cooked his meals, bore his babies and managed his home, and that seems the extent of it; there is no evidence she was treated as his equal and she seldom traveled with him, except when moving house. He never spoke of her in his speeches and their thirty year difference in age, a whole generation, would have been a barrier to personal closeness and intimacy. One is left with the conclusion that theirs was a remote relationship much like and adult and adolescent. Following the General's death, the *Carrollton Republican=Record* described Mary as a "patient, kind and sympathetic little woman... whose sole ambition was not to shine socially, but to minister to the wants and needs of her husband and family."[26]

The few windows available for glimpses into the General's married quarters show that he tended to ignore his wife and go his own way whenever he wanted, which Mrs.

Shields apparently accepted with equanimity. Certainly, this was the conclusion of Maria Daly, who did not note Mary objecting to such offhand treatment. The perceptive and catty Maria would certainly have commented upon any resistance that Mary might have registered, had she done so. Mary was reluctant to have her picture taken, either with the General or without. William Condon noted "I regret that I cannot induce Mrs. Shields to sit for her picture."[27] Mrs. Shields remained in the background at the unveiling of various Shields statues and had her children out in front. She did not undrape any of his likenesses, even though she appeared for unveilings and it would have been appropriate for her to have done so. Following the General's death, Mary, free from his powerful influence, appears to have shed her cocoon somewhat, according to Condon. He stated "In 1894, when I last saw her, she was bright and active, drove her own phaeton, from which she alighted as briskly as her daughter could, and everywhere cordially greeted the best people of Carrollton."[28] The General's personal letters to his family are revealing of the relationship more for what they did not say, than for what they did. The General almost never mentioned Mary when he wrote to his family in Ireland and, if he did, it was to carp, albeit affectionately, about her. In a letter to Patrick, fifteen years into their marriage, the General wrote "My children are going to school and Mary goes to school with them and is learning, though I fear she is like most of the others, she does not take to study."[29]

This statement is telling for two reasons. The first is the inescapable conclusion, that Mary's education was lacking and she sought to improve it. In this, she may have wanted to keep up with her children, satisfy some need of her own, or perhaps she was going to school to please her husband. Since he was such a stickler for education, it is not improbable that she was going to school at his bidding. As can be seen from his comment, like a schoolmaster with a slacker student, he was unhappy that she was not applying herself better and suggests that he had a paternalistic relationship with her. The second revelation about their state of marriage comes from Shields choice of words as he alluded to his wife and children. In the letter, he spoke of "my" children in a sentence that was mostly about his wife. An equal partner, is more likely to speak of "our" or "the" children and not as though they exclusively belonged to him. Another observation is that the General never included his wife's name alongside his own when he signed the family letters. Since there are no letters by Mary, it is not known if she included his name next to hers on her correspondence and, there are no samples of her writing to come to conclusions about her personality.

Mary was comfortable in her role as homemaker and housewife. She participated in church activities, stood as godmother for neighbors and nursed them when they were sick. Following the baptism of Mary Pattison, Alice said, "Mrs. Shields was so happy over her new godchild that she and the General took Mary home with them for a few day's visit."[30] Also in 1870, when Mrs. Pattison, the judge's wife, was seriously ill with pneumonia, Alice later wrote that Mrs. Shields "came and stayed several days and nights, taking care of mother till the crisis had passed."[31] For all that, the marriage appears to have suited the General's and Mary's needs and given them both what they wanted. It may not have been different from many marriages of the time and one may reasonably conclude that theirs was a relatively tranquil and harmonious relationship.

In 1873, the US Senate seat of Frank P. Blair was up for grabs in Missouri and the opportunistic Shields had his eye on it. Blair, originally a conservative Republican, had switched parties to run unsuccessfully for Vice President on the Democratic ticket with Horatio Seymour in 1868 and, his prickly personality and strongly anti-Reconstruction views made him politically controversial. The Democrats wanted new or possibly old blood, which gave the redoubtable General Shields an opportunity and, he was "named as among the aspirants and probable candidates for Frank P. Blair's seat in the U.S. Senate."[32] Unfortunately, Shields could not garner sufficient support this time around and the nomination went to Lewis V. Bogy, a prominent St. Louis lawyer, railroad president and former Commissioner of Indian Affairs who was elected. Despite that setback, Shields continued to function as a loyal Party man in the state and in 1874 was elected to the state Legislature as the representative from Carroll County.

When Shields first moved to Missouri, he was able to support himself and his family on his military pension of $30 a month and the limited produce from his farm. But by the 1870s his financial state, like his state of health, was hard pressed. As Koerner observed "he was in old age as poor almost as when he started life as a school teacher in the ancient town of Kaskaskia." The financial failures of the country in 1873 made times tough for everyone and, it was no different for Shields. He had suffered a series of health setbacks that restricted his mobility but somehow his indomitable spirit enabled him to carry on. He remained optimistic about himself and America.

"I have wonderful energy and resources of mind... The land is so full of real wealth that the money pressure is only temporary... We are not a country like any of...Europe but the best part of a virgin Continent and the richest region of the globe...["][33] he wrote to Patrick.

General Shields sustained a compound fracture of his thigh when he was knocked down by a runaway team of wagon horses in St. Joseph, Missouri in 1873.[34] Initially, the leg was knitting well and his bounciness showed through. He wrote "I am getting well, slowly and surely. The leg will be as strong as ever but a little shorter so that I will have to submit to a limp which is not much at my time of life."[35] But the following Spring, misfortune struck again when he tripped and fell at the home of a friend, Col James M. Barnes and refractured his femur once again.[36]

At that juncture, life was not treating the Shields family well. The Shields had five children and more than their share of misfortune; only three of the children were to survive to adulthood. Mary, the eldest, was the first go; she succumbed suddenly to pneumonia in 1870. As neighbor Alice Pattison recalled "One day little Mary was taken sick with a congestive chill and died in a few hours."[37] The child was buried on the Shields farm, because there was no Catholic cemetery in Carrollton at that time. Her body was later exhumed and reinterred in the Shields family plot in St. Mary's Cemetery after it became available. That heart rending scene was described by Alice Pattison "One evening we were waiting near the church door 'till time for services. Mrs. Shields came. A sympathetic young lady went to meet her and was condoling (sic) with Mrs. Shields who was crying and told of her little girl's second internment, that the coffin had been opened and there was only a little shoe."[38]

A year after Mary's death the Shields had a second daughter, Katherine, and then two boys, Charles and Daniel. The Shields eldest son, James, died in 1874 also from a congestive illness of the lungs. Charles, a University of Notre Dame graduate, went on to attend Washington and Lee University in Virginia, where he became a lawyer. He served in the Spanish-American War of 1898 and became ill after it. He and Alice Pattison had been classmates at the Sisters of Mercy School in Carrollton. She wrote of him "After the

Spanish War, Charles, poor boy, was an invalid... he was admitted to a veteran's institution in an Eastern city."[39] He was hospitalized in St. Elizabeth's Hospital, a psychiatric institution in the nation's Capital, and died in Washington. He is the only member of the family not interred in the family plot in Carrollton. Katherine, or "Kitty" as she was called by the family, graduated from the Boston Conservatory of Music and became the organist in the St. Mary's Church in Carrollton. She was "a bright eyed, rosy cheeked girl, the picture of health in her early young womanhood and she died, aged 30, of consumption in 1901."[40] The only child to live a full lifespan was the youngest, Daniel, who attended Georgetown University in Washington. He subsequently became an Ear Nose and Throat surgeon in New York City and passed away on April 28, 1960. He was the only family member to visit Ireland, which he did in 1931, three years after his mother's death.

Despite having to walk with a cane after breaking his leg, Shields continued his lecture tours, albeit at a less frenetic pace. His restricted travel schedule kept him closer to home where politics continued to sustain him. When General Shields took his seat in the Missouri Assembly in 1874, he was greeted by Lt. Gov. Charles P. Johnson who had known him as a boy in Sparta, Illinois in 1853. Johnson noted how much Shields had aged and commented: "Time had greatly changed him in every respect except in his military bearing and the brilliancy of his eyes... The first sentence he spoke was in reference to Kaskaskia. He said and this is the son of Elvira (meaning my mother) whom I knew as a girl in Kaskaskia. His conversation continued reminiscent and was highly interesting to me" wrote Johnson in his memoirs.[41]

In the State Assembly, Shields pushed for a state railroad commission and when it passed was appointed a commissioner. By now he was a senior statesman and was well regarded by his fellow legislators, since he was not the lightening rod he once was. He did not engage in controversial politics and was described as an "affable Irishman."[42] In 1876, General Shields campaigned for Presidential candidate Samuel Tilden on both sides of the Mississippi. Then, in what must have taken a major effort, he visited both the East and West coasts in a triumphal tour that would become his "swan song."[43] Shields was loudly acclaimed wherever he went. In New York and South Carolina Shields professed himself to be "not prepared" for the enormous State receptions afforded him.[44]

The bitterness of post Civil War reconstruction was very much rampant and Shields was one of the few national figures able to cross the Mason-Dixie divide and find acceptance on both sides. At a reception in his honor by the Shields Guards in Auburn, South Carolina in 1877, Governor Wade Hampton stated "I came, as I said, to do honor to my distinguished friend, General Shields. He wore the blue and I wore the gray, but we can let the curtain drop over those years and go back to the time when the flag borne by him waved alike over men of the South and men of the North. And I say this to you - a Southern man and a rebel, who fought as hard as he knew how against you... that flag shall be the symbol of liberty and equality and justice to all the states and to every man in every state..."[45] Shields responded "Now I am coming in for a large share of praise for all this, and that bewilders me. I am not a Governor, or a distinguished citizen. I am simply a private citizen living in retirement and almost in obscurity; I am a kind of a farmer in Carroll County. Twenty five years ago this company... assumed my name and emblazoned it on its standard. It has kept up that name for twenty-five years... Sixty seven years ago I was born to the inheritance of that name. I have borne it for sixty-seven years through all the trials of peace and war. Your gathering to-day is a certificate to all the world that the name you bear and the name I bear is still unsullied. Such a certificate is well worth a visit to Auburn." Afterwards more than 4000 Southerners waited patiently to file slowly through the room and shake Shields' hand.

Audiences "up north" were equally enthusiastic. Describing a reception for the General in Brooklyn, New York, a reporter wrote "The space in front of the Academy is black with people, and from opposite directions come diverging streams, the doors are thrown open and in twenty minutes the house is packed. The stage, too, presently fills up, civilians, military, lay and clerics, take their places. The rattle of drums, the clashing of cymbals and the notes of the ear-piercing fife float in from without. The General with his escorts enters. All is hushed. He is very pale, very attenuated. Silence reigns. All eyes and all hearts turn toward him. Simultaneously all on the stage rise to their feet. A voice; Three cheers for General Shields!" The great audience rose and the band played "Hail to the Chief", recollections of the victories he had helped to win from Buena Vista, to Winchester, flashed back; then as the chieftain who had a generation ago, led in triumph the citizenry soldiery of New York into the City of Mexico, stood before the remnants of his comrade in arms; then as the only man who had ever successfully crossed swords with Stonewall Jackson came in sight, then when General Shields, now a feeble, sick man presented himself before the people of Brooklyn, then went up a tempest of ringing cheers such as never before resounded within the four walls of that house."[46]

All this adulation did little to improve Shields' shaky financial condition and he was constantly living hand to mouth. How he and his family survived is not clear and, it is hard not to come to a conclusion that privation and poor nourishment were not factors in his children's deaths, since they succumbed to "consumption." They were living in rural surroundings and not crowded into poorly ventilated slums and malnutrition may have reduced their resistance to disease. By 1878, there was genuine concern about the General's impecunious state, though some were skeptical that he was as poor as he claimed. The St. Paul Dispatch noted "There is a paragraph going the rounds of the newspapers now-a-days about the destitution of General James Shields. No one ever knew the General to be rich, or to be poor, much less destitute. He has always kept the happy medium described in Agar's prayer in the bible. His personal wants were and are now probably few and simple, and he always had an almost morbid aversion to debt... He has a pension for services and honorable wounds in the Mexican war. Inasmuch as his arm was again shattered by the explosion of a shell at the battle of Winchester rendering it well-nigh useless, he ought to have an extra pension for this, or an increased one for all his martial scars... As he is the only officer who successfully met and defeated Stonewall Jackson in the late war, it would seem as if the Government might look into his claims, if he be really destitute and reward his services to the State, as a brave soldier and an incorruptible politician in his day."[47]

The campaign to improve his pension succeeded in the House of Representatives, which granted him a generous $3,000 annually. The *St. Paul Globe* approved, noting that friends of the "old hero.. will rejoice that he is at last raised above want" and went on to say "No foreign-born citizen, in the half century just passed, became so thoroughly a United States citizen, and so much a distinguished part of the new nationality as Gen. Shields. No man has been braver on the field of battle nor more beloved in the political and social circle... He is the Sir Roger de Coverly of politics and society, beloved by all who know him, not only for his patriotism and heroic deeds on the field of battle but for a kindly nature endearing him to all alike."[48] The passage of Shields pension bill depended not only on approval by the House but the Senate as well and, the Republican controlled Senate balked. Democrats tried to add an amendment on his behalf to the pension bill for U.S. Grant but failed, as did a motion by General Benjamin Butler of Massachusetts to name Shields doorkeeper of the House. Naming him doorkeeper was done without Shields' knowledge or consent and, he was mortified as he hobbled away from the chambers of Government, where he had once introduced legislation and served two

different States. Showing some his old spark, he denounced the "door-keeping business," saying "Sooner than have accepted the humiliation I would have trudged on foot to my little forty-acre farm,

Shields family home, North Main Street, Carrollton. In 1878, the Shields moved into the town from their farm in Eugene Township about ten miles away. The home today is owned by Mr. John Scott.

and with my ox team spent my days in a hazardous attempt to provide for my bodily wants."[49]

Shields was not alone in his anger at the Senate's stinginess; his supporters were furious too. They saw it as a slap in the face and renewed their efforts on his behalf. In the face of such pressure, Congress relented and on June 18, 1878, the national assembly granted Shields a regular army pension "as a mark of respect for his distinguished services and to relieve his necessities," which was richly deserved.[50] Shields monthly income rose from $30, not to $250 as the House had approved, but to $100 per month and certainly made the last year of his life more comfortable.

In the fall of 1878, Shields stumped for R. Graham Frost in his successful campaign for national office in a closely divided Third Missouri district. The previous year, Lewis V. Bogy, the man who had defeated Shields for the Senate 1873, had died while still in office. This created a vacancy and Missouri Democrats were debating how to fill Bogy's seat, when the previous runner up, Shields was suggested. His was a popular choice and Shields was elected Senator by the full Missouri Legislature on January 22, 1879. He immediately went to Washington where he took the oath of office five days later. The Irish-American was delighted to be back in the old familiar setting and, on Feb 20, delivered his maiden speech as Senator from Missouri. In it, he supported the military, and came out in favor of war pensions for survivors of the Civil War and widows of the Mexican War.

Shields was not expected to run for reelection and, when his term ended on March 4th 1879, did not do so. His election to the Senate from a third state rekindled interest in him and his career again took off and he became a sought after speaker. He began lecture tours again. One of his most popular presentations was "Recollections of Distinguished Statesmen" with whom he had served. There were many from which to choose: household names like Lincoln, Calhoun, Clay, Douglas and Davis. It was on one of these lecture tours that he succumbed, possibly to complications from his old war wounds.

On Monday May 26, Shields traveled from Carrollton to Ottumwa, Iowa to deliver a lecture even though he had been in declining health; many were eager to hear him and he did not want to disappoint his audience. "It was not a hard task to induce the General to come" Fr. Kreckel pastor Ottumwa Catholic Church recalled afterward. According to the *Ottumwa Weekly Courier,* on his arrival "The townspeople provided a civic reception, greeting the distinguished soldier and patriot with a marching band and a volunteer militia honor guard. Some noticed that even though General Shields mental faculties were as sharp as ever, his physical health was failing. They commented that war wounds received "under the old flag tell quite grievously upon his physical frame but his piercing, keen eyes still retain their brightness and show that the mind from which their inspiration is derived is yet full of vigor."[51]

A few days later he would be dead.

A St. Louis newspaper in describing what happened said that General Shields "had been suffering from the effects of a severe cold or an affectation of the lungs. He complained not a little of soreness of the chest, and at times his usually buoyant and cheerful spirit would fail him and a feeling of apprehension of danger take its place. In those moments of acriousness he had been heard to remark that he believed that this ailment had come to carry him off. But then he was a man of strong will and great courage.... With the warm and bright days of May he seemed to gain in strength and feel better and his active mind - never at ease when forced to rest - sought the excitement attending travel... On Wednesday evening he delivered his lecture on "Reminiscences of the Mexican War" to a large audience and, the remaining days of the week he spent there, meeting new faces and observing what there was to be seen in that thriving little city. When Sunday came he attended religious services and appeared unusually bright and happy."

Shields had been staying at the Sisters of Humility convent where his cousin Mary Talley and his young niece Mary T. Shields were living. Mrs. Talley had retired to Ottumwa - land of rippling waters - from New York. On the Sunday evening of his death, Shields retired for the night and a short time later his niece Mary heard a rapping from his room. She rushed there and found him gasping for breath. "Mary I'm dying" he said. According to reports "Mary gave him a drink of water and bathed his face and he began to feel a little better. This seemed to give him some relief and partially dressing himself, he walked over to a window, opened it and sat down in a chair where he could breathe the fresh, cool atmosphere. A physician and priest were at once sent for. They came promptly but nothing in his medicine could help the General. It was his system had given way and his life was fast fading. His spiritual comforter, however, was not too late, as the General retained his consciousness to the last. In about half an hour from the time that the rapping was heard in his room, Gen. Shields, sitting in a chair and holding the hands of his niece breathed his last..."[52] The following morning a telegram announcing the General's death arrived in Carrollton.

News of the General's demise hit the small town like a thunderbolt. For one thing, no one had been anticipating it, and another, no one knew how much he had been ailing, since the General had hidden it well. Even sixty years later Alice Pattison could still recall her shock on hearing the grim news. "I remember my father coming home one day and telling us of the death of General Shields, and of my mother's fervent ejaculation and horrified exclamation that any one should be called from life so suddenly."[53] she said.

The Carrollton newspaper also carried an account of Mrs. Shields' and the town of Carrollton's reaction. "It was about half-past seven o'clock on Monday morning when a telegram reached Carrollton, directed to Dr. Wm. Tull announcing Gen. Shields' death. It was sad and unexpected news, as our people had no previous intimation of the lamentable fact. Little it was thought when the General left home that in less than a week he would be a corpse. Mrs. Shields was on the street attending to some business when the telegram came, and it was in front of the dry goods store of Messrs Day and Clinkscales that she was met and informed of her husband's death. It is impossible for us to describe her feelings when she learned the sad news. Only the heart of a devoted wife, suddenly bereft of her dearest treasure, can appreciate her anguish. One instant the morning sun shone brightly and cheerfully upon her; the next her very soul was enveloped in a cloud of darkness and grief. But she was not alone in her sorrow. The whole community mourned with her, although none could feel as she. In the afternoon a meeting of citizens was held at the court house to take action on the matter of receiving the remains and conducting the funeral.[54] Arrangements were made for a large funeral, the biggest event the town had ever witnessed and, it had to be held in the open air and a special altar constructed because St. Mary's Church could not accommodate the enormous crowd.[55]

Mourners, estimated at more than 10,000, included political and military dignitaries, veterans of the Mexican and Civil Wars and local citizens. The funeral mass was said by three priests, Frs Ascherie, Pastor of Carrollton, Kreckel from Ottumwa and Henry of St. Louis. All had assembled to pay tribute to a unique individual and it was a somber group that wound its way after mass to St. Mary's Cemetery on the outskirts of town. The General was buried with full military honors and as his body was lowered into the grave, the Nineteenth U.S. Infantry Regiment fired a salute and a bugler played "Taps." Obituaries in local newspapers were highly laudatory, but the *New York Times* had reservations about the magnitude of Shields' contributions to the country.

According to the *Times*, Shields "was just the bold, brave, dashing man to conquer a striking success where any other man would have hesitated to venture" but it also dismissed him as merely a "Soldier of Fortune." The report also conceded "Although foreign-born, and never placed where he could command the full strength of a large Irish vote, he was always an office-holder... It cannot be said however, that he was a brilliant statesman or politician."[56]

General Shields estate consisted of his jeweled swords, valued at $3246.66, and the farm in Eugene Township, which was sold in two lots in 1885 for $3246.60 for a total estate of $6493.20. This small amount did not bode well for Shields' widow and it was good that Congress generously continued his pension. She was able to move to a new house on North Main Street, Carrollton where she remained for the next twenty years. Even with her pension and the proceeds from the sale of the farm, Mary, strapped for cash to support herself and pay for her children's education, was forced to sell her husband's jeweled swords to the Government.[57] After her youngest child, Daniel, became a surgeon and moved to New York, Mary joined him, and spent her remaining years there. Mary survived until October 8, 1928 and upon her death, her body was returned to Carrollton, where she was laid to rest next to her husband.

General Shields' death did not end his involvement in politics. There were debates in various legislatures about acknowledging his achievements, and erecting lasting memorials to him. The State of Illinois, in recognition of his services to the "Prairie State", appropriated $9000 for a bronze statue placed in the US Capitol in 1893. That statue no longer sits inside Statuary Hall where it was first situated, and, after 40 years of standing in the same spot, the roving Irish-American was moved in 1934, to the neighboring Hall of Columns, following concerns that the floor would collapse. Today, his is the third statue on the left, inside the second floor south entrance to the Capitol. The U.S. Government, for its part, erected a Federal memorial to the General in St. Mary's Cemetery, Carrollton after Shields body had lain unacknowledged in the quiet country cemetery for nearly 30 years. That memorial, consisting of a polished rose granite bust, resulted from the efforts of J.M. Meade, a man who had supported the South in the Civil War and who happened to pass through Carrollton by chance, where, he learned to his amazement, that General Shields was lying in an unmarked grave.

"How could that happen?" he asked incredulously, about the only man to defeat the legendary Stonewall Jackson.

"Dead soldiers like dead politicians carry no clout" he was told.

Meade prevailed on Congress to authorize funds for a memorial marker. Congress then allocated more money for him in death than in life. They designated Shields' family plot a national monument, the only one in the country in a private cemetery according to local sources. The bust over his grave, by sculptor Jerome Conners was presented to the people by US Congressman W.W. Rucker and accepted by Archbishop Glennon at a large gathering in the graveyard on Nov 12, 1910.

The State of Minnesota, not to be outdone, erected a statue of Shields at the state Capitol in St. Paul which was unveiled on October 20, 1914 and the State of Missouri also thought it appropriate to honor James Shields with a similar bronze likeness. Upon a motion introduced by Senator William G. Busby, $10,000 was authorized for an eight and a half foot statue on a nine and a half foot base. Fourteen sculptors competed for the assignment and Frederick C. Hibbard was awarded the commission. That statue was erected in the town square of Carrollton on November 12, 1914. All these memorials proved confusing to some townspeople, especially those who were not sure what Shields had done to deserve such adulation.[58]

Most assessments of Shields life were more favorable than the one provided by the *New York Times,* and according to his biographer Moran "His life in America was a grand one. He was the first foreign-born Catholic Irishman to be elected to the United States Senate. He remains to this day, the only American politician elected to the United States Senate from three different states. He may well be the most unique of Americans."[59]

The *History of Sangamon County* concluded "James Shields strictly speaking, was neither a great nor learned man, yet his abilities were far above the average, and no one ever made a better display than himself, of those talents with which the Creator endowed him. He was, in a certain sense, his own ancestor, and not for him was intended the Latin maxims, *avito viret honora.* As a politician, jurist, warrior, orator and Senator, he possessed many useful, many noble and many brilliant qualities; and despite the transitory nature of that which we call fame, his name and exploits will not soon be forgotten by his admiring countrymen."[60] James E. Myers, an author who had been critical of Shields in his monograph of Shields' near duel with Lincoln, later posed this rhetorical question: "What might Shields have done had he been less restless? He was a state legislator, state auditor, state Supreme Court justice, commissioner of the General Land

Office, US Senator from Illinois, then Minnesota, then Missouri, (brevet) Major General in the Mexican War, Brigadier General in the Civil War. And he once declined a chance to be Governor of Oregon. Short of the Presidency, what was left?"[61] What indeed?

James Shields, elder statesman and United States Senator from Missouri. In office for only six weeks, his election made him the only person to serve as US Senator from three different States.

Footnotes

Foreword

1.   The Presbyterians were living in Evanston near Chicago and wanted to distance themselves from newly arriving German and Irish immigrants. Seeking an abstemious environment, the Presbyterians were concerned that the Germans picnicked and drank beer on Sundays, while the Irish, frequenting saloons on their way home from work, drank every day.

2.   A History of Lake County Illinois. Halsey, JJ. p 115. Bates Pub. Chicago. 1912.

3.   History of Sangamon County. p 102. Inter-State Publishing Co, Chicago. 1881.

4.   The inn belonged to Mrs. William Dwyer, another immigrant from Ireland. A widow, she operated a farm and a stage coach relay station close to the site of the present-day Great Lakes Naval Training Center. Her establishment, first licensed to her husband William on March 12, 1838, stood on the old Military Road which ran northward along the lakeshore from Chicago to Milwaukee and on to Green Bay, Wisconsin. The Dwyer inn stood on the west side of Green Bay Road just north of Illinois State Route 176 in present day Lake Bluff.

5.   History of Sangamon County. p 102. Inter-State Publishing Co, Chicago. 1881.

6.   Carrolton Daily Democrat, Feb 28, 1989.

Introduction

1. Twentieth Century History of Carroll County,MO. Turner, SK. & Clark, SA. p 422/24. Bowen & Co, Indianapolis.

2. Illinois State Hist. Transactions. 21:113-23. 1915.

3. American Portrait Gallery, Buttre, LC. p 420-31. Vol. 2, #77, New York.. 1880.

4. Brigadier General James Shields. Missouri Monument Commission Record. Castle, HA. p 33. 1913. Copy in Carrollton Courthouse.

5. Century Magazine, p 973. 33:6. Apr. 1887.

6. Century Magazine, p 385. 33:3, Jan. 1887.

7.. Dr. Revel W. English. Obituary, Kansas City Times, Feb 1894.

8. General Washington's Son of Israel and Other Forgotten Heroes of History. Hart, CS. p 201. JB Lipincott, Philadelphia. 1936.

9. Statuary Hall of American Heroes, America's Hall of Fame, honors the country's greatest citizens on a State by State basis. It was created by an Act of Congress, signed into law by President Lincoln in 1864. On April 19th of that year, Representative Justin S. Morrill asked: "To what end more useful or grand, and at the same time simple and inexpensive, can we devote it [the former Chamber of the House that became Statuary Hall] than to ordain that it shall be set apart for the reception of such statuary as each

State shall elect to be deserving of in this lasting commemoration?" His proposal to create a National Statuary Hall became law on July 2, 1864. The Shields statue, commissioned by the State of Illinois and cast in bronze by Leonard W. Volk, was originally displayed in the Illinois pavilion at the Columbian Exposition in Chicago from May to October 1893. It was then transported to Washington DC and placed in Statuary Hall, where it was unveiled on December 6, 1893. There it stood until 1934, when it was relocated to the Hall of Columns next to Statuary Hall. Until recently, states were not allowed to change their statues once they had made their two statue selection. In 2000, Congress changed the law so that statues may now be removed and replaced. It is possible that General Shields' statue may once again be moved some time in the future.

10. The other Illinois statue was a marble figure of Francis E Willard placed there in 1905. The entire collection now consists of 97 statues contributed by 50 states. Forty-seven states have contributed two statues each. Nevada, New Mexico and North Dakota have donated one.

11. Life of Major-General James Shields.Hero Of Three Wars and Senator From Three States. Condon, WH. p 344. Blakley Printing Co. Chicago. 1900.

12. Ibid, p 348.

13. Brigadier General James Shields Missouri Monument Commission Record. Castle, HA. p 33. 1913. Copy in Carrollton Courthouse.

14. Ottumwa Democrat and Times, June 5, 1879.

15. Sacramento Daily Union, Oct 2, 1860.

16. Judge Kevin R. O'Shiel, Family History. I am deeply grateful to Eda Sagarra, Dublin, for providing me with a copy of this text.

17. Life of Major-General James Shields.Hero Of Three Wars and Senator From Three States. Condon, WH. Blakley Printing Co. Chicago. 1900.

18. Donaghmore started out as a Christian monastery founded by St. Patrick in the fifth century AD.

19. History of Effingham County. p 139. 1883.

20. Memoirs of Gustave Koerner, ed McCormack, TJ. (2 Vols) p 415. Torch Press, Cedar Rapids, IA. 1909

21. The Government of Ireland did not start a General registry of births until 1864. Tyrone (Tir Eoin or Eoghan in Irish) means land of the Eoins, an old Irish tribe from whom the O'Neills are descended.

22. Francis Shields Family History. I am deeply grateful to Eda Sagarra, Dublin, for providing me with a copy of this text.

23. Full-time mercenary soldiers.

24. Essex, the reputed paramour of Good Queen Bess, paid a high price for his less than fruitful forays into the Land of the Shamrock. Because of his reversals in Ireland, and other indiscretions, the Earl lost face, his fortune, and finally his head in the bloody fashion of the day; Good Queen Bess, finding him out of favor, had him executed on Ash Wednesday 1601. His passing did not go unremarked, and, he was lamented in an anonymous seventeenth century English poem entitled *"A Lementable New Ballad upon the Earle of Essex Death on Ashe Wednesday 1601. "Would god that he had ne'ere Ireland knowne,*
Nor set his feete in Flaunders ground
Then might we well injoyde our owne

Where nowe our Jewell will not be found;
Which makes our woes still to abound
Trickling with salt teares in my sight,
To heare his name in our eares to sound
-Lord Devreux took his last good-night.
(in The Common Muse, de Sola Pinto V. Rodway AE eds. Penguin Books, London, 1965.)
25. The O'Neills have two argent lions rampant, combatant gules supporting a dexter hand couped at the wrist. There are three estoiles and in the base is a naitant mullet with silvery scales. On the crest is an embowed arm in armor holding an angled sword. The O'Neill motto states "Lamh dearg Eireann," - "the red hand of Ireland."
26. Life of Major-General James Shields Hero Of Three Wars and Senator From Three States. Condon, WH. p 344. Blakley Printing Co. Chicago. 1900

Chapter 1

1. Francis Shields Papers, Omagh, Co. Tyrone, nephew of the General. I am deeply grateful to Eda Sagarra, Dublin, for providing me with a copy of this text.
2. The Career of James Shields An Immigrant Irishman in Nineteenth Century America. Moran Curran, J. p 21. Ed. D. diss. Columbia Univ. Teachers College. NY. 1980.
3. Date obtained from Catherine's gravestone in Galbally Cemetery. This contradicts 1842 date noted by both Condon and Moran.
4. A side-note of the Act of Union was that Sir John Stewart, Attorney General for Ireland at the time of Union, the man who actually drafted the articles for the Act, was a distant cousin of Shields. That family connection came through the General's great-great-grandmother. She was the daughter of Captain Thomas Morris, the officer in command of Mountjoy Castle, a fortress on Lough Neagh. Her sister married Hugh Stewart, son of a 16th century plantation owner and the Attorney General was a direct descendant of hers. Initially, Protestants welcomed the Act of Union and Catholics abhorred it. But as it turned out, the Act, which Catholic historian-solicitor Francis Shields termed "that unfortunate measure," marked the beginning of the end of Protestant hegemony in Ireland. In the century that followed, the British Parliament in Westminister enacted more progressive legislation benefiting Irish Catholics than probably would ever have been authorized by an Irish Legislature in Dublin, made up exclusively of land owning Irish Protestants. The legislation included Catholic emancipation in 1829, disestablishment of the Protestant Church of Ireland in 1869, Gladstone's land act of 1870, the Land Act of 1896 and the Local Government Act of 1898.
5. Life of Major-General James Shields Hero Of Three Wars and Senator From Three States. Condon, WH. p. 11. Blakley Printing Co. Chicago. 1900.
6. The Destruction of Lord Raglan. Hibbert, C. p 21, Penguin Books, London. 1963.
7. Life of Major-General James Shields Hero Of Three Wars and Senator From Three States. Condon, WH. p. 21. Blakley Printing Co. Chicago. 1900
8. Shields letter to Patrick Shields. Aug 2, 1874.
9. The Britons. Colley, L. p. 321. Yale U. Press. New Haven. 1992
10. The Penal Laws, enacted during the reign of William and Mary, restricted the right of Roman Catholics to practice their faith openly, to bear arms, to purchase Protestant land and, to educate their children in their own faith. Despite that, committed Roman

Catholics often defied the Government by sending their children abroad to study in Continental seminaries, expecting them to return to Ireland as priests. Generally they did return, often with a price on their head. Uncle James, one such prospect, attended a French seminary for a while, but did not complete his studies.

11. In America, Uncle James became a professor of classical Latin and Greek at a college or university in South Carolina. Judith Moran wrote she could not find his name listed on the rolls of the University of South Carolina. But that does not mean he was not a professor or tutor, since records are often incomplete and he could have worked at a different institution or privately. There is no doubt that Uncle James lived in the Charleston area, because his will, executed on December 10 1827, was probated there the following year. Uncle James, it appears, was a man of weapons as well as words. According to William Condon he struck some mighty blows for American freedom by taking up arms in the American War of Independence. Later, he fought alongside Andrew Jackson, at the siege of New Orleans in 1814 and, during a night attack against the British, Uncle James sustained a wound in the leg that lamed him for life. Afterwards he walked with a cane.

12. As it turned out, even though young James subsequently traveled to America, he never got the watch. Uncle James died in 1827 and left the prized time piece to a different nephew, a first cousin of James, who had immigrated to America before him. Young James probably considered that America itself was a richer reward. After Uncle James returned to Charleston he corresponded with Young James in Ireland. Uncle James always encouraged him to proceed with his studies, which the uncle said would be the hallmark of his success.

13. The Career of James Shields, An Immigrant Irishman in Nineteenth Century America. Moran Curran, J. Ed. D. diss. Columbia Univ. Teachers College. p 24. 1980.

14. History of Sangamon County. Inter-State Publishing Co. Chicago 1881

15. The Career of James Shields, An Immigrant Irishman in Nineteenth Century America. Moran Curran, J. Ed. D. diss. Columbia Univ. Teachers College. p 27/8. NY 1980. When Shields made the perilous transatlantic voyage, he certainly was not alone. He was one of the 30,000 Irish who immigrated into America between 1820 - 30. Mostly, they were Protestant and had originated in Ulster or present day Northern Ireland. It was not until the great famine and its aftermath in the 1840s that large numbers of Roman Catholics immigrated from the rest of the country. Eligible English or Irish emigrants received free passage to Canada, 100 acres of land and six months rations at low prices, or if they paid their own way, they found regular fares as low as three pounds ($15.) On the other hand, the cheapest fare to an American port from Belfast or Liverpool was more than three times that price at ten guineas. (Ten pounds and ten shillings.)

16. History of Effingham County. p 139. 1881.

17. Memoirs of Gustave Koerner, ed McCormack, TJ. (2 Vols) p 415. Torch Press, Cedar Rapids, IA. 1909.

18. Ottumwa Weekly Courier (Iowa) March 30, 1880. Mary, the daughter of James' Aunt Nancy, (his father's sister married to Daniel Quinn of Tolom, Co. Tyrone) was eight years older than James. She joined her cousin in Charleston when he was living there. When James went west to Illinois, Mary moved north to New York. There, she married Owen Tally, who was from the same part of Ireland as herself, and had four children, two boys and two girls. The boys died in infancy and the girls lived until 22 and 24

respectively. About ten years after marriage, Owen Tally's health failed and he decided to return to Ireland. He died at sea, leaving Mary a widow with two daughters. Mary started a market gardening business at Avenue A and Thirteenth Street on Manhattan's swampy southeastern bulge, at what was then the northern edge of the city. Later, she used the money she earned from vegetables to purchase rooming houses, where many newly arriving Irish lodged. She had remarkable business acumen and, over the years, became a woman of means. She kept in touch with her nomadic cousin and visited him on his Carrollton, Missouri homestead in his later years. While there, she learned that Carrollton had no Catholic place of worship. She reached into her purse and provided the funds to build a church and convent school. Befriended by the Sisters of the Order of the Humility of Mary, who operated the school, she took up residence with them. When the Sisters moved to Ottumwa, Wappello County, Iowa in 1877, in search of a fresh mission, Mary went too, via the newly opened Wabash railroad. In Wappello County, she continued as the Sisters' benefactress and provided additional funds for a convent and small hospital. The facility, completed in 1879, was known as Tally Hospital. Initially, it provided psychiatric care because mental patients were being denied admission to the Iowa State Asylum at Mount Pleasant, due to overcrowding. (Wapello County History, Sterling R. Ed. Sutherland Printing Co. Montezuma. IA. 1986.) When the county home opened in 1881, the psychiatric patients were transferred there and Tally Hospital became an acute care facility. Later, it was renamed St Joseph's Hospital, which grew to become a large teaching institution and, the hospital opened a highly regarded nursing school in 1914. St. Joseph's continued to provide care over the years, until it was consolidated into the Ottumwa Regional Health Center in 1986. Mary Tally spent her last years in Ottumwa, living with the Sisters until she died in 1880, a mere eight months after General Shields had passed away in the same building. Following her death, Mary's body was transported to New York, where she was interred in Calvary Cemetery, Woodside, next to her daughters and sons in the Tally family plot. Mary Tally left the bulk of her sizable fortune to charity and, following her death, two of her nephews John and Frank Quinn, who had arrived from Ireland a year previously, plus their siblings in Ireland, contested the terms of her will. They had been left a mere twenty five cents each and, the case, which dragged on for two years in three different counties, caused quite a stir. The Quinns, largely seen as undeserving opportunists, could not obtain witness support and, the terms of the will were upheld.

19. Today, almost nothing is left of Kaskaskia, the once thriving town that had been the pride of the prairie is no more. Only flat farmland meets the eye with almost no trace that it was once a major population center. A handful of houses with 18 inhabitants and the Church of the Immaculate Conception standing isolated among corn fields are all that remain. The church, which replaced the one originally built in 1675, is in disrepair and had to be moved back from the banks of the Mississippi because of repeated flooding. A small building next to the church houses the Liberty Bell of the West. The bell was presented to the citizens of Kaskasia in 1743 by King Louis XV of France, when the territory was a crown jewel of France's overseas dominions. It was renamed the "Liberty Bell of the West" after it rang out in joyous celebration on July 4, 1778, following the capture of Kaskaskia by American revolutionary Rogers Clark and his Virginian long knife militia. Rogers Clark was the brother of William Clark co-leader of the Lewis and Clark expedition. The explorers stopped at Kaskaskia on their way upriver in in

November 1803.

20. The Career of James Shields, An Immigrant Irishman in Nineteenth Century America. Moran Curran, J. Ed. D. diss. Columbia Univ. Teachers College. p 35. NY. 1980.

21. Randolph County had been organized in 1795 and the original Irish Settlement contributed greatly to its early success. An Illustrated Historical Atlas Map of Randolph County, published in 1875, at the time of the Centenary, states that those Irish "founded families of vigorous and healthy growth including a large number of the best men of Randolph County." (An Illustrated Historical Atlas Map of Randolph County. IL. p 19. W.R. Brink, IL 1875.) These included Robert Foster, who erected a steam distillery and horse-mill, and the parents of John Reynolds, a political rival of Shields, who became Governor of Illinois in 1832. In his memoirs, Governor Reynolds commented that his parents had immigrated in 1785, his father, Robert, from County Monaghan and his mother from Dundalk, County Louth. Gov. Reynolds recounted that when his father first arrived in Illinois he wanted to settle across the Mississippi in St. Francis, which was then Spanish territory. After crossing the river, he asked the authorities for permission to move there. They said that he could on one condition: that Robert raise his children in the Roman Catholic faith! That was too much for the staunch Ulster Presbyterian; Robert had not left the discrimination against religious dissenters in Ireland for religious tyranny across the sea. He refused the French terms, returned to Illinois, and established the Irish Settlement at Plum Creek.

22. A History of Illinois From Its Commencement as a State in 1818 to 1847. Ford T. Shields James ed. p. 94. Springfield. 1854.

23. Ibid, p. 94

24. Eoin Kerr, Donaghmore, who heard it from his grandfather. (Personal communication. 2000.)

25. Memoirs of Gustave Koerner ed McCormack TJ.(2 Vols) p 372-75. Torch Press, Cedar Rapids, IA. 1909.

26. Shields seldom alluded to his teaching career afterward, apart from mentioning that one of his pupils had been Leonidas Polk, a future Episcopalian bishop and General in the Confederate army. Why Polk would have attended Shields' school is unclear, since he was an 1827 graduate of West Point Military Academy. Later, he became Episcopal bishop of Louisiana and he died at the Battle of Pine Mountain in June 1864. Polk donated the land for Maury County's Saint John's Church with a cemetery so idyllic that Confederate General Patrick Ronayne Cleburne, from County Cork, Ireland remarked "It is almost worth dying for to be buried in such a beautiful place." Cleburne, known as the "Stonewall of the West" got his wish. He was killed a few days later at the Battle of Franklin, and was buried there, until his body was disinterred in 1870, and reburied in the Confederate portion of Maple Cemetery in Helena, Arkansas. Cleburne, a lawyer, was born on St. Patrick's Day 1828, about twelve miles from Cork City. He became Major General during the course of the war and had a brother on the opposite side in Union service. It is believed that Cleburne would have risen even higher in the ranks of the Confederacy except that he was foreign born, did not graduate from West Point, was trained in British Service, and his friends were political enemies of Jefferson Davis. The most damaging item against Cleburne was his suggestion that slaves be enlisted in the Confederate army to close a manpower gap late in the war.

Chapter 2

1. US Census 1835.
2. Belleville, IL Town website world wide web. Belleville.net
3. Memoirs of Gustave Koerner, ed McCormack TJ. (2 Vols) p 415, Torch Press, Cedar Rapids, IA. 1909.
4. Koerner was the junior partner in the firm. He lived a long life afterward and went on to become one of Illinois' most distinguished members of the Bar and political leaders. Koerner became Lieutenant Governor of Illinois, Justice of the Supreme Court and, during President Lincoln's term, was Minister Plenipotentiary at the Court of Spain. He also became a close friend and astute observer of James Shields. When Shields moved to Springfield in 1839, he continued to dabble in law in partnership with another attorney, James C. Conkling, but he was more active in legislative affairs. Conkling and his wife Mercy were good friends and confidantes of Abraham & Mary Lincoln. He was Mayor of Springfield in 1845 and then a member of the state Legislature. He read the famous "Conkling Letter" from Lincoln at a mass meeting in Springfield in September 1863, in which Lincoln defended so eloquently his policies in the war and the Emancipation Proclamation. He was a member of the "long nine," members of the Illinois Legislature, so called because they averaged over 6 feet in height, uncommon in that day and age.
5. Century Magazine, p 974, 33:6, Apr. 1887, New York.
6. Sketch of James Shields. Wallace, J. p 37. Unpubs. Ms. Il. State Historical Lib.
7. A History of Illinois From Its Commencement as a State in 1818 to 1847. Ford T. Shields Jas. Ed. p. 246. Springfield. 1854.
8. Life of Major-General James Shields.Hero Of Three Wars and Senator From Three States. Condon, WH. p 42. Blakley Printing Co. Chicago. 1900.
9. Shields Family Papers. I am deeply grateful to Frank Shields, Dungannon, for providing me with a copy of this text.
10. The Career of James Shields,An Immigrant Irishman in Nineteenth Century America. Moran Curran, J. Ed. D. diss. Columbia Univ. Teachers College. p 44. NY. 1980.
11. Memoirs of Gustave Koerner, ed McCormack, TJ. (2 Vols) p 415, Torch Press, Cedar Rapids, IA. 1909.
12. General James Shields of Illinois. O'Shaughnessy, F. Il State Hist. Soc. Transactions p 113-23. 21:1915.
13. Life of Major-General James Shields Hero Of Three Wars and Senator From Three States. Condon, WH. p 41. Blakley Printing Co. Chicago. 1900.
14. Adam W. Snyder and his Period in Illinois History. p 226. Snyder JF. Needam, Virginia, IL. 1906.
15. Brigadier General James Shields. Missouri Monument Commission Record. Castle, HA. p 33. 1913. Copy in Carrollton Courthouse.
16. Memoirs of Gustave Koerner. ed McCormack, TJ. (2 Vols) p 414, 417/18. Torch Press, Cedar Rapids, IA. 1909.
17. Ibid, p 414.
18. History of Sangamon County. p 102. Inter-State Publishing Co, Chicago. 1881. English born Baker, who grew up in America, was charismatic and controversial—a forceful speaker with an unusually good memory for people he had met. He moved west from Illinois and his oratorical abilities helped carry California and Oregon for Lincoln.

He was Senator from Oregon and was killed while serving in the Union army at the battle of Balls Bluff, Aug 1, 1861. He is the only sitting Senator to have died on active duty.
19. Sacramento Daily Union, July 28 1877.
20. Life of Major-General James ShieldsHero Of Three Wars and Senator From Three States. Condon, WH. p 23. Blakley Printing Co. Chicago. 1900.
21. Two examples: we would never have Marco Polo's account of his remarkable twenty four year journey to China in the thirteenth century had he not been imprisoned for a full year by the Genoans following his return. Nor would Sir Walter Raleigh be remembered as a fine Elizabethan author and poet, had he not been incarcerated in the Tower of London for thirteen years before being beheaded in 1618.
22. Grapho-Therapeutics. de Sainte Colombe, P. p 1-10, Bay Port Press, Chula Vista, CA. 1966.
23. Critical and Miscellaneous Essays: The State of German Literature Carlyle, T. 1827.
24. It includes whether the whole page is used or just part of it, and if letters are well formed and neat, or coarse and sloppy.
25. Shields letter to Breese, October, 28th, 1843 in Illinois State Historical Lib.. Springfield.
26. Letter to Patrick January 29, 1858.
27. Ibid.

Chapter 3

1. Encyclopedia Americana. Vol. 15, p 642. New York. 1971.
2. Sacramento Daily Union, Jan 11, 1861.
3. Ibid.
4. The Career of James Shields, An Immigrant Irishman in Nineteenth Century America. Moran Curran, J. Ed. D. diss. Columbia Univ. Teachers College. p 44. NY. 1980.
5. Sangamo Journal, Sept 9, 1837.
6. Illinois State Register, Aug 4, 1837.
7. Letter from Douglas to Shields. April 12th, 1841. IL State Historical Library.
8. Life of Stephen A. Douglas. Stevens, IL St. Hist J. p 299. Oct 1923-Jan 24.
9. Century Magazine, p 974, 33:6, Apr. 1887, New York.
10. Memoirs of Gustave Koerner, ed McCormack, TJ. (2 Vols) p 416. Torch Press, Cedar Rapids, IA. 1909.
11. Sangamo Journal,.July 12, 1839.
12. Memoirs of Gustave Koerner. ed McCormack, TJ. (2 Vols) p 448. Torch Press, Cedar Rapids, IA. 1909.
13. Sangamo Journal, Sept. 1842.
14. Century Magazine, p. 974, 33:6, Apr. 1887, New York.
15. A History of Illinois From Its Commencement as a State in 1818 to 1847. Ford T. ed Shields J. Griggs & Co. Chicago. 1854 Today, the book is recognized as a classic, both because of its candor and Ford's keen insight into the dynamics of frontier life. It provides an unrivaled account of the first thirty years of Illinois history. Described as both cynical and self-serving, Ford was a native of Uniontown, Pennsylvania, and served as Illinois state's attorney, circuit judge, and Supreme Court Justice before he was elected Governor. Constitutionally prohibited from succeeding himself, Ford retired when his term of office ended in 1846. His book describes in detail the persecution and ouster of

Mormons from the state, the Black Hawk War the prevailing attitudes of the Illinois people toward slavery, the murder of Elijah Lovejoy and the larger issues of violence and vigilantism on the American frontier.

16. Sangamo Journal, Nov 5, 1841.

17. Sangamo Journal, Nov 12, 1841.

18. Sangamo Journal, Nov 12, 1841.

19. Lincoln's Preparation for Greatness, Simon, P. p 205. U of I Press, 1971

20. Johnson, a war hero, had gained a brilliant victory over the British and Indians in 1813 at the Battle of the Thames and it was by his hand that the Indian leader, Tecumseh, was said to have fallen. Reynolds, also an old Indian fighter, thought Johnson would make an excellent leader and wanted the Belleville Democrats to come out for him. Shields thought differently and, to the chagrin of Reynolds, swayed the Belleville contingent away from Johnson to Van Buren.

21. Sangamo Journal, Mar 30, 1843.

22. Sangamo Journal, Apr 20, 1843.

Chapter 4

1. Sangamo Journal, Sept 16, 1842.

2. Eve of Conflict, Milton p. 23 in The Career of James Shields, An Immigrant Irishman in Nineteenth Century America. Moran Curran, J. Ed. D. diss. Columbia Univ. Teachers College. NY. 1980.

3. Letter to Mary Jane Wells, Chicago, Dec 6th 1865. Mary Lincoln: Biography of a Marriage, Randall, RP. p 65-69, Little, Brown Co. Boston 1953.

4. Mary Todd Lincoln: Her life and letters. Turner, J & Turner, L. p 292-93, 297-98) Knopf, New York. 1972.

5. Fraulein Knoebel later married a wealthy German lawyer.

6. General Washington's Son of Israel and Other Forgotten Heroes of History. Hart, CS. p 195. Lipincott, Philadelphia. 1936.

7. Butler was one of the "long nine," and when Abraham Lincoln moved to Springfield in 1837, he boarded at the Butler home. In 1859, Governor Bissell appointed Butler to the position of State Treasurer, and in 1860 he was reelected for 2 more years.

8. Century Magazine, p. 974, 33:6, Apr. 1887, New York. Merriman had been involved in a potential duel between Congressman John A. McClernand and the Honorable Theophilus W. Smith, a Supreme Court judge, where Merriman "penned in such discreet language that it might be construed into a challenge or not." That affair involving rifles at a distance of 40 paces was aborted when "the pugnacious gentleman of the judicial ermine was arrested and placed under bonds to keep the peace."

9. A Complete History of Illinois from 1673 to 1873. Davidson. A. & Stuve, B. p 622. IL Journal Company, Springfield. 1874.

10. Bennett's horse had trespassed repeatedly on Stuart's land and, despite Stuart's complaints, Bennett did nothing about it. Stuart had the horse shot and, Bennett was incensed which lead to the duel. The two combatants met in 1819 on a street in Belleville outside the home of Adam Snyder, General Shields' first law partner. Stuart was killed and Bennett was arrested, but broke out of the St. Clair County jail, and fled. He made his way to the Arkansas Territory but, the long arm of Illinois law stretched that far, and brought him back. Bennett was convicted of murder, and sentenced to be hung by Judge

John Reynolds later Governor of the state and General Shields' political foe. According to an eyewitness "The [Bennett] execution was held in public and was witnessed by one of the largest assemblages brought together in this county."

11. A Complete History of Illinois from 1673 to 1873. . Davidson. A. & Stuve, B. p 619 IL Journal Company, Springfield . 874.

12. Lincoln in Springfield. Nicolay, JG. p 385. 33:3. Century Magazine, NY.1887

13. The Astonishing Saber Duel of Abraham Lincoln. Myers, JE, p 14. Lincoln-Herndon Pubs. Springfield. IL. 1968.

14. Sketch of James Shields. Wallace, J. Unpubs. Ms. Il. State Hist. Lib.

15. Hardin was destined to die at the Battle of Buena Vista in Mexico five years later.

16. Alton Telegraph.

17. American Statesmen. Abraham Lincoln. Morse, JT. Jr. p 66. Houghton, Mifflin & Co. Boston & New York, 1893.

18. Memoirs of Gustave Koerner. ed McCormack, TJ. (2 Vols) p 418. Torch Press, Cedar Rapids, IA. 1909.

19. Sacramento Union, Mar 1, 1861.

20. Council   of Conservative Citizens. World wide web.cofcc.org/linc.htm.

21. Letter to Josiah G. Holland, Chicago, Dec 4, 1665.

22. Letter to Mary Jane Wells, Chicago, Dec 6, 1865 in Mary Todd Lincoln. Her Life and Letters. Turner, J. & Turner, L. p. 295. Knopf, New York. 1972.

Chapter 5

1. American Statesmen. Abraham Lincoln.. Morse, JT Jr. p 66. Houghton, Mifflin & Co. Boston & New York. 1893.

2. The Astonishing Saber Duel of Abraham Lincoln. Meyer, JL Lincoln-Herndon Bldg. Pubs p 30. Springfield, IL. 1968. 3.   American Statesmen. Abraham Lincoln. Morse, JT Jr. p 64. Houghton, Mifflin & Co. Boston & New York. 1893.

4. Letter to Mary Jane Wells, Chicago, Dec 6th 1865.

5. Letter to Francis Bicknell Carpenter, Chicago, Dec 8th 1865.

6. The Astonishing Saber Duel of Abraham Lincoln. Meyer, JL Lincoln-Herndon Bldg. Pubs p 28. Springfield, IL. 1968.

7. Honor's Voice. The Transformation of Abraham Lincoln. Wilson, DL. p 265. Knopf. NY. 1998.

8. Citizen Magazine, Nicolay JG, p 385/6, 33:3, Jan. 1887. New York.

9. American Statesmen. Abraham Lincoln. Morse, JT Jr. p 62/63. Houghton, Mifflin & Co. Boston & New York. 1893.

10. Ibid

11. Ibid

12. Herndon quoted in The Life of Abraham Lincoln. Tarbell, IM. p 201. McClure, Phillips & Co. NY. 1928.

13. Mary Lincoln. Randall, RP. p 44, Little Brown Co. Boston. 1953.

14. Abraham Lincoln. The Prairie Years. Sandburg, C. p 53 Harcourt Brace. NY. 1926.

15. ibid p 49.

16. The Life of Abraham Lincoln. Tarbell. IM. p 199. McClure, Phillips & Co. NY. 1928.

17. History of Carrollton. World wide web: carolnet.com/cced/history.html. Carrollton Area Chamber of Commerce Membership Directory and Buyer's Guide. p 48, Standard

Herald. 2001.

18. One historical writer who uses meticulously researched historical accuracy in her novels postulated that very situation. She quoted Mary as saying "Other young men in our coterie were dear Edward Baker, handsome James Shields (courting me, but too in love with himself) Lyman Trumbull and James Conkling, the beau of my best friend... in My Name Was Mary, Rogers, G. extract at www. Gayle.rogers.com. May 2003.

19. Honor's Voice. The Transformation of Abraham Lincoln. Wilson, DL. p 265. Knopf. NY. 1998.

20. Raymond, Incidents in the Life of Mrs. Benj. S. Edwards, p 16 in Mary Lincoln. Biography of a Marriage, Randall, RP. p 10. Boston. 1953.

21. Honor's Voice. The Transformation of Abraham Lincoln. Wilson, DL p 271. Knopf. NY. 1998.

22. Letter from Mary Lincoln to Francis G. Carpenter, Dec 8, 1865.

23. A Complete History of Illinois from 1673 to 1873. p 618. Davidson, A. & Stuve, B. IL Journal Company, Springfield. 1874.

24. Statement of Mrs. N.W. Edwards to Herndon July 27, 1887, Herndon-Weik MS in Mary Lincoln. Biography of a Marriage, Randall, RP. p 43, Little Brown Co. Boston. 1953.

25. Life of Major-General James Shields Hero Of Three Wars and Senator From Three States. Condon, WH. p. 368. Blakley Printing Co. Chicago. 1900.

26. Columbia Magazine, Gurn, J. p 6. September 1928.

27. Honor's Voice. The Transformation of Abraham Lincoln. Wilson, DL. p 284/5. Knopf. NY. 1998.

28. American Statesmen. Abraham Lincoln. Morse, JT Jr. p 64. Houghton, Mifflin & Co. Boston & New York. 1893.

29. Honor's Voice. The Transformation of Abraham Lincoln. Wilson, DL P 292. Knopf. NY. 1998.

30. Alton Telegraph and Review, Oct 1, 1842.

31. A Complete History of Illinois from 1673 to 1873. p 627. Davidson. A. & Stuve. B. IL Journal Company, Springfield. 1874.

32. Sangamo Journal, Mar 19, 1841.

33. The Career of James Shields,An Immigrant Irishman in Nineteenth Century America. Moran Curran, J. Ed. D. diss. p138 Columbia Univ. Teachers College. NY.1980.

34. Shields letter to Breese Feb 19, 1845 in David Davis papers.

35. Life of Major-General James Shields, ero Of Three Wars and Senator From Three States. Condon, WH. p 51. Blakley Printing Co. Chicago. 1900.

36. American Statesmen. Abraham Lincoln. Morse, JT Jr. p 67. Houghton, Mifflin & Co. Boston & New York. 1893.

37. Life of Major-General James Shields Hero Of Three Wars and Senator From Three States. Condon, WH. p 51. Blakley Printing Co. Chicago. 1900.

38. Shields biographer Henry A. Castle. Faribault Daily News, Mar 1, 1932.

39. Mankato Historical Society, Aug 24, 1924 in Minn State Hist Lib.

40. Century Magazine, p 973. 33:6. Apr. 1887.

41. The Law in an Illinois Corner. The Impact of the Law on an Antebellum Family. McDermott, SP. W.Press.uillinois.edu/epub/books/stowell/ch6.html.

42. Lincoln to Samuel Marshall, 11 Nov, 1842. 375

43. American Statesmen. Abraham Lincoln. Morse, JT Jr. p 81. Houghton, Mifflin & Co.Boston & New York. 1893

Chapter 6

1. Our Landed Heritage: The Public Domain, 1776-1936. Robbins, RM. p 143 NY. 1950.
2. The War With Mexico, Morris, RB. ed. p 193 Encyclopedia of American History. Harper & Bros, NY. 1953.
3. ibid.
4. Ibid.
5. Ibid, p 196.
6. Ibid.
7. James Polk Papers, 1775-1891, Book I: 386-390 Library of Congress, Manuscript Division, Washington.
8. Ibid.
9. Mr. Polk's Army. The American Military Experience in the Mexican War. Winders, RB. Texas A& M Press. 1997.
10. The Mexican War, Nevin, D. p 60. Time-Life Books, NY. 1973.
11. Memoirs of Gustave Koerner. ed McCormack, TJ. (2 Vols) p Torch Press, Cedar Rapids, IA. 1909.
12. Journal of Francis Collins. Quarterly Publications of the Historical and Philosophical Society of Ohio. p 43. April -July. 1915.
13. The Mexican War, 1846-1848. Bauer, J. p 147-48. Macmillan, NY. 1974.
14. Shields to Buchanan. Buchanan Collected Papers. Penn. Hist. Soc.
15. Sangamo Journal, Jan 14, 1847.
16. General Order No. 20.
17. Sacramento Daily Union, Oct 2, 1860.
18. Life of Major-General James Shields Hero Of Three Wars and Senator From Three States. Condon, WH. p 57. Blakley Printing Co. Chicago. 1900.
19. In that battle in 480 BC, 300 Spartans held off 30,000 Persians for 3 days and were overcome only when a peasant showed the Persians a back way through the mountains.
20. Life of Major-General James Shields Hero Of Three Wars and Senator From Three States. Condon, WH. p 57. Blakley Printing Co. Chicago. 1900.
21. Vindication of Santa Anna by Manuel Maria Jimen, El Diario del Gabierno, May 1847 in Life of Major-General James Shields Hero Of Three Wars and Senator From Three States. Condon, WH. p 74. Blakley Printing Co. Chicago. 1900.
22. Memoirs of Gustave Koerner. ed McCormack, TJ (2 Vols) p 418, Torch Press, Cedar Rapids, IA. 1909.
23. Columbia Magazine, Gurn J. p. 6. September. 1928.
24. Burnett, WB. Offical Reports: Misc. Manus. Mex. War. New York Hist. Soc.
25. Sacramento Union, Oct 2, 1860.
26. The War With Mexico, Morris, RB. ed. p 206 Encyclopedia of American History. Harper & Bros, NY. 1953.
27. Campaign of General Scott in the Valley of Mexico. Semmes, R. p 270-271. Moore & Anderson. Cincinnati. 1852.
28. Battle of Churubusco, p 107. Vol. XLIII, Southern Quarterly Review. Warren & Richards, Charleston, SC July 1852.
29. Ibid p 108.

30. Ibid p 109.

31. Life of Quitman, Clairborne. JH. I. p 357. NY. 1860.

32. Battle of Churubusco, p 109. Vol. XLIII, Southern Quarterly Review. Warren & Richards, Charleston, SC July 1852.

33. Official Report of the 1st Regt. Burnett, NY Historical Society.

34. History of the Mexican War, The Deserters from Both Sides. Wilcox, CM. p 395. Church News Publishing Co. Washington DC. 1892. Some Irish had changed sides because they disliked life in the American army or preferred to fight for a Catholic country, Mexico. Led by Capt. John O'Reilly from Clifden, Connemara, the *San Patricio* brigade had 200 men in two companies and three artillery batteries and performed courageously for Mexico before being captured. San Patricio casualties at Churubusco were high: when the battle began, the two companies were apparently at full strength with 102 men each. Three hours later 60 percent of the men were either dead or had been captured by the enemy; 85 were taken prisoner, 72 of whom were accused of deserting the US Army and the remaining up to 90 men had escaped. A history of the war states "Their deportment deserves the greatest eulogies, for throughout all the battles they maintained the fire with extraordinary courage. A great number of them fell in the action, while those who survived, more unfortunate than their companions suffered soon after a cruel death, or horrible torments, improper in a civilized age, and from a people who aspire to the title of illustrious and humane." From inside the fort the San Patricios had manned three of seven cannons. (Later some said that their gunfire was aimed at former officers.) As the Americans pressed, the second company of San Patricios and other Mexican soldiers were forced into the convent. Reportedly, Mexican soldiers inside the convent tried three times to raise the white flag, but the San Patricios, desperate because of their fate if captured, tore it down. At last Capt. James M. Smith of the Third Infantry entered and put his own handkerchief on the pole. Once back with the United States Army, the San Patricio company did not fare well. Gen. Winfield Scott issued General Orders 259 and 263 establishing two courts martial for seventy-two deserters. Col. John Garland convened the first court martial on August 23, 1847, in Tacubaya. Col. Bennet Riley, an Irish Catholic officer, convened the second court martial at San Angel on August 26. Following the American victory, seventy one of the captured *San Patricios* were sentenced to be hung as deserters and traitors. Only two defendants did not receive the death sentence, one excused because of improper enlistment in the United States Army, the other because he was deemed insane. Some fifty were executed; of the others, most received fifty lashes and were drummed out, two were pardoned because their sons or brothers had remained true to the American flag and a few were excused because of their youth when they changed sides. As for John O'Reilly, their leader, his life was spared because he had switched to the Mexican side before declaration of war, but the letter "D," for deserter, was branded on his cheeks. General Scott signed the orders of execution. It is not known what role, if any, Shields played in the punishments inflicted on the *San Patricios*.

35. During the battle some of the cadets threw themselves over a cliff rather than surrender. Today, a monument to the boy heroes stands in their honor at the foot of Chapultepec Hill.

36. Shields reported in the Irish World in 1879.

37. Then & Now, History of Rice County Minn. p 9. Rice County Bi-Centennial

Commission, Modern Printers, Faribault MN. 1977.

38. This enormous painting (nearly 8 by 18 feet) has been on view at the Historical Center/Museum at the Washington, DC, Navy Yard as part of an exhibit on Marine Corps history since 1982. According to Jamie Arbolino, Registrar, US Senate Commission on Art, the painting's massive size made it prohibitive for display or storage at the Capitol. When the painting was first received in the late 1800s, it was displayed in the west staircase of the newly added Senate wing of the Capitol. Subsequently, it was replaced with a portrait of Abraham Lincoln, the "First Reading of the Emancipation Proclamation by Lincoln." The Senate still has the original frame of Chapultepec in its off-site storage facility in Maryland. When the Senate's a new Visitor Center opens, the painting will be recalled from it's current long-term loan to be hung there.

39. Illinois Historical Society Transactions vol. 21. P. 118. The Mexican war was the first conflict anywhere in the world to be photographed.

40. The Illinois, Gray, J. p 148 Farrar and Rhinehart, NY, 1940.

Chapter 7

1. The Career of James Shields, An Immigrant Irishman in Nineteenth Century America. Moran Curran, J. Ed. D. diss. p 91. Columbia Univ. Teachers College. NY. 1980.

2. The Illinois, Gray, J p 146. Farrar and Rhinehart, NY, 1940.

3.Sangamo Journal, Jan 20, 1848.

4. James Polk Papers, 1775-1891, Book III 4 Jan 1848. p. 283 - 4 Library of Congress, Manuscript Division. Washington.

5. Letter from Shields to Buchanan, Oct 20, 1848. Buchanan Papers.

6. Glimpses of the Past. Vol. 7, p 19. Missouri Hist Soc, Jefferson Memorial.1940.

7. Ibid.

8. Duyckinch, Mexican War and Its Heroes, II, 125 in The Career of James Shields, An Immigrant Irishman in Nineteenth Century America. Moran Curran, J. Ed. D. diss. p 90. Columbia Univ. Teachers College. NY.1980.

9. To Conquer a Peace. The War Between the United States and Mexico. Weems, JE. p 442. Texas A & M University Press. College Station, TX. 1974. Scott, who was not a West Pointer earned his nickname by riding into Mexico City in full dress uniform with all brass and buckles to accept its surrender. Those who saw him said he was a complete parade by himself.

10. Century Magazine, Nicolay J. p. 387. Vol 33. Issue 3. Jan 1887.

11. Centennial History of Illinois, Vol. 3. The era of the Civil War: p 62. IL Centennial Commission, Springfield. 1919.

12. Plato to Breese in IL State Historic Library, Springfield.

13. The Illinois. Gray, J p146. Farrar and Rhinehart, NY. 1940.

14. History of Oregon. Bancroft, HH. Vol. I. p 776, San Francisco. 1890.

15. Letter from Quitman to Shields Sept 9, 1848. in Life & Correspondence of John A. Quitman, Major General USA & Governor of Mississippi, Claiborne, JF, p 15. New York. 1860.

16. Letter from Ebenezer Z. Ryan to McLean Jan 15th 1849 in Il State Historical Library, Springfield.

17. James Polk Papers, 1775-1891, Diary Vol. IV. p. 350 Library of Congress, Manuscript Division. Washington.

18. Sangamo Journal, Jan 24, 1849.

19. Congressional Quarterly's Guide to Congress, Biographical Directory of the American Congress 2nd Edition, 5 p 685/6. US Gov. Pubs. Washington DC.

20. Pub in National Intelligencer, Feb 28, 1849. Washington.

21. Centennial History of IL. Vol. 3. The Era of the Civil War. P. 63. IL Centennial Committee, Springfield. 1919.

22. Sangamo Journal, Mar 29, 1849.

23. Life of Major-General James Shields Hero Of Three Wars and Senator From Three States. Condon, WH. p 123. Blakley Printing Co. Chicago. 1900.

24. History of California Vol. 19 p 173. Cal. Hist Soc. Pubs, San Francisco.

25. Biographical Directory of the US Congress 1774-1989, Bicentennial Ed. p 1805. Washington.

26. History of Cal Vol. 19 p. 345. Cal. Hist Soc. Pubs, San Francisco.

27. Shields to Buchanan Dec 8, 1849. Buchanan Papers.

28. Life of Major-General James Shields Hero Of Three Wars and Senator From Three States. Condon, WH. P 156. Blakley Printing Co. Chicago. 1900.

29. A History of Illinois From Its Commencement as a State in 1818 to 1847. Ford T. Shields Jas. Ed. p. 234. Springfield. 1854.

30. The editorials that first got Lovejoy labeled an intolerant and quarrelsome bigot were not attacks on slavery, but screeds on the Roman Catholic Church and "Popists."

Chapter 8

1. Centennial Hist. of Illinois. The Era of the Civil War p. 134. Springfield. 1919.

2. Douglas to Lampire, Dec 18 1854. Il State Historical Lib, Springfield.

3. In those days Douglas spelled his name with a double "s" at the end.

4. Alton Weekly Courier, Oct 12, 1854.

5. Chicago Tribune, The Rise of a Great American Newspaper. Wendt, L. p 56 Rand McNally, Chicago. 1979.

6. Philadelphia American, 1855 in Il State Historical Lib, Springfield.

7. Centennial History of Illinois. The Era of the Civil War p 135. Centennial Comm. Springfield. 1919.

8. Trumbull had a distinguished career. He became a Republican shortly after his election and would later change parties again. He proposed and wrote the 13th amendment to the Constitution abolishing slavery.

9. Officially called the American Party, the Know-Nothings were a loose-knit anti-Catholic and anti-immigrant organization. They got their name because of the "I don't know" password used by members of secret lodges. In 1855, they were at their zenith and active in every state. The Party called for the exclusion of Catholics and foreigners from public office and for a 21 year residence for immigrants as qualification for citizenship. When the Know-Nothing Party fizzled out a few years later, many of its members became Republicans.

10. Chicago Tribune, The Rise of a Great American Newspaper. Wendt, L. p 56 Rand McNally, Chicago. 1979.

11. Memoirs of Gustave Koerner. ed . McCormack, TJ. (2 Vols) p 417. Torch Press, Cedar Rapids, IA. 1909.

12. Shields letter to Patrick Shields, January 29, 1858.

13. Chicago Tribune, Dec 23, 1853.

14. Centennial History of Illinois. The Era of the Civil War. p 22/3. IL Cent. Comm. Springfield. 1919.

15. New York Morning Post, 27 Dec. 1845.

16. Shields letter to Patrick Shields, Oct 3, 1873.

17. The Irish Diaspora in America, McCaffrey, LJ. Catholic University of America Press. Washington, DC 1976. The Career of James Shields, An Immigrant Irishman in Nineteenth Century America. Moran Curran, J. Ed. D. diss. p 14 Columbia Univ. Teachers College. 1980.

18. Shields letter to Patrick Shields, Jan 29, 1858.

19. The Reminiscences of Carl Schurz, Schurz, C. II 21-22. McClure, NY. 1907.

20. Letter from Zarachious C. Lee to Shields, Dec 24, 1845, Dreer Collection.

21. Memoirs of Gustave Koerner. ed McCormack, TJ. (2 Vols) p 571. Torch Press, Cedar Rapids, IA. 1909.

22. The Fenians began in New York in 1855 in the law offices of Michael Doheny a former Young Irelander. (Lecture by Michael O'Donnell. World wide web. Fethard.com/people/doheny.html) Irish-Americans funded the Fenian movement, which sought to overthrow English rule in Ireland. In 1866, a group of Fenians invaded Canada from Buffalo, New York and captured Fort Erie but went no farther. A Fenian revolt in Ireland a year later also failed. While the Fenians did not prosper in their day, their actions and ideas provided a road map embraced by others, which eventually led to an Irish revolution and freedom. For more information see: The Story of the Irish Race, MacManus, S. Devon-Adair Co. NY. 1974.

23. Shields letter to Patrick Shields, January 29, 1858.

24. Resolution Expressive of Sympathy for the Exiled Irish Patriots, Jan 29, 1852.

25. A Committee of His Fellow Citizens, Washington Aug 5, 1852.

26. Meagher subsequently became a Brigadier General leading the Irish Brigade in the Civil War. He was appointed acting Governor of Montana in 1865, and drowned two years later, when he apparently fell overboard into the Missouri river at Fort Benton.

27. Life of Major-General James Shields. Hero Of Three Wars and Senator From Three States. Condon, WH. p 335. Blakley Printing Co. Chicago. 1900.

28. Shields letter to Patrick Shields. January 29, 1858.

29. History of Rice and Steele Counties Minnesota, Curtiss-Wedge, F. Vol II, p 321. Cooper, Chicago. 1910.

30. From New York Tribune in *Faribault Democrat,* February 14, 1879.

31. History of Rice and Steele counties. Curtiss-Wedge, F. Vol II, p 330. Cooper, Chicago. 1910.

32. Then & Now, History of Rice County, Minn. p 10. Rice County Bi-Centennial Commission, Modern Printers, Faribault, MN. 1977.

33. ibid p 264.

34. Life of Major-General James Shields Hero Of Three Wars and Senator From Three States. Condon, WH. p 53. Blakley Printing Co. Chicago. 1900.

35. Shields letter to Patrick Shields, Jan 29, 1858.

36. History of Rice and Steele counties. Curtiss-Wedge, F. Vol II, p 330. Cooper, Chicago. 1910.

37. Then & Now History of Rice County, Minn p 10. Rice County Bi-Centennial

Commission, Modern Printers, Faribault, MN. 1977.

38. ibid. p 263. 389

39. Life of Major-General James Shields Hero Of Three Wars and Senator From Three States. Condon, WH. p 269. Blakley Printing Co. Chicago. 1900.

40. History of Rice and Steele counties. Curtiss-Wedge, F. Vol II, p 330. Cooper, Chicago 1910. Shieldsville's first officers included: supervisors, Joseph Hagerty and Patrick Cuniff. constables, Michael Hanley and Patrick McKenna; justices of the peace, Timothy Doyle and James Roach.

41. Faribault Pilot, March 17, 1910.

42. Carrollton Daily Democrat, February 29, 1932.

43. Letter in Minn. Hist. Library. Shields came to an accommodation with the Indians and permitted them to use a spot adjoining Shieldsville known as General's island, as a campground. In 1862, after Shields had left Minnesota, another confrontation took place between the settlers and the Indians. About 100 whites descended on the Indian village and demanded that they leave the area. They refused to do so, producing a letter from General Shields with a permit for them to occupy Shields Island as their home. A spokesman for the pioneers informed the Indians that if "General Shields was there a gun would be put in his hands and he would be forced to fight" indicating that General Shields was no longer in charge. This ended the matter of words, and the pioneers began knocking the tepees right and left and evicted the Indians. They were last seen carrying crying children and dragging their meager possessions as they headed west along Dodd Road.

44. Shields letter to Patrick Shields, Jan 29, 1858.

45. The railroad was built eventually, but that was long after Shields had left Minnesota. It reached Rochester in 1864 and was linked to Faribault by stage route. When it got to Northfield the following year at the close of the Civil War, its name was changed to the Minnesota Railway Company. The railroad made money afterward, but not for Shields.

46. A History of Minnesota: Folwell, WW. Vol. 2. p 7. Minn Hist Soc, St Paul. 1961.

47. ibid

48. Then & Now: History of Rice County, Minn. p 8. Rice County Bi-Centennial Commission, Modern Printers, Faribault, MN. 1977.

49. Minneapolis Sunday Tribune, May 1, 1927.

50. ibid.

51. Then & Now: History of Rice County, Minn. p 8. Rice County Bi-Centennial Commission, Modern Printers, Faribault,MN 1977.

52. Life of Major-General James Shields Hero Of Three Wars and Senator From Three States. Condon, WH. p 269. Blakley Printing Co. Chicago. 1900.

53. A History of Minnesota: Folwell, WW Vol. 2. P. 12/13 Minn Hist Soc, St Paul. 1961.

54. Shields letter to Patrick Shields, Jan 29, 1858. 391

55. Letter of Shields to McGroarty, March 4, 1858. McGroarty papers. Minn. Hist. Society Library.

56. Shields letter to Patrick Shields, Jan 29, 1858.

57. Shields letter to Sibley, May 24, 1858, Sibley Papers. Minn. Hist. Society Library.

58. Rice letter to Sibley, June 22, 1858, Sibley Papers Minn. Hist. Society Library.

59. Congressional Globe, 35th Congress, 1st Session, p 2426. in The Career of James Shields, An Immigrant Irishman in Nineteenth Century America. Moran Curran, J. Ed. D.

diss. p 176 Columbia Univ. Teachers College. NY 1980
60. Minneapolis Sunday Tribune, May 1, 1927.
61. Ibid.
62. Kingsbury letter to Sibley Oct 1, 1859, Sibley Papers. Minn. Hist. Society Library.
63. Letter to William P. Murray Mar 28, 1860, in ibid P.177.
64. Ibid.
65. Life of Major-General James Shields, ero Of Three Wars and Senator From Three States. Condon, WH. p 269. Blakley Printing Co. Chicago. 1900.

Chapter 9

1. The author of this song is unknown. It was brought from Ireland to America by Irish-speaking immigrants in the 18th century. It is a young girl's lament for her sweetheart, who left Ireland to fight on foreign fields, as a member of the "Wild Geese." The song became Americanized to "Johnny Has Gone for a Soldier" in the US Civil War, even though it retained its phonetic Gaelic refrain. The author of this book has translated the refrain from Irish as follows:

My Precious! Bide safely with me.
Come steal away, My Love, with me,
Tread softly, gently, quietly.
Elope My Dear! Step through the door!
Be safe with me, evermore.

Irish authors were associated with songs of the South as well as the North. Dan Emmett, who was born in Ohio, wrote *Dixie's Land*, the most popular song of the war and Harry B. McCarthy, an Irish actor, composed *The Bonnie Blue Flag* while performing in Jackson, Mississippi in 1861. He set the verses an old Irish air *"The Irish Jaunting Car,"* and the refrain goes *Hurrah! Hurrah! For Southern rights hurrah! Hurrah for the Bonnie Blue Flag that bears a single star.*

2. Constructed in 1835 as the home of Isaac Williams, a New England merchant who moved to Los Angeles three years earlier, the hotel was originally a one story adobe building, which became the last Capitol of Alta California during the Mexican era when Governor Pio Pico purchased it for his office. A second story was added in 1851 and on October 7, 1858, the first Butterfield Overland Mail stage from the East arrived 21 days after leaving St. Louis. After the occupation of Los Angeles by American forces in 1847, the building was used to house American troops and, when they left, it became a saloon. By early 1850, the building was operating as the Bella Union Hotel. Later that year, it became the county's first courthouse and beginning in 1858, it was the region's transportation hub. The Overland Mail Company operated by John Butterfield (the founder of American Express) rented space in it for a station until Overland built new quarters in 1860 at Second and Spring—the present location of Mirror Building. The Wells, Fargo Company also had their office here and Phineas Banning operated coaches to Wilmington and San Bernardino from the hotel.

3. Sixty Years in Southern California. 1853-1913, Newmark, H. p 271. New York. 1926.
4. Hist. of Cal 31:13. Cal. Hist Soc. Pubs, San Francisco.
5. Broderick and Terry dueled over the Lecompton amendment on the foggy shores of

Lake Merced in the southwest corner of San Francisco. In the face-off, Broderick's hairspring triggered pistol discharged prematurely. He then remained perfectly still, as required by the *Code Duello* while Terry took deliberate aim and shot him in the right breast. He died shortly afterward. Broderick himself was no stranger to dueling. In an earlier encounter, his life was spared when a bullet ricocheted off his pocket watch.

6. San Francisco Alta, Aug 2, 1860.

7. San Francisco Directory 1861.

8. The Annals of San Francisco, II Chap XXVIII, Soule, F et al. Internet May 17, 2003.

9. Encyclopedia of American History. Morris, RB. ed. p 228. Harper & Bros, New York. 1953.

10. Journals of Charles E. De Long. p 284. Cal. Hist Soc. Pubs. San Francisco.

11. California Historical Society Quarterly, Vol. X, #3, p 296. Sept 1931, San Francisco.

12. Sacramento Daily Union March 1, 1861.

13. Memoirs of Gustave Koerner. ed McCormack, TJ.(2 Vols) Torch Press, Cedar Rapids, IA. 1909.

14. Sacramento Daily Union, Jan 11, 1861.

15. A Catholic house of worship of that name now stands in the University of San Francisco, but it is not the same site where the marriage took place. The original, a parish church near the city center, was destroyed in the great earthquake of 1906. No records remain from the Shields-Carr ceremony, because they were destroyed in the fire that followed the earthquake. According to the Carrollton *Republican = Record*, of Nov 17, 1910, the Shields' wedding was officiated by Rev. Father Maraski, S.J., assisted by Rev. Fr. Colby, S.J.; Judge Calkery was bestman and Miss Susie Sweeney was bridesmaid.

16. Life of Major-General James Shields Hero Of Three Wars and Senator From Three States. Condon, WH. p 269. Blakley Printing Co. Chicago. 1900.

17. Carrollton Daily Democrat, 1988. Castle, HA. General James Shields Soldier, Orator, Statesman. Minn. Monument Commission. 1914.

18. Republican=Record, Carrollton, Nov 17, 1910.

19. Judge Daly (1816 - 99) was of Irish descent. His parents had immigrated from Cork in the late 18th Century. But one would never have known that from his wife, Maria Lydig Daly, an engaging but snooty New York socialite. Judge Daly had done well; he was a Justice of the Court of Common Pleas, the highest court in New York, for 42 years and its Chief Justice for 27.

20. Diary of a Union Lady. Hammond, HH. Ed. p xxvii. Bison Bks. New York. 1962. It is possible that when Mrs. Daly was fostering Shields' career she was thinking not only of him, but also of her husband's future. Harold E. Hammond, who edited Mrs. Daly's diaries for publication, wrote "According to his wife, the Judge deserved a much higher position than his own ambitions allowed and Mrs. Daly was unceasing in her efforts to promote him through her many highly placed friends and acquaintances. Her particular ambition was that the Judge should serve on the US Supreme Court." If Shields were a successful Senator her reasoning may have run, he would be well placed to assist in the nomination of her husband to the highest court in the land.

21. Ibid p 56.

22. Shields to Scott Oct 14, 1861, National Archives. Shields to John F. Callan, June 18, 1861, Dreer Collection.

23. Shields to Maria Daly, June 10, 1861.

24. Letter to Alta newspaper, Dec 1861.

25. San Francisco Alta, Dec 11, 1861.

26. Diary of a Union Lady. Hammond, HH. Ed. Bison Bks. New York. 1962.

27. Shields to Maria Daly, Jan 22, 1862.

28. Lt. Dick Dowling and an artillery battery of 42 Irish "dockwallopers" turned back more than 15,000 Yankees in the Battle of Sabine Pass. Afterwards Confederate President Jefferson described the victory as being "without parallel in ancient or modern warfare." Carl Wittke in *The Irish In America* reported, "Confederate Generals spoke highly of Irish soldiers. Some preferred them as clean, fearless fighters who were loyal to their leaders and whose irrepressible humor did not fail them even in moments of greatest danger." See also General Richard Taylor's book Destruction and Reconstruction, Appleton, New York, 1879. On the Federal side, The Irish Brigade included the 63rd, 69th, and 88th New York Infantry Regiments as well as the 28th Massachusetts and 116th Pennsylvania.

29. Shields to McClellan, Jan 10, 1862. Brigadier General Shields Monument Commission Record. Castle, HA. p. 50. Carrollton, MO. Jan. 30, 1913.

30. Shields to Maria Daly Feb 7, 1862.

31. Republican=Record, Carrollton, Nov 17, 1910.

32. Like Shields, Jackson had Irish antecedents from Ulster. His great grandfather had emigrated in 1748 from Beragh, twelve miles from Altmore, where Shields had grown up, and Jackson's great grandmother Elizabeth Cummings hailed from the neighboring county of Derry. Upon arrival in the U.S., the couple settled in Cecil County, Maryland.

33. The New York Freeman's Journal, p 3. March 12 1910.

34. Carrollton Daily Democrat. Dec 12, 1914.

35. The crack-shot Phillips lived until 1904, when he died peacefully in his native town of Berryville, Virginia.

36. The New York Freeman's Journal, p 3 March 12, 1910.

37. Ibid

38. ibid

39. Jackson never again held a commanders conference after his Winchester defeat. He was on personal reconnaissance following victory at Chancellorsville, Virginia, when his own troops, mistaking him for a Yankee, opened fire and shot him. He died a week later from his wounds, a victim of "friendly fire."

40. Stonewall Jackson as Military Commander. Selby, SM. Van Nostram, Princeton, 1968.

41. Life of Major-General James Shields Hero Of Three Wars and Senator From Three States. Condon, WH. p 207. Blakley Printing Co. Chicago. 1900.

42. Richmond Whig, Apr 9, 1862.

43. Carrollton Daily Democrat, Nov 18, 1910. After the war, Huron became a prominent attorney and newspaper publisher in Topeka, Kansas. He had been a member of the 7th Indiana and claimed that he invented the verse in John Brown's Body about hanging Confederate President Jeff Davis to a tree, during Shields' campaign against Stonewall Jackson. According to Huron, the soldiers in his division had been marching for some time singing "John Brown's body lies a moulderin' in the grave." He suggested they give John Brown a rest and sing about hanging Jeff Davis "to a sour apple tree." He said he based the verse on an old song from his childhood, "A sick monkey in a sour apple tree."

The verse eventually was transformed into the more familiar "We'll hang Jeff Davis to a sour apple tree," but there is some controversy about how this verse reached its final form.

44. Mr. Lincoln's Army. Catton, B. p 105. Anchor Books. NY. 1951.
45. The New York Freeman's Journal, p 3. March 12, 1910. The water route to Richmond up the James River was guarded by the ironclad *Merrimac* renamed the *Virginia*. After sinking the *Cumberland* and *Congress* off Hampton Roads the *Merrimac* sailed out next day to complete the destruction of the Union flagship *Minnesota*, which had run aground. En route, the *Merrimac* was met by the U.S.S. *Monitor*, an armored raft-like craft with a revolving turret amidships, which had rushed to the rescue. The ensuing 5-hr. battle, the first naval engagement between ironclads, resulted in a draw. Although the *Merrimac* was forced to return to Norfolk for repairs, its threat kept the Union fleet bottled up in port and saved Richmond. The Merrimac was scuttled by its crew to prevent her falling into enemy hands when Norfolk fell to Union forces later that year.
46. The Fiber of Character, Gregory, T. quoted in address delivered at annual meeting of Illinois State Bar Association, June 4, 1948. Illinois Bar Journal, Oct. 1948.
47. Within a couple of days he accused General Garnett with a long list of failures at Kernstown, removed him from command, and put him under arrest. The army was stunned, and most officers openly rebelled. General Garnett was a brave, aggressive officer who did not deserve Jackson's charges. He had resigned his commission in the US Army to join the army of Virginia. General Richard Taylor (a Confederate commander and son of former President Zachary Taylor) wrote: "I have never met an officer or soldier, present at Kernstown, who failed to condemn the harsh treatment of Garnett after that action." It was almost as if Jackson, unable to bear the torment of defeat, needed to purge himself with a scapegoat. Richmond agreed with the troops, for Jackson was ordered to release Garnett from arrest and assign him to duty. Jackson was uncompromising and refused to reinstate General Garnett. Garnett eventually returned to duty and died later in the war, leading a brigade in Pickett's charge at Gettysburg, just weeks after he had been a pallbearer at Jackson's funeral. Jackson also wrestled with his conscience on whether he had properly attacked the enemy on Sunday, the Sabbath, rather than on Monday.
48. Shields to Maria Daly, Mar 26, 1862.
49. The New York Freeman's Journal, March 12 1910. P. 3.
50. Ibid
51. ibid
52. Lincoln to Hooker, 10 June 1863 in The Collected Works of Abraham Lincoln. Basler, RM. ed. Vol VI p. 257. The Rutgers Press, New Brunswick, NJ. 1953.
53. Lincoln to James C. Conkling in ibid p. 407.

Chapter 10

1. New York Herald, Apr 8, 1862.
2. Shields to Col Lewis, April 7, 1862 in IL State Historical Library.
3. The Collected Works of Abraham Lincoln. Basler, RP. ed. Vol V p 272-73. The Rutgers Press, New Brunswick, NJ. 1953. Life of Major-General James Shields Hero Of Three Wars and Senator From Three States. Condon, WH. p 236. Blakley Printing Co.

Chicago. 1900.

4. Life of Major-General James Shields Hero Of Three Wars and Senator From Three States. Condon, WH. P 367/8. Blakley Printing Co. Chicago. 1900. The number of Brigadier-Generals was capped at 200 by Congress.

5. General Washington's Son of Israel and Other Forgotten Heroes of History. Hart, CS. p 204. JB Lipincott, Philadelphia. 1936.

6. The Illinois. Gray J. p 148. Farrar & Rhinehart, NY 1940.

7. One hundred years after her daring espionage activities for the Confederacy, a Front Royal gas station attendant, when asked if he knew who Belle Boyd was, responded in a conspiratorial whisper: "She wuz th' Suth'run lady that made luv to th' Yune-yun Gin-rul."That 'Yune-yun Gin-rul' was none other than General Shields. Of course, that may have been an exaggeration; Belle and Shields may never have 'made luv' but their paths certainly crossed. The proprietress of a Front Royal restaurant sporting Belle's name had a different take on the beautiful Miss Belle's wartime activities. "Belle Boyd was the girl who ran down the street in her underwear to warn General Andrew Jackson the Yankee's were coming" affirmed the restaurateur, when asked about her. As far as we know, Belle Boyd did neither but she did a lot for the South, judging from her own colorful account. Belle Boyd in Camp and Prison. Davis C. ed Introduction. p 55. Yoseloff pub, Cranbury, NJ. 1968.

8. Stonewall Jacksons Valley Campaign. Gingrich, S. p 37 Air War College Thesis, Maxwell AFB, AL. 1995.

9. The play, a civil war romance set in the Valley of Virginia, told the story of a heroine who gathered critical intelligence for "Stonewall" Jackson, which was exactly what Belle Boyd did against the unsuspecting General James Shields. Boyd was feted in England because of considerable sympathy there for the Southern cause. English upper classes were closely allied with Southern aristocracy and, British manufacturers and shippers, irked by the high tariffs imposed by the Union, looked forward to the opening of a vast free-trade market in the Confederacy, as a separate country. Because of that, Britain seriously considered recognizing the South early on. Consequently, Belle's memoirs, published in London in 1865, enjoyed considerable acclaim.

10. General Shields came out looking more gullible than gallant in the hands of the manipulative Miss Belle, especially when his enemies in high places learned of his involvement with her. Correspondent Paige, in a private letter to his managing editor in far-off New York, mentioned that Belle had been "closeted four hours" with General Shields, the Union Commander. Paige said he did not believe Belle was a "camp cyprian" as the New York *Herald* and the Philadelphia *Inquirer* had labeled her but, it did not look good for the General. Neither was General Shields' military career enhanced when the Washington *Evening Star* in August 1862 reported luridly that "One of the Generals formerly stationed in the Shenandoah Valley is mentioned rather oddly as association with her, and Belle boasts of having once wrapped a rebel flag around his head." (BB P. 72-3.)

11. Not all Southerners cottoned to Miss Belle "playing the game of flirt," nor trucking with Yankees, even if it was all for the cause of the South. Tom Ashby, a Southern chronicler accused her of "lowering the dignity of her sex." Ashby, who was 14 when he first saw the flighty Miss Belle, wrote in his reminiscences, *The Valley Campaigns*, that Belle was "a young woman of some personal beauty, vivacious, attractive and spirited in

manner, and a skilled rider of spirited horses. Nor was she wanting in energy, dash and courage… She was as far below the standard of the pure and noble womanhood of the South as was a circus rider" he sniffed.

12. Belle Boyd in Camp and Prison. Davis C. ed Introduction. p 149. Yoseloff pub, Cranbury, NJ. 1968.

13. Ibid p 150.

14. Ibid p 67.

15. Belle Boyd in Camp and Prison. Boyd, B. Blelock. NY. 1865.

16. Turner Ashby was 34 and had fought in 28 battles in the preceding 35 days. Afterwards, Jackson wrote "As a partisan officer I never knew his superior. His daring was proverbial, his tone of character heroic, his power of endurance almost incredible, and his sagacity almost intuitive in divining the purposes and movements of the enemy."

17. Stonewall Jackson Portrait of a Soldier, Bowers, J. p 64 Wm Morrow, NY. 1989.

18. Tom to Dick (last names not identified) in Shields box, Minnesota State Historical Society Library. June 8th, 1862.

19. Stonewall Jackson in the Shenandoah. p 30 - 31, Century Magazine, June 1885. NY.

20. Irish Rebels Confederate Tigers. A History of the 6th Louisiana Volunteers, Gannon, J. p 57, Savas, Campbell, CA. 1998.

21. Stonewall Jackson's Valley Campaign. Gingrich, S. p 53/54 Air War College Thesis, Maxwell AFB, AL 1995.

22. Destruction and Reconstruction. Personal Experiences of the Late War. Taylor, R. Appleton, New York, 1879.

23. ibid

24. The Career of James Shields, An Immigrant Irishman in Nineteenth Century America. Moran Curran, J. Ed. D. diss. Columbia Univ. Teachers College. p 198. 1980

25. It was largely believed that Shields was relieved of command, not because he was defeated by Jackson, but because he failed to destroy the remaining bridge still standing at Port Republic which allowed Jackson to escape. General Shields had ordered Col. Sam Carroll, with four regiments the 84th and 110th Pennsylvania, 8th Ohio and 7th Indiana, to destroy the bridge and, Carroll reported his order for burning the bridge to McDowell at Front Royal, whereupon McDowell sent an order by courier mounted upon a fleet horse to Col Carroll direct, ordering him to take his brigade at once to Port Republic, not to burn the bridge but to hold it at all hazards. Arriving at the bridge in the early morning of June 9th, Carroll placed his troops for its defense but was over run by Jackson's forces and the bridge became Jackson's route of retreat. Shields explanation of what had happened was not accepted, since that would have made McDowell, a West Point graduate, culpable, which was not acceptable to higher command. Afterwards, Shields sharply condemned Sam Carroll's "blunders": "Colonel Carroll neglected to burn the bridge at Port Republic. . . . He held it three-quarters of an hour and wanted the good sense to burn it. They took up an indefensible position afterward instead of a defensible one." Carroll was hurt during the battle when his wounded horse fell on him.

26. Carrollton Republican=Record, Nov 17, 1912.

27. The Civil War Diaries of Salmon P. Chase: Inside Lincoln's Cabinet. Donald, D. ed p 104-05. Longmans Green & Co. NY. 1954.

28. An infamous military prison in New York, known as the American Bastille. The fort was built on a small rock island lying in the Narrows between the lower end of Staten

Island and Long Island, opposite Fort Hamilton.

29. Diary of a Union Lady. Hammond, HH. Ed. Bison Bks. New York. 1962.

30. Life of Major-General James Shields Hero Of Three Wars and Senator From Three States. Condon, WH. p 337. Blakley Printing Co. Chicago. 1900.

31. Diary of a Union Lady. Hammond, HH. Ed. P. 221. Bison Bks. New York. 1962. 32. Supreme Command: Leadership in Wartime. Cohen, EA. p 34/5. Simon & Schuster, New York, 2002.

32. Century Magazine, Nicolay, J. p. 386. Vol 33, Iss. 3 Jan 1887. Memoirs of Gustave Koerner. ed Thomas J. McCormack (2 Vols) Torch Press, Cedar Rapids, IA. 1909.

33. Shannon R. St Louis Republic, Feb 19, 1913.

34. General James Shields of Illinois. O'Shaughnessy F. llinois State History Transactions, Vol. 21. p 113 - 23. 1915.

35. Carrollton Republican=Record, Nov 17, 1912.

36. Life of Major-General James Shields Hero Of Three Wars and Senator From Three States. Condon, WH. p 80/82. Blakley Printing Co. Chicago. 1900.

37. Ibid p 28

38. Sacramento Daily Union, Oct, 2, 1860.

39. Diary of a Union Lady. Hammond, HH. Ed. Bison Bks. New York. 1962.

Chapter 11

1. Irish for "My Beloved."

2. Irish for "Bright Vein of My Heart," which the poet, Doheny, is using as a pet name for Ireland.

3. Carrollton Daily Democrat, Feb 28, 1989.

4. Letter from Alice Pattison to Grace Peltier, Feb 16, 1938, in Carrollton Public Library.

5. Ibid

6. The Carrolls, an Anglo-Irish Catholic family, originally settled in Maryland near Baltimore in 1688. Charles, grandson of the original immigrants, had been an American patriot who signed the Declaration of Independence in 1776.

7. Letter from Alice Pattison to Grace Peltier, Feb 16, 1938, in Carrollton Public Library.

8. Republician=Record, Carrollton, Nov 17, 1910.

9. Shields letter to Rev. John J. Hogan Aug 9, 1869 in Carrollton Public Library.

10. Shields letter to Patrick Shields, Oct 3, 1873.

11. Shields letter to Patrick Shields, May 16, 1875.

12. Letter from Alice Pattison to Grace Peltier, Feb 16, 1938, in Carrollton Public Library. Both of the General's brothers had sons named Patrick and James. John, who visited from Ireland, was son the General's brother Patrick who started the Altmore Loan Fund in 1852 and lived in Altmore House. Litton was son of the General's other brother Daniel who lived in Barracktown House on Altmore mountain. Litton became a wealthy rail road contractor in St. Paul, Minn and died in 1933. He was present in the Minnesota Capitol when his daughter, Florence, unveiled the statue of General Shields in 1914. John, moved west to Utah and settled in Park City, where he became mayor. According to Judge Kevin O'Shiel "One of his sons, Dan B., a lawyer, was Attorney-General for Utah under the Woodrow Wilson regime."

13. Life of Major-General James Shields Hero Of Three Wars and Senator From Three States. Condon, WH. p 288. Blakley Printing Co. Chicago. 1900.

14. Ibid.
15. New York Times. Oct 16, 1866.
16. The oath required an individual to specify that he had never borne arms against the United States or exercised authority hostile to the Government. That was a tall order in post-Civil War Missouri.
17. Life of Major-General James Shields Hero Of Three Wars and Senator From Three States. Condon, WH. p 368. Blakley Printing Co. Chicago. 1900.
18. Ibid p 288 411
19. Ibid p 285/6.
20. Apparently Grant did not care much for Shields either. In his memoirs, Grant pointedly omitted mentioning, Shields even though the two had fought in Mexico. Grant spent so much time in the Hotel Washington across the street from the White House that people went there to see him and gave rise to the term "lobbyist."
21. Ibid p 292-95
22. The Felon's Track. A History of the Late Attempted Outbreak in Ireland, Doheny, M. Holbrook, NY. 1850.
23. Shields letter to Patrick Shields, Oct 3, 1873.
24. Shields letter to Patrick Shields, May 16th 1875.
25. Ibid
26. Republician=Record, Carrollton, Nov 17, 1910.
27. Life of Major-General James Shields Hero Of Three Wars and Senator From Three States. Condon, WH. Blakley Printing Co. Chicago. 1900.
28. Ibid
29. Shields letter to Patrick Shields, May 16th 1875.
30. Letter from Alice Pattison to Grace Peltier, Feb 16, 1938, in Carrollton Public Library.
31. ibid
32. Faribault Republican, Nov. 27, 1872.
33. Shields letter to Patrick Shields, Oct 3, 1873.
34. Faribault Republican, May 14, 1873. 412
35. Shields letter to Patrick Shields, Oct 3, 1873.
36. Blair had a checkered career. Before the war, he and his brother Montgomery were law partners in St. Louis and he served as Attorney General for the New Mexico Territory. Though his family owned slaves, he was instrumental in keeping Missouri in the Union in 1861. Appointed Maj-General by Lincoln without Senate approval, he fought at the Siege of Vicksburg. His irascible personality made him controversial in Missouri and across the country and doomed his family's long-held dream to elect him President.
37. Letter from Alice Pattison to Grace Peltier, Feb 16, 1938, in Carrollton Public Library. Charles was reportedly buried at Arlington National Cemetery but the Cemetery reported no record of him.
38. ibid
39. Ibid
40. Ibid
41. Johnson Memoirs p.40. Hist. Lib. Il. 1904.
42. Conrad in The Career of James Shields An Immigrant Irishman in Nineteenth

Century America. Ed. D. diss. p 219. Columbia Univ. Teachers College. Moran Curran, J. 1980.

43. History of Carroll County, p 497. St. Louis Hist. Co. 1881.

44. Life of Major-General James Shields Hero Of Three Wars and Senator From Three States. Condon, WH. p 281. Blakley Printing Co. Chicago. 1900.

45. Ibid p 281.

46. Brig-Gen Jas. Shields Monument Commission Record. p 49. Jan 30, 1913. Carrollton, MO. The reporter erroneously included Shields as being present at the Battle of Buena Vista when he had not.

47. St. Paul Dispatch in the Faribault Republican, Jan 23, 1878.

48. St. Paul Globe in the Faribault Democrat, April 12, 1878.

49. Faribault Democrat, Oct 11, 1878.

50. Life of Major-General James Shields Hero Of Three Wars and Senator From Three States. Condon, WH. p 272. Blakley Printing Co. Chicago. 1900. Memoirs of Gustave Koerner. ed Thomas J. McCormack (2 Vols) p 480. Torch Press, Cedar Rapids, IA. 1909. Hx of Sang. County. P102, Interstate Publishing Co. 1881

51. Ottumwa Weekly Courier, June 4, 1879.

52. St. Louis Republic Newspaper.

53. Letter from Alice Pattison to Grace Peltier, Feb 16, 1938, p 7 in Carrollton Public Library.

54. Carrollton Daily Democrat, June 9, 1879.

55. History of St. Mary's Catholic Church, Carrollton. Pattison, CR. Mss in Carrollton Public Library. 1938.

56. The New York Times.

57. The swords are now stored at the Armed Forces History Division of the National Museum of American History and may be viewed by special appointment. The museum is located between 12th & 14th Streets on Constitution Ave NW in Washington. DC.

58. Following the unveiling of the second Carrollton statue, C. M. Morrison, a reporter for the St. Louis *Republic* newspaper, on 13th November 1914, described the scene at the unveiling. Shields would probably have been among the first to chuckle at Morrison's amusing account. "It is not every pretty little country town that can claim the grave of a national hero, and in these last four years Carrollton has made the most of its opportunity" wrote Morrison. "I tells you, boss" said one of Carrollton's ancient and dusky citizens Thursday, as he watched the Third Regiment of the Missouri Guards swing through the square, "dis am the third time I've gone to that General man's funer-al. I was dar when they sho-nuff buried him, den I was out to that graveyard foah yeahs ago, when they had the big cannons heah, and we-all are buryin' him agin." This last "funer-al" was the most splendid of them all. Carrollton rose to its opportunity, and amid the thunder of salutes, the blare of regimental bands, and the outpourings of oratory from the representatives of three States, the big bronze figure presented by the State of Missouri was formally unveiled." (Republic newspaper. November 15, 1914.) The newspaper also noted that citizens in Kansas were thinking of erecting a statue of Shields in Swope Park, Kansas City. That statue never materialized.

59. The Career of James Shields, An Immigrant Irishman in Nineteenth Century America. Moran Curran, J. Ed. D. diss. p 223. Columbia Univ. Teachers College. NY 1980.

Footnotes

60. History of Sangamon County. p 102. Inter-State Publishing Co, Chicago. 1881.
61. This Irishman Made History. Myers, JE p 18/9, 38. American Legion Magazine, March 1977.

Appendix

Appendix A.

Letter to newspapers from Gov. Carlin, Auditor Shields and Treasurer Carpenter
suspending the use of State Bank bills for payment of taxes until further notice.
STATE REGISTER.
EXTRA.
SPRINGFIELD:
Monday, August 22, 1842

Executive Department Illinois,
August 15th, 1842.

We, the undersigned officers of the State being of the opinion that there will be danger of
loss by receiving the bills of the State Bank of Illinois and branches in payment of the
revenue of the state and of the different counties in the State for the year 1842 and in
payment of college, school, and seminary debts and interest, do hereby prohibit the
reception of said bills for the purposes aforesaid after the 12th day of September until
next otherwise provided by law.

Given under our hands the day and year above written.

Tho. Carlin, Gov.
Jas. Shields, Auditor
Milton Carpenter, Treas.

All the publishers of newspapers in this State are requested to publish the above notice
for three successive weeks and send their bills for the same to the Auditor's office.
Jas. Shields, Auditor.
****

Appendix B.

*Letter to state tax collectors from auditor Shields informing them of the Governor,
Treasurer's and his own decision to suspend the use of State Bank bills for payment of
taxes until further notice.*

AUDITOR'S OFFICE, ILLINOIS \
Springfield, August 20, 1842.

Appendix

To the collector of the County of:

DEAR SIR: The Governor, Auditor, and Treasurer have prohibited the reception of the bills of the State Bank of Illinois and branches in the payment of the revenue of 1842, and of debts due the school fund. The bills of the Bank of Illinois at Shawneetown would have been included in the prohibition also, if the law had only invested us with such powers. The object of this measure is to suspend the collection of the revenue for the current year, which would otherwise commence in September next, until the next Legislature may have an opportunity of acting on the subject. Without some such suspension act a large portion of the revenue of 1842, particularly that portion payable by non-resident land owners and large land companies would be paid to collectors before the meeting of the Legislature; and that body would be consequently prevented for the space of another year, not only from making any change in the system, but from dissolving the degrading connection now subsisting between the State and a bankrupt institution. The restoration of a sound currency which is so essentially needed at present in this State can only be effected by the joint efforts of the Government and the people, and the first step toward the accomplishment of this object, is the rejection of depreciated paper by the State. - It is folly to hope for a sound circulation while the Government is patronizing a worthless one. To prevent this change from operating oppressively the Legislature will have it in its power, by the reduction of salaries and the curtailment of all expenses not absolutely indispensible for the existence of Government, to make a material reduction in the taxes for the next two years.

By this means a sound currency can be gradually, though perhaps slowly, introduced without increasing the burdens of the people. The exigency of the present crisis requires a common sacrifice, and if it be wisely and firmly made, both by the people and their agents, a few years will suffice to lift our young State out of its present prostration. - Once more I take the liberty of repeating that the object and intention of the present notification is to suspend the collection of the revenue for the year 1842 until the meeting of the Legislature, at which time that body can provide for the payment of taxes in such funds as it may deem advisable, and effect such reduction in the amount of revenue as it may deem practicable.

Your obedient servant

JAS. SHIELDS, Auditor.

****

Appendix C.

First Rebecca of Lost Townships letter which Lincoln admitted writing.

Lost Townships, Aug. 27, 1842

Dear Mr. Printer:

I see you printed that long letter I sent you a spell ago - I'm quite encouraged by it, and can't keep from writing again. I think the printing of my letters will be a good thing all round, - it will give me the benefit of being known by the world and give the world the advantage of knowing what's going on in the Lost Townships and give your paper respectability beside. So here comes another. Yesterday afternoon I hurried through cleaning up the dinner dishes, and stopped over to neighbor S— to see if his wife Peggy was as well as might be expected, and hear what they called the baby. Well, when I got there, and just turned round the corner of his log cabin, there he was setting on the door-step reading a newspaper.

'How are you Jeff,' says I, - he sorter started when he heard me, for he hadn't seen me before. 'Why,' says he, 'I'm mad as the devil, aunt Becca.'

'What about,' says I, 'ain't his hair the right color? None of that nonsense, Jeff - there aint an honester woman in the Lost Township than - ' 'Than who?' says he, 'what the mischief are you about?' I began to see I was running the wrong trail, and so says I, 'O nothing, I guess I was mistaken a little, that's all. But what is it you're mad about?'

'Why' says he, I've been tugging ever since harvest getting out wheat and hauling it to the river, to raise State Bank paper enough to pay my tax this year, and a little school debt I owe; and now just as I've got it, here I open the infernal Extra Register, expecting to find it full of "glorious democratic victories," and "High Comb'd Cocks," when, lo and behold, I find a set of fellows calling themselves officers of State, have forbidden the tax collectors and school commissioners to receive State paper at all; and so here it is, dead on my hands. I don't now believe all the plunder I've got will fetch ready cash enough to pay my taxes and that school debt. 'I was a good deal thunderstruck myself; for that was the first I had heard of the proclamation, and my old man was pretty much in the same fix with Jeff. We both stood a moment staring at one another without knowing what to say. At last says I, 'Mr. S— let me look over at that paper.' He handed it to me, when I read the proclamation over. 'There now,' says he, 'did you ever see such a piece of impudence and imposition as that?' I saw Jeff was in a good tune for saying some illnatured things, and so I tho't I would just argue a little on the contrary side, and make him rant a spell if I could.

'Why,' says I, looking as dignified and thoughtful as I could, 'it seems pretty tough to be sure, to have to raise silver when there's none to be raised, but then you see "there will be danger of loss" if it aint done.' 'Loss, damnation!' says he, 'I defy Daniel Webster, I defy King Solomon, I defy even you, aunt Becca, to show how the people can lose any thing by paying their taxes in State paper.' 'Well,' says I 'you see what the officers of State say about it, and they are a desarnin set of men.' 'But,' says I, 'I guess you're mistaken about what the proclamation says; it don't say the people will lose anything by their paper money being taken for taxes. It only says "there will be danger of loss" and though it is tolerably plain that the people can't lose by paying their taxes in something they can get easier than silver, instead of having to pay silver; and though it is just as plain, that the State can't lose by taking State Bank paper, however low it may be, while she owes the Bank more than the whole revenue, and can pay that paper over her debt, dollar for dollar; still "there is danger of loss to the officers of State," and you know Jeff, we can't get along without "officers of State."

'Damn officers of State,' says he, 'that's what you whigs are always hurraing for.' 'Now don't swear so Jeff,' says I, 'you know I belong to the meetin, and swearin hurts my feelings.' 'Beg pardon, aunt Becca,' says he, 'but I do say its enough to make Dr. Goddard swear, to have tax to pay in silver, for nothing only that Ford may get his two thousand a year and Shields his twenty four hundred a year, and Carpenter his sixteen hundred a year, and all "without danger of loss" by taking it in State paper.' Wonder if we don't have a proclamation before long, commanding us to make up this loss to Wash in Silver.'

And so he went on, till his breath run out, and he had to stop. I couldn't think of anything to say just then; and so I begun to look over the paper again. 'Aye! Here's another proclamation, or something like it,' another! Says Jeff, 'and whose egg is it, pray?' I looked to the bottom of it, and read aloud, 'Your obedient servant, Jas Shields, Auditor.' 'Aha!' says Jeff 'one of them same three fellows again. Well read it, and let's hear what of it.' I read on till I came to where it says, "The object of this measure is to suspend the collection of the revenue for the current year." 'Now stop, now stop,' says he, 'that's a lie already, and I don't want to hear of it.' 'O may be not,' says I. "I say it-is-a-lie, - Suspend the collection, indeed! Will the collectors that have taken their oaths to make the collection dare to suspend it?' Is there anything in the law requiring them to perjure themselves at the bidding of Jas. Shields? Will the greedy gullet of the penitentiary be satisfied with swallowing him in stead of all of them if they should venture to obey him? And would he not discover some "danger of loss" and be off, about the time it came to taking their places? 'And suppose the people attempt to suspend by refusing to pay, what then? The collectors would just jerk up their horses, and cows, and the like, and sell them to the highest bidder for silver in hand, without valuation or redemption. Why, Shields didn't believe that story himself - it was never meant for the truth. If it was true, why was it not writ till five days after the proclamation? Why didn't Carlin and Carpenter sign it as well as Shields? Answer me that, aunt Becca. I say it is a lie, and not a well told one at that. It grins out like a copper dollar. Shields is a fool as well as a liar. With him truth is out of the question, and as for getting a good bright passable lie out of him, you might as well try to strike fire from a cake of tallow. I stick to it, its all an infernal whig lie.' 'A whig lie, - Highty! Tighty!!' 'Yes, a whig lie: and its just like everything the cursed British whigs do. First they'll do some devilment, and then they'll tell a lie to hide it. And they don't care how plain a lie it is; they think they can cram any sort of one down the throats of the ignorant loco focos, as they call the democrats.'

'Why, Jeff, you're crazy - you don't mean to say Shields is a whig?' 'Yes I do.' 'Why, look here, the proclamation is in your own democratic paper as you call it.' 'I know it and what of that? They only printed it to let us democrats see the deviltry the whigs are at.' 'Well, but Shields is the Auditor of this loco - I mean democratic State. 'So he is, and Tyler appointed him to office.' 'Tyler appointed him?' 'Yes (if you must chaw it over) Tyler appointed him, or if it wasn't him it was old Granny Harrison, and that's all one. I tell you aunt Becca, there's no mistake about him being a whig - why his very looks shows it - everything about him shows it - if I was deaf and blind I could tell him by the smell. I seed him when I was down in Springfield last winter. They had a sort of gatherin there one night, among the grandees, they called it a fair. All the galls about town was there, and all the handsome widows, and married women finickin about, trying to look like galls, tied as tight in the middle, and puffed out at both ends like bundles of fodder that hadn't been stacked yet, but wanted stacking pretty bad. And then they had tables all around the house kivered over with baby caps, and pin-cushions, and ten thousand such little nick-nacks, trying to sell 'em to the fellows that were bowin and scrapin, and kungeerin about 'em. They wouldn't let no democrats in, for fear they'd disgust the ladies, or scare the little galls, or dirty the floor. I looked in at the window, and there was this same fellow Shields floatin about on the air, without heft or earthly substance, just like a lock of cat-fur where cats had been fightin. He was paying his money to this one and that one, and tother one, and suffering great loss because it wasn't silver instead of State paper; and the sweet distress he seemed to be in, - his very features, in the ecstatic agony of his soul, spoke audibly and distinctly- "Dear girls, it is distressing, but I cannot marry you all. Too well I know how much you suffer; but do, do remember, it is not my fault that I am so handsome and so interesting." 'As this last was expressed by a most exquisite contortion of his face, he seized hold of one of their hands and squeezed, and held onto it about a quarter of an hour. O, my good fellow, says I to myself, if that was one of our democratic galls in the Lost Township, the way you'd get a brass pin let into you, would be about up to the head. He a democrat! Fiddle-sticks! I tell you aunt Becca, he's a whig, and no mistake; no body but a whig could make such a concity dunce of himself.'

'Well,' says I, 'may be he is, but if he is, I'm mistaken the worst sort.

'May be so; may be so; but if I am I'll suffer by it; I'll be a democrat if it turns out that Shields is a whig; considerin you shall be a whig if he turns out a democrat.' 'A bargain, by jingoes,' says he, 'but how will we find out.'

'Why,' says I, 'we'll just write and ax the printer.' 'Agreed again,' says he 'and by thunder if it does turn out that Shields is a democrat, I never will————'

'Jefferson, - Jefferson - ' 'What do you want, Peggy.' 'Do get through your everlasting clatter some time, and bring me a gourd of water; the child's been crying for a drink this live-long hour.'

'Let it die then, it may as well die for water as to be taxed to death to fatten officers of the State.' Jeff run off to get the water though, just like he hadn't been sayin anything any thing spiteful; for he's a rall good hearted fellow, after all, once you get at the foundation of him.

I walked into the house, and 'why Peggy,' says I, 'I declare, we like to forgot you altogether.' 'O yes,' says she, 'when a body can't help themselves, everybody soon forgets 'em; but thank God by day after tomorrow I shall be well enough to milk the cows and pen the calves, and wring the contrary one's tails for 'em and no thanks to nobody.' 'Good evening, Peggy' says I, and so I sloped, for I seed she was mad at me, for making Jeff neglect her so long.

And now Mr. Printer, will you be sure to let us know in your next paper whether this Shields is a whig or democrat? I don't care about it for myself, for I know well enough how it is already, but I want to convince Jeff. It may do some good to let him, and others like him, know who and what these officers of State are. It may help to send the present hypocritical set to where they belong, and to fill the places they now disgrace with men who will do more work, for less pay, and take a fewer airs while they are doing it. It ain't sensible to think that the same men who get us into trouble will change their course; and yet it is pretty plain, if some change for the better is not made, its not long that neither Peggy, or I, or any of us, will have a cow left to milk, or a calf's tail to wring.

Yours truly, Appendix

Rebecca————.

****

Appendix D.

Second Rebecca of Lost Townships letter apparently written by Mary Todd alone.

LOST TOWNSHIPS, SEPT. 8, 1842

Dear Mr. Printer: I was a standin at the spring yesterday a washin out butter, when I seed Jim Snooks a ridin up towards the house for very life like, when jist as I was a wonderin what on airth was the matter with him, he stops suddenly and ses he, aunt Becca, here's somethin for you, and with that he hands out your letter. Well you see I steps out towards him, not thinkin that I had both hands full of butter, and seein I couldn't take the letter you know without greasin it, I ses, Jim, jist you open it and read it before me. Well, Jim opens it and reads it; and would you believe it, Mr. Editor, I was so completely dumfounded and turned into stone, that there I stood in the sun, a workin the butter, and it arunnin on the ground while he read the letter, that I never thunk what I was about till the hull ont run melted on the ground and was lost. Now, sir, its not for the butter nor the price of the butter, but the Lord have massy on us, I wouldn't have sich another fright for a whole firkin of it. Why, when I found out that it was the man what Jeff seed down to the fair, that had demanded the author of my letters, threatnin to to take personal satisfaction of the writer, I was so skart that I tho't I should quill-wheel right where I was. You say that Mr. S. is offended at being compared to cat's fur, and is as mad a March hare, (that aint fur) because I told about the squeezin. Now I want to tell Mr. S. that rather than fight I'll make any apology, and if he wants personal satisfaction, let him only come here and he may squeeze my hand as I squeeze the butter, and if that ain't personal satisfaction, I can only say that he is the fust man that was not satisfied with squeezin my hand. If this should not answer, there is one thing more that I would do rather than get a lickin. I have all a long expected to die a widow, but as Mr. S. is rather good looking than otherwise, I must say I don't care if we compromise the matter by-really: Mr. Printer, I can't help blushin-but I- it must come out- I-but widowed modesty- well, if I must, I must- wouldn't he-may-be-sorter, let the old grudge drap if I was to consent to be-be-h-i-s-w-i-f-e? I know he's a fightin man, and would rather fight than eat; but isn't marrying better than fightin, though it does sometimes run into it? And I don't think upon the whole that I'd be sich a bad match neither-I'm not over sixty, and am just four feet three in my bare feet, and-not much more round the girth, and for color I wouldn't turn my back to any gal in the Lost Townships. But after all may-be I'm countin my chickins before they're hatched-and dreamin of matrimonial bliss when the only alternative reserved for me may be a lickin. Jeff tells me the way these fireeaters do is to give the challenged party choice of weapons, &c, which bein the case I'll tell you in confidence that I never fights with anything but broom-sticks or hot water, or a shovel full of coals, or some such thing: the former of which being somewhat like a shillalah, may not be very objectionable to him. I will give him choice, however, in one thing, and that is whether, when we fight, I shall wear breeches or the petticoats; for I presume that change is sufficient to place us on an equality.
Yours, & c,
REBECCA P. S. Jist say to your friend if he concludes to marry, rather than fight, I shall only inforce one condition, that is, if he should ever happen to gallant any young galls home of nights from our house, he must not squeeze their hands.
****

Appendix E.

FOR THE JOURNAL
Ye jews-harps awake! The A(uditor)'s won-
Rebecca the widow, has gained Erin's son.
The pride of the North from the emerald isle
Has been woo'd and won by a woman's sweet smile;
The combat's relinquished, old love's all forgot,
To the widow he's bound, oh! Bright be his lot
In the smiles of the conquest so lately achieved,
Joyful be his bride, 'widowed modesty' relieved
The footsteps of time tread lightly on flowers-
May the cares of this world neer darken their hours.
But the pleasures of life are fickle and coy
As the smiles of a maiden, sent oft to destroy;
Happy groom! In sadness far distant from thee
The FAIR girls dream only of past times of glee
Enjoyed in the presence, whilst the soft blarnied store
Will be fondly remembered as relics of yore,
And hands that in rapture you oft would have prest,
In prayer will be clasp'd that your lot may be blest.
Cathleen
****

Appendix F.

First Shields letter to Lincoln in Tremont requesting that he retract the offensive Rebecca letters.

Tremont, Sept 17, 1842
A. Lincoln, Esq.

I regret that my absence on public business compelled me to postpone a matter of private consideration a little longer than I could have desired. It will only be necessary, however, to account for it by informing you that I have been to Quincy on business that would not admit of delay. I will now state briefly the reasons of my troubling you with this communication, the disagreeable nature of which I regret - as I had hoped to avoid any difficulty with anyone in Springfield while residing there, by endeavoring to conduct myself in such a way amongst my political friends and opponents, as to escape the necessity of any. Whilst thus abstaining from giving provocation, I have become the object of slander, vituperation and personal abuse, which were I capable of submitting to, I would prove myself worthy of the whole of it.
In two or three of the last numbers of the Sangamo Journal, articles of the most personal nature and calculated to degrade me, have made their appearance. On inquiring I was informed by the editor of that paper, through the medium of my friend, Gen. Whiteside, that you are the author of those articles. This information satisfies me that I have become by some means or other the object of your secret hostility. I will not take

the trouble of inquiring into the reason of all this, but I will take the liberty of requiring a full, positive and absolute retraction of all offensive allusions used by you in these communications, in relation to my private character and standing as a man, as an apology for the insults conveyed in them.

This may prevent consequences which no one will regret more than myself.

Your ob't serv't
Jas. Shields.
****

Appendix G.

First Lincoln response to Shields letter in Tremont.

Tremont, Sept. 17, 1842
Jas. Shields, Esq.

Your note of today was handed to me by Gen. Whiteside. In that note you say you have been informed, through the medium of the editor of the Journal, that I am the author of certain articles in that paper which you deem personally abusive of you: without stopping to enquire whether I really am the author, or to point out what is offensive in them, you demand an unqualified retraction of all that is offensive; and then proceed to hint at consequences.

Now, sir, there is in this so much assumption of facts, and so much of menace as to consequences, that I cannot submit to answer that note any farther than I have, and to add, that the consequence to which I suppose you allude, would be a matter of great regret to me as it possibly could to you.

Respectfully,
A. Lincoln.
****

Appendix H

Second Shields letter to Lincoln in Tremont asking if Lincoln was the author of the Rebecca letters and, if he was, that he withdraw the allegations about Shields' character contained in them.

Tremont, Sept 17, 1842
A. Lincoln, Esq.

In reply to my note of this date, you intimate that I assume facts, and menace consequences and that you cannot submit to answer it further. As now, sir, you desire it, I will be a little more particular. The editor of the Sangamo Journal gave me to understand you are the author of an article which appeared I think in that paper on the 2nd of Sept. inst., headed the Lost Townships and signed Rebecca or Becca. I would therefore take the liberty of asking whether you are the author of said article or any other over the same signature, which has appeared in any of the late numbers of that paper. If so, I repeat my request of an absolute retraction of all offensive allusion contained therein in relation to my private character and standing. If you are not the author of any of the articles your denial will be sufficient. I will say further it is not my intention to menace but to do myself justice.

Your ob't serv't
Jas. Shields.

****

Appendix I.

Lincoln two part letter from Springfield; the first admitting he wrote one of Rebecca letters and the second stating terms and conditions for the duel.

September 19, 1842.

In case Whitesides shall signify a wish to adjust this affair without further difficulty, let him know that if the present papers be withdrawn, and a note from Mr. Shields asking to know if I am the author of the articles of which he complains, and asking that I shall make him gentlemanly satisfaction, if I am that author, and this without menace, or dictation as to what that satisfaction shall be, a pledge is made that the following answer shall be given-
I did write the 'Lost Township' letter which appeared in the Journal of the 2nd. Inst., but had no participation, in any form, in any other article alluding to you. I wrote that purely for political effect. I had no intention of injuring your personal or private character or standing as a man or a gentleman; and I did not then think, and do not now think that article could produce or has produced that effect on you, and had I anticipated such an effect I would have forborne to write it. And I will add that your conduct towards me, so far as I knew, has always been gentlemanly; and that I had no personal pique against you, and no cause for any.
If this should be done, I leave it with you what shall and what shall not be published.
If nothing like this is done - the preliminaries of the fight are to be-
1st. Weapons - Cavalry broad swords of the largest size, precisely equal in all respects - and such as now used by the cavalry company at Jacksonville.
2nd. Position - A plank ten feet long, & from nine to twelve inches broad to be firmly fixed on edge, on the ground, as the line between us which neither is to pass his foot over upon forfeit of his life. Next a line drawn on the ground on either side of said plank and parallel to it, each at the distance of the whole length of the sword and three feet additional from the plank; and the passing of his own such line by either party during the fight shall be deemed a surrender of the contest.
3rd. Time - On Thursday evening at five o'clock if you can get it so; but in no case to be at a greater distance of time than Friday evening at five o'clock
4th. Place - Within three miles of Alton on the opposite side of the river, at the particular spot to be agreed on by you.
Any preliminary details coming within the above rules you are at liberty to make at your discretion; but you are in no case to swerve from these rules, or to pass beyond their limits.
****

Appendix

Appendix J.

Hardin and English letter written at Bloody Island suggesting that the dispute between Lincoln and Shields be referred to a mutually agreeable panel of gentlemen for resolution.

Alton, Sept 22, 1842

Messrs. Whiteside and Merriman: As the mutual personal friends of Messrs. Shields and Lincoln, but without authority from either, we earnestly desire a reconciliation of the misunderstanding which exists between them. Such difficulties should always be arranged amicably, if it is possible to do so, with honor, to both parties. Believing ourselves that such arrangements can possibly be effected, we respectfully but earnestly submit the following proposition for your consideration: Let the whole difficulty be submitted to four or more gentlemen, to be selected by yourselves, who shall consider the affair, and report thereon for your consideration.

John J. Hardin,
R.W. English.

****

Appendix K.

One of several eyewitness accounts of what transpired during negotiations on Bloody Island.

"I watched Lincoln closely while he sat on a log awaiting the signal to fight. His face was grave and serious. I could discern nothing suggestive of 'Old Abe,' as we knew him. I never knew him to go so long before without making a joke, and I believe he was getting frightened. But presently he reached over and picked up one of the swords, which he drew from its scabbard. Then he felt along the edge of the weapon with his thumb, like a barber feels the edge of his razor, raised himself to his full height, stretched out his long arms and clipped off a twig from above his head with the sword. There wasn't another man of us who could have reached anywhere near that twig, and the absurdity of that long-reaching fellow fighting with cavalry sabers with Shields, who could walk under his arm, came pretty near making me howl with laughter. After Lincoln had cut off the twig he returned the sword to the scabbard with a sigh and sat down, but I detected the gleam in his eye, which was always the forerunner of one of his inimitable yarns, and fully expected him to tell a side-splitter there in the shadow of the grave - Shields's grave.

****

Appendix L.

Letter from Whiteside ten days after the episode describing the sequence of events leading up to the near duel and how the matter got resolved.

Springfield, Oct 3, 1842

To the Editor of "The Sangamon Journal."

Sir -, To prevent misrepresentation of the recent affair between Messrs. Shields and Lincoln, I think it proper to give a brief narrative of the facts of the case as they came within my knowledge; for the truth of which I hold myself responsible, and request you to give the same publication. An offensive article in relation to Mr. Shields appeared in "The Sangamon Journal", of the second of September last, and, on demanding the author, Mr. Lincoln was given up by the editor. Mr. Shields, previous to this demand, made arrangements to go to Quincy on public business; and before his return Mr. Lincoln had left for Tremont to attend court with the intention of as we learned, of remaining on the circuit several weeks. Mr. Shields, on his return, requested me to accompany him to Tremont; and, on arriving there. We found that Dr. Merryman and Mr. Butler had passed us in the night, and got there before us.

We arrived in Tremont on the 17th ult; and Mr. Shields addressed a note to Mr. Lincoln immediately informing him that he was given up as the author of some articles that appeared in "The Sangamon Journal", (one more, over the signature having made its appearance at this time), and requested him to retract the offensive allusions contained in said articles in relation to his private character. Mr. Shields handed me this note to deliver to Mr. Lincoln, and directed me, at the same time, not to enter into any verbal communication, or be the bearer of any verbal explanation, as such were always liable to misapprehension. The note was delivered by me to Mr. Lincoln, stating at the time, that I would call at his convenience for an answer.

Mr. Lincoln, in the evening of the same day, handed me a letter addressed to Mr. Shields. In this he gave or offered no explanation, but stated therein that he could not submit answer further, on the ground that Shields's note contained an assumption of facts and also a menace. Mr. Shields then addressed him another note, in which he disavowed all intention to menace, and requested to know whether he (Mr. Lincoln) was the author of either of the articles which appeared in "The Journal" headed "Lost Townships and signed "Rebecca and if so, he repeated his request for a retraction of the offensive matter in relation to his private character; if not, his denial would be held sufficient. This letter was returned to Mr. Shields, unanswered, with a verbal statement, "that there could be no further negotiations with Mr. Shields until first note was withdrawn."

Mr. Shields then sent a note designating me as his friend to which Mr. Lincoln replied by designating Dr. Merryman. These last three notes passed on Monday morning, the 19th.

Dr. Merryman handed me Mr. Lincoln's note when by ourselves (Line missing) …that I would propose that he and myself should pledge our words and honor to each other to try to agree upon terms of amicable agreement, and compel our principles to accept them. To this we readily assented and we shook hands upon the pledge. It was then mutually agreed that we should adjourn to Springfield and there procrastinate the matter, for the purpose of affecting a secret arrangement between him and myself. All this I kept concealed from Mr. Shields

Our horse had got a little lame in going to Tremont and Dr. Merryman invited me to take a seat in his buggy. I accepted the invitation more readily as I thought that leaving Mr. Shields in Tremont until the horse would be in better condition to travel would facilitate the private agreement between Dr. Merryman and myself. I traveled to Springfield part of the way with him and part of the way with Mr. Lincoln; but nothing passed between us on the journey in relation to the matter at hand. We arrived in Springfield on Monday night, about noon on Tuesday, to my astonishment, a proposition was made to meet in Missouri within three miles of Alton on the next Thursday! The weapons, cavalry broadswords of the largest size; the parties to stand on each side of a barrier, and to be confined to a limits space. As I had not been consulted at all on the subject, and considering the private understanding between Dr. Merryman and myself, and it being known that Mr. Shields being left in Tremont, such a proposition took me by surprise. However, being determined not to violate the law of the state, I declined agreement upon terms until we should meet in Missouri. Immediately after, I called upon Dr. Merryman and withdrew the pledge of honor between him and myself in relation to the secret agreement. I started after this to meet Mr. Shields and met him about twenty miles from Springfield. It was late on Tuesday night when we both reached the city and learned that Dr. Merryman had left for Missouri, Mr. Lincoln having left before the proposition was made as Dr. Merryman himself had informed me. The time and place made it necessary to start at once. We left Springfield at eleven o'clock on Tuesday night and traveled all night and arrived in Hillsborough on Wednesday morning, where we took in General Ewing.

From there we went to Alton where we arrived on Thursday; and as the proposition required three friends on each side, I was joined by Gen Ewing and Dr. Hope, as the friends of Mr. Shields; we then crossed to Missouri where a proposition was made by Gen Hardin and Dr. English (who had arrived there in the meantime as mutual friends) to refer the matter to I think, four friends for a settlement; this I believed Mr. Shields would refuse, and declined seeing him; but Dr. Hope who conferred with him on the subject, returned and stated that Mr. Shields declined settling the matter through any other than the friends he had selected to stand by him on that occasion. The friends of both parties finally agreed to withdraw the papers (temporarily) to give the friends of Mr. Lincoln an opportunity to explain. Whereupon the friends of Mr. Lincoln, to wit: Messrs. Merryman, Bledsoe and Butler, made a full and satisfactory explanation in relation to the articles which appeared in "The Sangamon Journal", of the 2nd, the only one written by him. This was all done without the knowledge or consent of Mr. Shields; and he refused to accept it until Dr. Hope, Gen Ewing and myself declared the apology sufficient and that we could not sustain him in going any further. I think it necessary to state further that no explanation or apology had been previously offered on the part of Mr. Lincoln to Mr. Shields and that none was ever communicated to him by me, nor was any ever offered unless a paper read to me by Dr. Merryman after he had handed me the broadswords proposition on Tuesday. I heard so little of the reading of the paper that I do not know fully what it purported to be, and I was inclined to inquire, as to Mr. Lincoln was then gone to Missouri, and Mr. Shields had not yet arrived from Tremont. In fact, I could not entertain any offer of the kind unless upon my own responsibility; and that I was not disposed to do after what had already transpired.

I make this statement as I am about to be absent for some time, and I think it due to all concerned to give a true version of the matter before I leave.

Your obedient servant,
John D. Whiteside.

****

Appendix M.

Eyewitness accounts of Lincoln and Shields getting along amicably following their potentially deadly confrontation.

"We all returned on Chapman's ferry boat. On the way across the river Jake Smith, then City Marshal, about the same height and shape of Lincoln, was laid on the bows of the boat. Three or four with their coats off were fanning them with their hats. I stood near Lincoln and Shields, who were talking. They had become quite friendly again. The latter remarked to Lincoln, 'As that fellow on the bench is about your size, they will think it was you. I did not hear Lincoln's reply…" (The Life of Abraham Lincoln. I. Tarbell, IM.p.218 McClure, Phillips & Co. NY 1928)

A second eyewitness account of same from the riverbank stated that Smith had not really been injured and was merely playing a joke: "It was not very long until the boat was seen returning to Alton. As it drew near I saw what was presumably a mortally wounded man lying in the bow of the boat. His shirt appeared to be bathed in blood. I distinguished Jacob Smith, a constable fanning the supposed victim vigorously. The people on the bank held their breath in suspense, and guesses were feebly made as to which of the two men had been so terribly wounded. But suspense soon turned to chagrin and relief when it transpired that the supposed candidate for another world was nothing more or less than a log covered with a red shirt. The ruse had been resorted to in order to fool the people on the levee; and it worked to perfection. Lincoln and Shields came off the boat together, chatting in a nonchalant but pleasant manner." (The Life of Abraham Lincoln. I, Tarbell, IM p.219. McClure, Phillips & Co. NY 1928)

****

Appendix N.

Letter from Shields seconds noting withdrawal of Shields' original letters and requesting that Lincoln provide an explanation for the Rebecca letters. Letter notes that issue was defused by the intervention of Hardin and English.

Missouri, Sept 22, 1842

Gentlemen: - All papers in relation to the matter in controversy between Mr. Shields and Mr. Lincoln, having being withdrawn by the friends of the parties concerned, the friends of Mr. Shields ask the friends of Mr. Lincoln to explain the offensive matter in the articles which appeared in the Sangamo Journal of the 2nd, 9th and 16th of September, over the signature of Rebecca and headed 'Lost Township.'
It is due to Gen. Hardin and Mr. English to state that their interference was of the most courteous and gentlemanly character.

John D. Whiteside
Wm. Lee D. Ewing,

T. M. Hope.

****

Appendix O.

Letter from Lincoln seconds admitting that Lincoln had written first Rebecca letter but he had not meant to harm Shields character. Letter also notes that Hardin and English had helped resolve the matter.

Missouri, Sept. 22, 1842

Gentlemen: All papers in relation to the matter in controversy between Mr. Lincoln and Mr. Shields having been withdrawn by the friends of the parties concerned, we, the undersigned, friends of Mr. Lincoln, in accordance with your request, that an explanation of Mr. Lincoln's publication in relation to Mr. Shields in the Sangamo Journal of the 2nd, 9th and 16th of September, be made, take pleasure in saying that although Mr. Lincoln was the writer of the article signed Rebecca in the Journal of the 2nd, and that only, yet he had no intention of injuring the personal or private character or standing of Mr. Shields as a gentleman or a man, and that Mr. Lincoln did not think, nor does he now think, that said article could produce such an effect, and had Mr. Lincoln anticipated such an effect he would have forborne to write it; we will further state that said article was written solely for political effect, and not to gratify any personal pique against Mr. Shields, for he had none, and knew of no cause for any.
It is due to Gen. Hardin and Mr. English to say that their interference was of the most courteous and gentlemanly character.

E. H. Merriman,
A. T. Bledsoe, Wm. Butler.

****

Appendix P.

Letter from Gustave Koerner to Century magazine in April, 1887 defending Shields after Shields actions had been distorted by Lincoln biographer Nicolay in previous issue of magazine.

To THE EDITOR (Century Magazine):
As a friend of the late General Shields, who has intimately known him from the time he made his first appearance in Illinois until his death a few years ago, I trust to your known impartiality for allowing me to make a few observations on the harsh judgment which the biographers of President Lincoln have passed on the character of General Shields in the January number of THE CENTURY.
Shields, while under age, came to this country, either at the instance or under the auspices of an uncle who settled in South Carolina. After reaching manhood he went North teaching school,— the beginning of so many of our most distinguished politicians and even statesmen. In 1835 or 1836 he opened a school at Kaskaskia which, though it had ceased to be the capital of the State, was still the residence of a highly intellectual and polished society. There lived the families of Elias K. Kane, then United States Senator from Illinois; of the eminent Judge Nathaniel Pope, United States District Judge; of the

able lawyer David J. Baker, of William and Robert Morrison, of Governor Menard, of the Maxwells, and of many other prominent citizens.

General Shields had not received a thorough classical education; but he had some knowledge of Latin and French. He was an excellent English scholar, familiar with the best literature of England and America, and had a more than usual knowledge of history, particularly of that of modern times.

He was quick of perception, lively in conversation, ardent but by no means as touchy and irascible as the biographers represent him. His vanity was indeed inordinate, really so much so that it rather became amusing than offensive. The best evidence of his being an honorable gentleman and a man of superior parts, was that he was most kindly received and made much of in the families I have mentioned. Judge Pope was his most particular patron and spoke kindly and highly of him to the day of his death. Judge Breese, who had, however, left Kaskaskia shortly before, became well acquainted with him somewhat later, on the circuit, and formed as much of friendship for him at that time as lay in his nature. And what is a most remarkable circumstance, all these Kaskaskia people without exception were strong Whigs while Shields was a Democrat, though never a radical one. He did not seek to rise in his party, as a great many men of small caliber do, by professing ultra views, and to a certain extent be even despised popularity.

There was a special session of the Legislature called in 1837 owing to the suspension of our banks and to the embarrassment growing out of the monstrous system of internal improvements shortly before adopted by the State.

In the representation of Randolph County a vacancy had taken place, and Shields, though a Democrat, was elected in a county then largely Whig, he receiving the support of Judge Pope, David J. Baker, and other leading Whigs. Hardly any Irishmen were then living in that county. It was largely inhabited by French people, amongst whom Shields was always well liked for his vivacity and probably also for his knowledge of their language. Surely he was not put up as a candidate on account of his nationality. In the Legislature he made many warm friends and was considered an able reasoner and debater. He had studied law probably before he came to Illinois, continued it here, and was in fact very well grounded in the principles of law— rather more so than most of his rivals then at the bar. He argued closely and to the point, was much stronger before the court than before the jury, as he had not the gift of the gab, and hardly ever tried to be rhetorical or pathetic. When he did try, it was generally a bad failure. His language was always chaste and grammatically correct. He had a subtle and logical mind, though his impulsiveness made him sometimes act very illogically. He was ambitious, so much so that many people judged him to be too selfish. I, however, know of a great many instances when he acted very generously, and forgetful of himself. Very few ambitious men are free from the charge of egotism. He was careless about money matters and not the least avaricious. In 1837, at the instance of the late A. W. Snyder, then a member of Congress, who had taken a great liking to Shields, he settled in Belleville, Illinois, as a lawyer, and, forming a partnership, entered on a very successful practice. Traveling the then very large circuit, he became well known in all southern Illinois, and his sociability, warm temperament, sprightly and intelligent conversation made him hosts of friends. While he himself delighted in being flattered he took occasionally good advantage of the same weakness in others.

In Belleville he soon made many friends, particularly amongst the educated Germans, who found his conversation interesting and cosmopolitan. There were few Irishmen then in that county, and he was not particularly popular amongst those few.

His election for State Auditor in 1840, by the Legislature, was owing to the fact that he knew most of the members personally, to his social qualities, and to his reputation of an able and honest man. It is just barely possible that his nationality may have had some influence with some of the politicians; but it was his tact, and the friendship of Douglas, who was then Secretary of State, and of other leading Democrats, such as General Whiteside and Colonel W. H. Bissell late Governor of Illinois, that made him successful. As regards the contemplated duel with Lincoln, the biographers remark very rightly: "We have reason to think that the whole affair was excessively distasteful to Lincoln. He did not even enjoy the ludicrousness of it, as might have been expected." It could not fail that the noble-hearted and eminently just Lincoln would, as soon as he was out of the hands of his ill-advising friend, most deeply regret this episode of his life.

The articles, for which Mr. Lincoln had made himself generously responsible, "covered," as the biographers themselves say, "Mr. Shields with merciless personal ridicule." But they also charged him, together with Governor Carlin and Treasurer Campbell, who had instructed the Collectors of the State revenue not to receive the almost worthless bank paper for payment of State taxes, with the most sordid motives. No man of the least spirit could have taken those insults without seeking satisfaction, even by arms, if necessary. Dueling, particularly amongst public men, had at that time not so much faded out of fashion, either in England or in our country, as at present, and is not yet sunk into entire oblivion. The provocation was of the strongest, and no blame attached to Shields at the time. It is no proof of Shields's irascibility. He was a young man who had his reputation for honesty at stake; and to have in addition his personal features and peculiar habits ridiculed in a small but select society in which he daily moved was more than even a saint could have borne. But there was another reason why, as the biographers say, "Lincoln would have been glad to banish the matter from his memory." Both parties had been very unfortunate in the choice of their "friends." General Whiteside was a very brave man; he had seen some service in the Black Hawk War and was a good Indian-fighter. But he was no better qualified to manage an "affair of honor" than Black Hawk himself. Whatever the pretensions of Dr. Merryman might have been, he certainly was equally ignorant of the "code of honor," the first and foremost rule of which is that the combatants should, as much as possible, meet on an equal footing. Air and sun must be equally divided.

Mr. Shields was just about of medium height, of light weight at the time, by no means strong; while Mr.Lincoln was of towering height, heavy, and long armed, and of almost superhuman muscular strength.

In this respect the choice of arms, "cavalry broad-swords of the heaviest caliber," undoubtedly suggested by the Doctor, was an unfair one. The only excuse for him, and after all a bad one, might have been this, that as a friend of Lincoln he wanted to prevent a duel at all, and so he would propose such a sort of a fight as would bluff off Shields. But if he thought so, which is a mere surmise of the writer, he did not know the man Shields. But it would have been the duty of Whiteside to decline peremptorily such a combat, and to insist on pistols, a weapon with the use of which both parties might have been supposed to be somewhat acquainted, or with which by a few days' practice they could have familiarized themselves. Another rule of the code is that no unusual weapons must be used. Now, outside of army officers or students on the continent of Europe who are more or less trained in fencing-schools, the saber, or even the small sword, is never resorted to in dueling, and even with those classes pistols are the more customary arms. Amongst civilians it is an unheard-of thing. I am almost sure that Mr. Lincoln never before had handled a heavy cavalry sword; I am certain that Shields never had. If the duel had taken place, it would have been a ludicrous as well as a brutal affair. In the hands of novices a somewhat crooked heavy cavalry sword becomes no better than a flail or a stick. The strokes intended to cut head, shoulder, or breast in nine cases out of ten fall flat, and may knock a man down without ever drawing blood. The blame of this opera-bouffe affair falls properly on the seconds. It is plain, however, that none attached to Shields.

The letter to Judge Breese referred to is clearly indefensible. It was the worst mistake in Shields's life, though, strange to say, it did not hurt him with his constituents; for while he was rejected by the Senate on account of lack of constitutional qualification when he first offered himself in March, 1849, the moment that disqualification ceased, October, 1849, be was reelected Senator by the Legislature, called at a special session for that purpose. He seemed to have lost his head entirely on that occasion. He had been naturalized in 1840, in September, I believe. At the December session of Congress, 1849, he would have been a citizen of nine years' standing. But he hastened to Washington soon after his election, and presented his credentials in the Senate, which had been called for an extra session for Executive purposes after the 4th of March. An objection was made to his qualifications and sustained. The letter was written to frighten off Judge Breese from having the objection raised. Whatever his motive he committed an abominable error.

When in 1844 Governor Ford appointed Mr. Shields one of the Judges of the Supreme Court to fill a vacancy, it was surely not on account of his being an Irishman. Ford was not that sort of a man. He never cared about popularity. He only looked to the qualification of his appointees. Shields filled the office to the satisfaction of the people, and the few opinions he wrote during his short stay on the bench are lucid and forcible. As Logan in the civil war, so Shields in the Mexican war, was the most distinguished volunteer General. Severely wounded, when leading his Illinois Brigade at Cerro Gordo he led the Palmetto and another regiment with distinction at Contreras and received at the storming of Chapultepec a most painful and slowly healing wound in his right wrist. In the civil war he was again wounded in the arm by a ball at Winchester. He was not a great strategist, nor even a tactician; but he was always found in front, and the soldiers liked to follow him.

He may in older days have indulged too much in reminiscences of his former feats of arms, but there are few old soldiers who are not guilty of such a charge. The writer was very near him for several years after the Mexican war, and is not aware that he ever unduly prided himself on his military performances.

He was naturally very much opposed to slavery. It was with great reluctance he voted for the Kansas-Nebraska bill. But Mr. Douglas, his colleague in the Senate, had much influence over him, Douglas having always nobly supported him. He had taken the view which Mr. Webster had promulgated in his celebrated speech, that slavery could not exist in either of the territories, from climatic and other causes that nature had ordained, and that therefore the repeal of the Missouri Compromise could do no harm.

Earthly goods he never acquired. Before the generosity of Congress, not long before his end, relieved him, he spent many years in actual poverty. His mind, while eccentric, sometimes erratic, was essentially of a lofty nature. He could not have risen to all the high stations he filled except by some intrinsic merits. Were it otherwise, not he, but those who elected him; would have to bear the blame.

BELLEVILLE, ILLINOIS. Gustav Koerner.

(Century Magazine, p 973. 33:6. Apr. 1887.)

****

Appendix Q.

Letter in Alton newspaper defending Butler and poking fun at Shields for being so duel-happy.

October 5, 1842

Challenging to mortal combat is not uncommon here just now. The Auditor on Monday evening sent one of your satisfaction notes to Mr. Butler, the author of two of Rebecca's epistles to the Journal. Butler did not demur- appointed the next (Tuesday) morning-at sunrise for the meeting, at Allen's meadow, near the timber, with rifles-45 yards-firing to continue until one of the parties fell dead, or was disabled by wounds to level his piece. The Auditor declined the terms as it would be such a violation of the laws of the State as would deprive him of his office. Yesterday, Gen. Whiteside sent a sort of billet-doux challenge-not exactly a challenge but having an awful squinting that way-for something growing out of the mornings proceedings, to Dr. Merryman. The Doctor, nothing loathe, took the hint, named pistols, and Louisiana, a little town opposite Quincy, for the meeting. The General preferred Planter's House, St. Louis, to settle preliminaries and thereabouts for the duel. How the matter stands now (10 o'clock, P. M.) or whether it has flown over, can't say. A street fight was expected this Morning:- there was terrible out-goings-nothing as yet, however has disturbed the peace. The name of the author on the "Lines" of the marriage of Rebecca and the Auditor was demanded.-Miss M. T. [Mary Todd wrote them in the Parlor of her friend, Miss J. J. [Julia Jayne] for fun. The latter snatched them and sent them to the printer. No challenge will be sent in this case, the author being female-the code does not require it.

Oct. 6; half past six morning-have just been around the square
- saw written notices stuck up of blank challenges for sale at Auditor's office. It is thought and I think there is a good prospect, that all our *honorable* affairs or rather our affairs of honor, will end in *fuma*."

****

Appendix R.

Alton newspaper editorial recommending that Lincoln and Shields be criminally prosecuted for agreeing to duel, thereby breaking Illinois law.

"We consider that these gentlemen have both violated the laws of the country and insist that neither their influence, their respectability nor their private worth should save them from being made amenable to those laws they have violated. Both of them are lawyers - both have been legislators of the State and aided in the construction of laws for the protection of society - both exercise no small influence in community - all of which, in our estimation aggravates instead of mitigating their offence.... Among the catalogue of crime that disgraces the land, we look upon none to be more aggravated and less excusable than that of duelling. It is the calmest, most deliberate, and malicious species of murder - a relict of the most cruel barbarism that ever disgraced the darkest periods of the world and one which every principle of religion, virtue and good order, loudly demands should be put a stop to. This can be done only by a firm and unwavering enforcement of the law, in regard to dueling, towards all those who so far forget the obligations they are under to society and the laws which protect them as to violate its provisions. And until this is done, until the civil authorities have the moral courage to discharge their duty and enforce the law in this respect, we may frequently expect to witness the same disgraceful scenes that were acted in our city last week. Upon a former occasion, when under somewhat similar circumstances our city was visited, we called upon the Attorney General to enforce the law, and bring the offenders to justice. Bills of indictment were preferred against the guilty...

The offenders in this instance, as in the former, comitted the violation of the law in Springfield, and we again call upon Mr. Attorney General Lamborn, to exercise a little of that zeal which he is continually putting in requisition against less favored but no less guilty offenders, and bring ALL who have been concerned in the late attempt at assassination to justice. Unless he does it, he will prove himself unworthy of the high trust that has been reposed in him.

How the affair finally terminated, not having taken the trouble to inquire, we are unable to say. The friends of Mr. Shields and Mr. Lincoln claim it to have been settled upon terms alike honorable to both, not withstanding the hundred rumours — many of which border on the ridiculous — that are in circulation. We are rejoiced that both were permitted to return to the bosom of their friends and trust that they will now consider, if they did not do it before, that rushing unprepared upon the untried scenes of Eternity, is a step too fearful in its consequences to be undertaken without preparation." [Alton Telegraph and Review. Oct 1, 1842]

****

Appendix S.

Extract from Belle Boyd in Camp and Prison, in which Miss Belle describes how she spied on Shields for the South.

When I found that the Confederate forces were retreating so far down the Valley, and reflected that my father was with, I became very anxious to return to my mother; and, as no tie of duty bound me to Front Royal, I resolved upon the attempt at all hazards.

I started in company with my maid, and had got safely without adventure of any kind as far as Winchester when some unknown enemy or some malicious neutral denounced me to the authorities as a Confederate spy.

Before, however, this act of hostility or malice had been perpetrated, I had taken the precaution of procuring a pass from General Shields; and I fondly hoped that this would, under all circumstances, secure me from molestation and arrest; for I was not aware that, while I was in the very act of receiving my bill of "moral health," an order was being issued by the Provost Marshal which forbade me to leave the town.

When the hour which I had fixed for my departure arrived, I stepped into the railway-cars, and was congratulating myself with the thought that I should ere long be at home once more, and in the society of those I loved, when a Federal officer, Captain Bannon, appeared. He was in charge of some Confederate prisonrs, who, under his command, were en route to the Baltimore prison. I was more surprised than pleased when, handing over the prisoners to a subordinate, he walked straight up to me, and said:
"Is this Miss Belle Boyd?
"Yes."
"I am the Assistant-Provost, and I regret to say, orders have been issued for your detention, and it is my duty to inform you that you cannot proceed until your case has been investigated; so you will, if you please, get out, as the train is on the point of starting."
"Sir," I replied, presenting him General Shields's pass, "here is a pass which I beg you will examine. You will find that it authorizes my maid and myself to pass on any road to Martinsburg."
He reflected for sometime, and at last said:
"Well, I scarcely know how to act in your case. Orders have been issued for your arrest, and yet you have a pass from the General allowing you to return home. However, I shall take the responsibility upon my shoulders, convey you with the other prisoners to Baltimore, and hand you over to General Dix.
I played my role of submission as gracefully as I could; for where resistance is impossible, it is still left to the vanquished to yield with dignity.
The train by which we travelled was the first that had been run through from Wheeling to Baltimore since the damage done to the permanent way by the Confederates had been repaired.
We had not proceeded far when I observed an old friend of mine, Mr. M., of Baltimore, a gentleman whose sympathies were strongly enlisted on the side of the South. At my request, he took a seat beside me, and, after we had conversed for some time upon different topics, he told me, in a whisper, that he had a small Confederate flag concealed about his person.
"Manage to give it me," I said; "I am already a prisoner; besides, free or in chains, I shall always glory in the possession of the emblem."
Mr. M. watched his opportunity, and, when all eyes were turned from us, he stealthily and quickly drew the little flag from his bosom, and placed it in my hand.
We had eluded the vigilance of the officer under whose surveillance I was travelling; and I leave my readers to imagine his surprise when I drew it forth from my pocket, and, with a laugh, waved it over our heads with a gesture of triumph.
It was a daring action, but my captivity had, I think, superadded the courage of despair to the hardihood I had already acquired in my country's service. The first emotions of the Federal officer and his men were those of indignation; but better feelings succeeded, and they allowed it was an excellent joke, that a convoy of Confederate prisoners should be brought in under a Confederate flag, and that flag raised by a lady.
Upon our arrival at Baltimore, I was taken to the Eutaw House, one of the largest and best hotels in the city, where, I must in justice say, I was treated with all possible courtesy and consideration, and permission to see my friends was at once and spontaneously granted. As soon as it was known that I was in Baltimore, a prisoner and alone, I was

visited, not merely by my personal friends, but by those who knew me by reputation only; for Baltimore is Confederate to its heart's core.

I remained a prisoner in the Eutaw House about a week; at the expiration of which time, General Dix the officer in command, having heard nothing against me, decided to send me home. I arrived safely at Martinsburg, which is now occupied in force by the Federal troops.

Here I was placed under a strict surveillance, and forbidden to leave the town. I was incessantly watched and persecuted; and at last the restrictions imposed upon me became so irksome and vexatious, that my mother resolved to intercede with Major Walker, the Provost-Marshal, on my behalf. The result of this intercession was, that he granted us both a pass, by way of Winchester to Front Royal, with a view to my being sent on to join my relations at Richmond.

Upon arriving at Winchester we had much difficulty in getting permission to proceed; for General Shields had just occupied Front Royal, and had prohibited all intercourse between that place and Winchester. However, Lieutenant- Colonel Fillebrowne, of the Tenth Maine Regiment, who was acting as Provost-Marshal, at length relented, and allowed us to go on our way.

It was almost twilight when we arrived at the Shenandoah River. We found that the bridges had been destroyed, and no means of transport left but a ferry-boat, which the Yankees monopolized for their own exclusive purposes.

Here we should have been subjected to much inconvenience and delay, had it not been for the courtesy and kindness of Captain Everhart, through whose intervention we were enabled to cross at once.

It was quite dark when we reached the village, and, to our great surprise, we found the family domiciled in a little cottage in the court-yard, the residence having been appropriated by General Shields and his staff.

However, we were glad enough to find ourselves at our journey's end, and to sit down to a comfortable dinner, for which fatigue and a long fast had sharpened our appetite. As soon as we had satisfied our hunger, I sent in my card to General Shields, who promptly returned my missive in person. He was an Irishman, and endowed with all those graces of manner for which the better class of his countrymen are justly famous; nor was he devoid of the humor for which they are no less notorious.

To my application for leave to pass instanter through his lines, en route for Richmond, he replied, that old Jackson's army was so demoralized that he dared not trust me to their tender mercies; but that they would be annihilated within a few days, and, after such a desirable consummation, I might wander whither I would.

This, of course, was mere badinage on his part; but I am convinced he felt confident of immediate and complete success, or he would not have allowed some expressions to escape him which I turned to account: In short, he was completely off his guard, and forgot that a woman can sometimes listen and remember.

General Shields, introduced me to the officers of his staff, two of whom were young Irishmen; and to one of these Captain K., I am indebted for some very remarkable effusions, some withered flowers, and last, not least, for a great deal of very important information, which was carefully transmitted to my countrymen. I must avow the flowers and the poetry were comparatively valueless in my eyes; but let Captain K. be consoled: these were days of war, not of love, and there are still other ladies in the world besides

286

the "rebel spy.".,

The night before the departure of General Shields, who was about, as he informed us, to "whip" Jackson, a council of war was held in what had formerly been my aunt's drawing-room. Immediately above this was a bed-chamber, containing a closet, through the floor of which I observed a hole had been bored, whether with a view to espionage or not I have never been able to ascertain. It occurred to me, however, that I might turn the discovery to account; and as soon as the council of war had assembled, I stole softly up stairs, and lying down on the floor of the closet, applied my ear to the hole, and found, to my great joy, I could distinctly hear the conversation that was passing below.

The council prolonged their discussion for some hours; but I remained motionless and silent until the proceedings were brought to a conclusion, at one o'clock in the morning. As soon as the coast was clear I crossed the court-yard, and made the best of my way to my own room, and took down in cipher everything I had heard which seemed to me of any importance.

I felt convinced that to rouse a servant, or make any disturbance at that hour, would excite the suspicions of the Federals by whom I was surrounded; accordingly I went straight to the stables myself, saddled my horse, and galloped away in the direction of the mountains.

Fortunately I had about me some passes which I had from time to time procured for Confederate soldiers returning south, and which, owing to various circumstances, had never been put in requisition. They now, however, proved invaluable; for I was twice brought to a stand-still by the challenge of the Federal sentries, and who would inevitably have put a period to my adventurous career had they not been beguiled by my false passport. Once clear of the chain of sentries, I dashed on unquestioned across fields and along roads, through fens and marshes, until, after a scamper of about fifteen miles, I found myself at the door of Mr. M.'s house. All was still and quiet: not a light was to be seen. I did not lose a moment in springing from my horse; and, running up the steps, I knocked at the door with such vehemence that the house re-echoed with the sound.

It was not until I had repeated my summons, at intervals of a few seconds, for some time, that I heard the response, "Who is there?" given in a sharp voice from a window above. "It is I."

"But who are you? What is your name?"

"Belle Boyd. I have important intelligence to communicate to Colonel Ashby: is he here?" "No; but wait a minute: I will come down."

The door was opened, and Mrs. M. drew me in, and exclaimed in a tone of astonishment - "My dear, where did you come from? And how on earth did you get here?"

"Oh, I forced the sentries," I replied, "and here I am; but I have no time to tell you the how, and the why, and the wherefore. I must see Colonel Ashby without the loss of a minute: tell me where he is to be found."

Upon hearing that his party was a quarter of a mile farther up the wood, I turned to depart in search of them, and was in the very act of remounting when a door on my right was thrown open, and revealed Colonel Ashby himself, who could not conceal his surprise at seeing me standing before him.

"Good God! Miss Belle, is this you? Where did you come from? Have you dropped from the clouds? Or am I dreaming?"

I first convinced him he was wide awake, and that my presence was substantial and of the earth - not a visionary emanation from the world of spirits - then, without further circumlocution, I proceeded to narrate all I had overheard in the closet, of which I have before made mention. I gave him the cipher, and started on my return.

I arrived safely at my aunt's house, after a two hours' ride, in the course of which I "ran the blockade" of a sleeping sentry, who awoke to the sound of my horse's hoofs just in time to see me disappear round an abrupt turning, which shielded me from the bullet he was about to send after me. Upon getting home, I unsaddled my horse and "turned in" -if I may be permitted the expression, which is certainly expressive rather than refined -just as Aurora, springing from the rosy bed of Tithonus, began her pursuit of the flying hour; in plain English, just as day began to break.

A few days afterwards General Shields marched south, laying a trap, as he supposed, to catch "poor old Jackson and his demoralized army," leaving behind him, to occupy Front Royal, one squadron of cavalry, one field battery, and the 1st Maryland Regiment of Infantry, under command of Colonel Kenly; Major Tyndale, of Philadelphia, being appointed Provost-Marshal. (Belle Boyd in Camp and Prison. Boyd, B. Blelock. NY. 1865.)

In June 1900, Belle died of a heart attack while performing in Wisconsin…penniless, but undaunted. She was buried in the scenic Wisconsin Dells, far from her beloved Virginia.
****

Appendix T.

Official description of Shields swords by T. Belote, curator of Smithsonian Museum.

General Shields swords were transferred from the War Department (now the Department of Defense) to the Smithsonian National Museum in 1890. A book published in 1932 by Theodore T. Belote, Curator of History at the museum, contains a complete description of the swords. Belote wrote "Two very interesting presentation swords in the National Museum were presented to Brig. Gen. James Shields United States Volunteers, by the State of Illinois and the State of South Carolina, respectively. The blade of the first (Length; 99 cm. Blade, 80 cm. long, 2.5 cm. wide) is of a somewhat antiquated type with a broad shallow groove extending about three-fourths its length. The obverse is decorated in gold chasing with a design showing American troops crossing the Rio Grande, the whole being flanked by floral and trophy designs. The reverse is decorated in silver chasing on a gold ground with a view of the American troops entering the City of Mexico, and the whole is flanked by floral and trophy designs. The grip of this sword, which is unusually large, is finished in gilt. The obverse side bears the figure of Mars standing and the reverse the figure of Ulysses standing. The pommel is formed by a medieval helmet with plume covering the end of the grip and in one piece with that portion of the hilt. The quillons are formed by two eagles standing with extended wings back to back on each side of the blade. Immediately below these on the obverse is a shield decorated with the head of Zeus and on the reverse with the United States shield. The scabbard, which is finished in gilt, bears two small mounts on the obverse, one of which is decorated with the head of Medusa and the other with a plain shield surrounded by a geometrical design. Between the two is engraved the inscription: "Presented by the State of Illinois to General James Shields for gallant services at Vera Cruz, , Cerro Gordo, Contreras, Churubusco, Chapultepec and the City, of Mexico." The remaining surface of the scabbard is engraved with large floral designs.

The sword presented to General Shields by the State of South Carolina (Length, 97.5 cm. Blade. 80.8 cm. long, 2.8 cm. wide. Marked "Ames Mfg. Co.") is of a more ornate and costly design than the one just described. The blade is of the regular type of the Mexican War period with two edges and a single, narrow, deep central groove. The obverse is decorated in silver chasing with trophies including quivers, cannon, drums, swords, and the United States shield surrounded by a sunburst and floral and scroll designs. The reverse is decorated in the same manner with the addition of the United States coat of arms. The grip is 8-sided, and is faced with alternate strips of gold plate and mother-of-pearl. The former are engraved with floral and scroll designs, and the latter are set with small gold globules. The pommel is vase-shaped, the sides are decorated with scroll designs, and the end is encircled with an oak wreath and set with a large emerald. The quillions are composed of four narrow flat scrolls bound together with oak and palm sprays. The center of the obverse of the quill ions is set with a ruby above a gold shield engraved with a scene showing the American troops attacking the City of Mexico. The scabbard is decorated on the obverse near the top with a palmetto tree in heavy relief bearing on the trunk two oval shields, one inscribed "Churubusco, Aug. 20, 1847" and other "Chapultepec, Sept. 11, 12, 13." A second design in relief shows the United States shield superimposed upon oak sprays, with an engraved design below showing a military trophy with a central shield inscribed "Mexico." Between the two relief designs is engraved the inscription, in five lines, with a scroll border: "From the State of South Carolina to General Shields in testimony of her admiration of his gallantry in the Mexican War and as in gratitude for his parental attention to the Palmetto Regiment." (American and European Swords in the Historical Collections of the United States Museum. Belote, T. Bulletin 163. US Government Printing Office, Washington, 1932.)

****

Appendix U.

Typescript of Shields letter.

Nashville (?) April 12th 1844

My Dear friend

I received your kind letter by our friend Mr. Browne. Since then I find there is a disposition here to defeat Smith at any rate. And if such is the case and it is likely to be done I have determined to accept if nominated - In Bond and Clinton and Washington delegates are appointed and though not instructed they will nearly all be for me - Your county wants to make the matter certain - and the opinion here is that Trumbull will beat Smith with almost all these if I be not nominated - I wish you and a few of my true friends would select good delegates and let them be return without any instructions. That is the course pursued by the other counties and you can make this a rule. When you meet at Kaskaskia you can do as you please.

The convention caucuses on next Monday week - Your county must be represented - I wish you move to cover yourself - Do if possible and get good men - My friends are urgent that I have to run they say if Smith is to be beat - it is great injustice to me to let others interruption (??.)

Let this be in confidence -

Your friend

Jas. Shields

P.S. Your county is entitled to 6 delegates I am told. The Democratic vote of 46 is the basis - and one to 200 Democrats - J.S.

Index

About the Author

Dr. J. P. Sean Callan is a psychiatrist-journalist who graduated from the National University of Ireland, former U.S. correspondent Irish Medical Times, former clinical assistant professor of psychiatry Chicago Medical School, and former contributing editor Journal of the American Medical Association. Dr. Callan served actively in the U.S. military during Vietnam and retired from the Air Force Reserve with the rank of Colonel. Dr. Callan's plays The Day Room and The Sixteenth Man have been produced in Chicago and, Hearthstone was a winner at Tara Circle, New York. Dr. Callan's books include Your Guide to Mental Health and The Physician, A Professional Under Stress. Courage and Country is Dr. Callan's first historical biography. Dr. Callan and his wife Clair, live in Lake Forest, Illinois.